THE LENGTHENING SHADOW

LIZ HARRIS

HEYWOOD PRESS

P rimrose Hill,
       May, 1917

DOROTHY STOOD in the centre of the nursery at the top of the
house, and stared around the room in which she and her
younger brother and sister had spent so much time in their
early years.

She'd wondered if she'd feel a sense of nostalgia for the
childhood she was now about to leave firmly behind her,
but she didn't. The speed of events in the past few days, and
the knowledge of where she was being sent, had left her
devoid of any emotion other than acute misery.

Unfastening her dark blue nurse's cape, she slid it from
her shoulders and holding it in her hand, went across to the
wall on the other side of the room and looked up at the wallpaper. Illustrations from the story of *Sleeping Beauty* looked
back at her.

Their colour had faded beneath the light that streamed

through the window after the heavy brocade curtains had been tied back. And parts of the pictures had been erased by the servants' attempts over the years at removing the grubby marks left by three children.

Her brother, Robert, had been the worst. Their nanny had never been able to stop him from drawing houses on the walls, and traces of his outlines could still be seen.

She glanced down at the large white dolls' house that stood against the wall, and moved over to it. Kneeling, she peered into one small room after another.

The tiny inhabitants of the house were a replica of her family: the father in a dark brown three-piece suit wore a bowler hat that was the same as her father, Joseph, had insisted on wearing to show that he was a working man, despite her mother's regular protestations that a man in his position should wear a top hat.

The mother wore an elegant long mauve dress with a high neck and puffed sleeves, a replica of her mother's favourite dress.

The two little girls, one older than the other, were both in long-sleeved white frocks and dark cotton stockings, and a little boy in a sailor suit, who came between them in age, had been arranged at the foot of the miniature staircase.

Whenever Nellie played at families, she always arranged the three children with Dorothy on one side, herself on the other, and Robert between them—the order in which they'd been born.

Smiling at the memory, she picked up the father figure, looked at it, and put it down again.

Standing up, she turned towards the metal toy pram that stood at the side of the cast-iron fireplace. A china doll dressed in a bonnet, cape and long white gown, was reclining in the pram. Its pale blue eyes wide open, it stared up at her in perpetual surprise. How Nellie had loved that doll!

And how Robert had loved his rocking horse!

She glanced at the large white rocking horse that stood motionless in front of the window. Its silvery mane, once long and luxurious, was threadbare now after the years of enthusiastic galloping with which Robert had greeted the start of almost every day.

She went across to the horse, pushed it backwards and forwards once or twice, and stood back, watching as it slowly creaked to a halt.

Then she turned and looked across at the child-sized table that stood against the far wall. Inevitably, the pink tablecloth had faded. After all, Nellie had chosen the cloth when she'd been no more than five years old. Their low wooden chairs were tucked under the table.

She gave a slight shake of her head. It was impossible to believe that the three of them had ever been small enough to sit on those chairs.

A set of alphabet blocks was piled neatly on top of the table.

But there was no sign of the tea set that she and Nellie had been given. Not that they'd often played with it. Being five years older than Nellie, she'd outgrown the desire to make tea for her dolls long before Nellie had reached that stage.

And Robert had shown no interest at all in participating in a tea party, not with her, not with Nellie. Over the years, all he'd ever really wanted to do was play with the set of blocks.

Her gaze lingered on the blocks, each of which had a beautifully engraved letter of the alphabet carved into one of its faces, and she smiled to herself.

They'd been given to Robert to help him learn his letters. But never once had he paid the slightest attention to the colourful letters, never once had he attempted to construct a word—his sole interest in the blocks had been as a means of building houses.

She looked at the walls again and at the pictures of *Sleeping Beauty* interspersed with traces of Robert's house designs, and in her mind she rolled back the years.

For the first three of her twenty years, the nursery had been hers alone. During those three years, a different wallpaper had covered the walls. It had illustrated the poem *This Is the House That Jack Built*, a poem she'd never liked with its endless list of animals, and its references to killing and to the maiden all forlorn.

As she'd grown older, she'd wondered several times whether to ask her parents if the wallpaper could be changed for something she'd like. But she didn't. She didn't want to remind them she was a girl.

She couldn't remember a time when she hadn't been aware that her parents, who'd chosen the wallpaper in the weeks before she'd been born, had wanted a boy. They hadn't for one moment considered that her mother, Maud, might give birth to a girl.

Having a girl had been a huge disappointment.

No one had needed to tell her that—she'd always sensed it.

And never had she been more conscious of it than three years later when Robert had been born. The sombre mood that had lain over the house had seemed to lighten overnight.

There'd been jubilation among her parents, uncles and aunts, and also among the servants. Even Nanny had smiled and looked happy.

It had been as if, with Robert's birth, all had felt that at last they could relax.

It wasn't that her parents didn't love her—she was sure that they did. It was just that being a girl, she was less important than Robert. But Nanny had explained why, so she hadn't blamed her parents for that. And she hadn't blamed Robert, either.

She'd asked Nanny why everyone kept on exclaiming that the baby was a boy, and Nanny had told her that her father had needed a son, who would one day take over from him the running of Linford & Sons, her family's successful construction company.

Robert was the longed-for son, and that was that.

And he was a sweet little boy and she loved him, even though his arrival had caused some changes in the routine of her day.

Before Robert had been born, Nanny used to take her downstairs every afternoon to see her parents, and she and her parents would sit together for a short period of time.

When she was old enough to reply to questions, her parents would ask her what she'd learned that day, and she would tell them. Apart from that, she'd sit quietly until it was time to be taken back up to the nursery.

But things had been very different after Robert's birth.

From that time on, Nanny would take both of them downstairs every afternoon to sit with their parents. Her parents would ask her the same sort of questions that they'd always asked, but their eyes had always been on Robert.

And they didn't sit straight-backed in the armchair as they'd always done before Robert came along. They'd often asked Nanny to put Robert between them, and they'd tickle him and make funny noises to make him laugh.

They'd never tickled her when she'd been little.

And they'd never visited the nursery during the day, either, which they'd started to do after Robert's arrival.

When Robert was two, Nellie was born.

Again, she'd felt her parents' disappointment at the birth of a girl. They'd wanted another boy, Nanny had told her, and she'd encouraged Dorothy to be extra good so as not to make her parents more upset than they already were.

But *she* wasn't upset.

She was overjoyed at having a sister, even though Nellie was five years younger. It meant that while her parents were paying attention to Robert, exclaiming with delight at every new word he'd learned, and at every misshapen house he'd drawn, she wouldn't have to sit there on her own, watching them—she'd have her baby sister next to her. And as Nellie got older, she'd have someone to talk to while her parents talked to Robert.

But it hadn't worked out like that.

Her parents had overcome swiftly their regret at having another daughter, and they'd soon clearly adored Nellie, who had large blue eyes, a mass of dark curly hair, and who was bold enough from an early age to make it clear that she, too, expected to cuddle up to her parents on their afternoon visits downstairs.

Gradually, she'd become aware that their father was paying almost as much attention to Nellie, both downstairs and in the nursery, as he did to Robert.

It wasn't just her parents who doted on Nellie—everyone in the family did, too. And so did she. It wasn't Nellie's fault that she was so lovable, and that the more delight Nellie's presence gave, the more ungainly it made her feel.

Seeing Nellie's success with her parents, she'd gone through a period of time in which she'd tried hard to think of clever things to say that would make her family notice her, too, and take an interest in her.

But whatever she attempted, it had always seemed to come out wrong.

In the end, she'd given up making the effort, and for years had sat back in the shadows, letting her brother and sister shine brightly in the light of the family's attention.

And then, when she was seventeen, war had broken out, and she'd stepped out of the shadows.

N o one had been more surprised than Dorothy herself when as soon as the country was officially at war, she'd announced to her parents that she was going to train to become a nurse.

She, who'd never before done anything impulsive, had done perhaps the first impulsive thing in her life. She didn't know where the words had come from, but from the moment that they'd been uttered, she knew that this was something she really wanted to do.

Later that evening, as she'd stood at her bedroom window and looked back at the moment at which she'd spoken out, she'd felt that behind her words, there'd been something stronger than a mere feeling that this was something she ought to do to, given the situation facing the country.

It had been as if Destiny had been speaking for her.

Because she wouldn't be twenty-one for four more years, she couldn't register as a Red Cross nurse, and having a generous allowance from her father, she had no need of money, so she'd gone to the local Red Cross and asked for advice about what she could do at her age to help.

As a result, she'd started volunteering in local hospitals and dispensaries, and in that way, had managed to obtain some teaching in the basics of first aid and home nursing, supervised by a doctor.

Months later, when she'd felt ready, she'd taken the elementary nursing examinations, passed them, and been given certificates in home nursing and first aid.

With the number of injured servicemen increasing daily, and the War Office calling for women to enter the medical profession, even though she was a little young, she'd been allowed to join the Voluntary Aid Detachment set up by her local Red Cross. Her duties, she knew, would be less technical than those of fully-trained nurses, but they'd be no less important.

SHE'D BEEN SENT ALMOST at once to work part-time in an auxiliary hospital in Highgate, where she'd been one of a contingent of full-time nurses, and of part-time VADs whose role it was to help the trained nurses care for wounded soldiers who'd been sent back home from abroad.

Although the hospital wasn't too far from the family home in Primrose Hill for her to be able to go back and visit them at times, she'd realised that it would be too far for her to commute on the days she worked, her shifts being either from seven thirty in the morning to eight at night, or from seven thirty in the morning to one in the afternoon, and then again from five in the evening until nine o'clock at night.

Her father had agreed, and had said at once that he'd pay for the hostel, food and accommodation. And a week after that, she'd moved into the hostel attached to the hospital.

Leaving the familiar surroundings of home, and the daily ministrations of the family's servants, had brought home to her that she really was a nurse at last, and she'd never forget the pride she'd felt when on her first morning, she'd donned the VAD apron with the large bright red cross in the centre.

Nor would she forget how she and the other two VAD nurses who were starting at the same time, had laughingly sprinkled themselves with carbolic in order to have a hospital smell about them, just to make absolutely sure that people would know they were nurses.

The hospital, which was located in a large house on a residential road, had been open for one year only when she started there.

With six large rooms, a good-sized recreation room that housed a piano and a small billiard table, and the operating theatre on the upper floor, there was a general feeling of light and airiness, which made it a comfortable place in which to work.

But it wasn't just the building that was pleasant. So, too, were the people with whom she was working. She'd been very surprised to find how friendly the trained nurses and masseuses were towards the VAD nurses.

During the years in which she'd been mastering the skills of nursing, she'd heard about the contempt in which some of the trained nurses held the VADs, and when she started at the hospital in Highgate, she'd been somewhat apprehensive as to how they'd all work together.

But to her great relief, she found nothing but friendliness.

Through throwaway remarks from the trained nurses,

she'd learned that some of the VADs with whom the nurses had worked in previous hospitals had attempted to avoid the worst of the tasks, such as redressing a suppurating wound.

But neither she nor any of her VAD colleagues in Highgate had acted in such a way. Rather, all of the nurses and VADs did their fair share of everything that had to be done, no matter how unpleasant, and this had clearly been noticed by the trained nurses.

So, even though the days were long and tiring, and the work relentless, and despite having to tend injuries that were frequently gruesome to see, the year she'd spent at the hospital had been fulfilling, and in so far as it could be, given the parlous situation of the country, it had been happy. She'd liked her colleagues and had felt needed and important to the work of the hospital.

But now, all that was about to end.

And that's what she'd come home to tell her family.

To her huge disappointment and despair, she was being transferred to the hospital in the Alexandra Palace Internment Camp.

It meant that she was going to have to say goodbye to her nursing colleagues, and to the patients she'd come to know very well and to care for, and go to a place she absolutely didn't want to go.

But she'd no choice in the matter.

Two days earlier, when Matron had called her to her office and told her about her imminent transfer, she'd instantly said that she wanted to stay where she was.

Her uncle Thomas was risking his life overseas, she'd said, and she couldn't bear the thought of looking after any Germans, even if they *were* only internees.

Every time she'd look at them, she'd think of her uncle,

and that she might never see him again, and she'd hate
them. That wasn't the way to feel about your patients, she'd
told Matron.

Matron had brushed aside her objections. She wasn't
the only one with a member of the family fighting the
Germans, Matron had told her somewhat acidly. Some of
the nurses came from homes where every single man was at
the front. The hospital at Alexandra Palace needed help,
and she'd been chosen to give them that help, and she
would do so.

Her distress had been further compounded when she
realised that she'd have to transfer to a hostel closer to
Alexandra Palace.

With the camp some distance across London, she'd be
unlikely to see her Highgate friends again, and between
the length of her working day and her distance from Primrose Hill, she'd hardly ever be able to see her family,
either.

A quiet knock on the nursery door brought her back to
the present, and she went quickly to the door and opened it.

The housemaid was standing there.

'Begging your pardon, Miss Dorothy,' the housemaid
said. 'Mr and Mrs Charles have arrived, and Mrs Morley is
about to serve tea. Mr Linford would like you to join them.'

'Of course, Ethel. Thank you.'

The housemaid gave a slight bob, and hurried back
down the stairs.

She went out on to the upper landing. Pausing a
moment, she looked back into the nursery. It belonged to a
world they were never going to see again, she thought in a
moment of sudden nostalgia. Whatever the outcome of the
war, the world in the future was bound to look very
different.

For a moment or two, she stood motionless. Then she stepped back, and closed the door firmly on her childhood.

THE MUFFLED sound of the conversation in the main reception room became louder as she reached the top of the final flight of stairs. She paused, her cape in one hand and her other hand resting lightly on the mahogany banister, not really in the mood to join in the conversation.

She couldn't make out the words they were saying, but she could imagine what they were.

Her father, Joseph Linford, Chairman of Linford & Sons, would inevitably be talking about houses and their latest wartime contracts; his banker brother, her uncle Charles, was bound to be discussing the pressure on money that was caused by the war; both would be expressing anxiety about the youngest of the three brothers, Uncle Thomas, who'd signed up as soon as war had been declared.

Her mother, Maud, would be reclining languidly against the back of the armchair, looking as elegant as ever; Uncle Charles's wife, Sarah, would be criticising something that Uncle Charles had said and done, or not done, which she habitually did.

Fifteen-year-old Nellie, whose lively voice could be heard above the others, would be trying to start a conversation with Aunt Sarah, to whom she was very close.

The one discordant note in the room would be that of her brother, Robert.

This was the first weekend for ages that Robert had stayed in London and not gone to Chorton House, the family's weekend retreat in the Cotswolds.

Staying in London every weekend, which he was going to have to do for a month, hadn't been his choice, and according to her father, Robert had been making his displeasure felt for the whole of the past week.

She could imagine him, therefore, sitting apart from the family, glowering.

The family had known for several weeks that Robert had fallen heavily for a Land Girl called Lily Brown, who worked on the farm that neighboured Chorton House, and they'd known that Joseph was furious about it.

When Robert, standing hand in hand with Lily, had first told his father that he loved Lily, Joseph had thundered that a woman who was older than Robert, who visibly lacked education, background and money, was completely unsuitable for the man who'd one day be Chairman of Linford & Sons.

And from that moment on, Joseph had loudly and vigorously opposed Robert's friendship with Lily, completely ignoring the advice of them all that his continued vocal opposition to the friendship would push Robert closer to Lily, which is what had inevitably happened.

In desperation, Joseph had concocted a thinly veiled reason connected with work as to why Robert must stay in London for four weeks, including the weekends.

He'd clearly been hoping, as Robert knew, that if he prevented Robert from seeing Lily for at least a month, he might forget her. And if, while in London, Robert met a woman who'd be a more suitable match, so much the better.

With that thought in mind, and fed up at seeing Robert moping around the house, snapping at everyone, Joseph had belatedly accepted an invitation to a charity dinner the following weekend, which was to be held at the tennis club.

All of the local businessmen involved in the war effort at home had been invited, along with their families, and

Joseph had ordered Robert, Maud and Nellie to accompany him.

Maud and Nellie had been delighted at a rare opportunity to dress up, even though it would be a somewhat subdued event.

Robert had been predictably resentful, and had told Dorothy how much he wished that he, too, would be working on the other side of London, and thus be unable to go.

On the other side of London.

Her stomach churned.

Yes, she'd have already started in Alexandra Palace. In one week's time—not even as long as that—she'd be surrounded by people who came from enemy countries, the countries her uncle Thomas was fighting.

And she was absolutely dreading it.

The very thought of having to touch such people, of having to do the most personal, intimate of things for them, sent a shudder through the length of her body.

Ice cold, she stood there.

Then she heard the door to the main reception room open, and someone pass through the doorway and move around within the room.

The timbre of the conversation in the room changed, and she heard the sound of wooden table legs scraping on the polished parquet floor.

The maid and housekeeper will have just taken in the afternoon tea, she realised. She must join her family for what she suspected would be her last family tea for a long while.

Gripping the banister tightly, she swallowed hard, and walked down the last few steps.

3

A lexandra Palace,
      May, 1917

DOROTHY MOVED through her first couple of weeks at
Alexandra Palace in a daze.

Daily, she found it a struggle to adjust to being in such a
large, cavernous building that, she was told, could accom-
modate well over three thousand interned prisoners.

For organisational purposes, it had been split into three
subdivisions, one for each battalion, with each sub-division
being large enough to contain a thousand men. She'd get
used to it, her nursing colleagues would say whenever she
commented on the size of the place, but she didn't think she
ever would.

Having just spent a year in a small, friendly hospital
with forty-two beds only, the number of people she now
encountered on a regular basis was overwhelming. And so,
too, was the deafening noise that was ever-present

throughout the day. Every single person seemed to shout rather than speak.

To her great dismay, she was frequently asked in the first few weeks to leave the wing that housed the hospital and go to the administrative area.

As this was on the other side of the building, she had to pass through all three battalion sub-divisions, and make her way between rows of men reclining on raised board-beds covered with a straw mattress, pillows and three blankets.

The men would invariably call out after her in words she couldn't understand, but of which the meaning was clear, and she'd felt acutely uncomfortable every minute of the time she was away from the hospital.

She was hugely relieved, therefore, when she was given her first two-month stint of night duty not too long after she'd started at the internment camp, as it meant that she wouldn't have to leave the hospital quite as often.

She was soon to discover another reason to be thankful that she'd been given her first block of night duty at that particular time.

Late one evening, while she was dressing a troublesome ulcer on the inside of an internee's leg, just above his ankle, the man whose leg she was tending suddenly spoke.

Startled, she stayed as she was, bent over his leg, and didn't move.

'This is ironic, is it not,' the man said, his voice rolling over her, 'that Alexandra Palace, originally intended to be a place of refuge and safety for Belgians fleeing the German invasion of their country, has now become a place of captivity for people of German origin?'

She glanced quickly up at him. He was lying partly on his back, propped up on his elbows, and was staring at her with deep blue eyes, his blond hair falling across his forehead in disarray.

She looked up at the information sheet on the wall above his bed and saw that his name was Franz Hartmann.

She turned her attention back to his leg.

'If you say so,' she said tersely, and resumed wiping the discoloured skin from around his ulcer.

'I do. When Germans, Austrians and Hungarians were all declared to be enemy aliens, even if they'd lived here for years, and were ordered to register with the police in their local district, it was obvious to all that it was only a matter of time before the British Government would decide to intern all the males from those countries, as they've now done for men between seventeen and fifty-five. So, yes, I do say that there's some irony in this. Would you not agree, Dorothy?'

She looked up sharply.

'How d'you know my name?'

He gave a slight shrug. 'I've heard the other nurses call you that.'

'They're allowed to call me by my name, but you should address me as Nurse.'

'Very well. Would you not agree, Nurse Dorothy?'

Hearing the laughter in his voice, she looked at him properly for the first time.

Her eyes met his eyes, and in them she saw open appreciation.

Why, he looks nice, she thought with a shock, and he's really handsome.

'It's Nurse Linford,' she said, injecting as much firmness as she could into her voice, and she turned quickly back to his leg.

Fighting the urge to look at him again, she forced herself

to concentrate on his ulcerous leg, while vowing that she'd avoid the man as much as she could in the future.

By the following evening, her resolve had failed, and she was acutely aware as she entered the hospital wing for her night shift, of how much she was looking forward to seeing Franz Hartmann again, and that she was going to make sure she did so.

By the end of the month, in the time that it had taken for his ulcer to clear up, she'd fallen deeply in love with him.

Although Franz had returned to his sub-division by then, he had continued to present his ulcer for her inspection every evening without fail.

He knew that by eight o'clock, she'd have finished consulting with the nurses from whom she'd taken over, would have read through the patients' notes and done her tour of the wards, and that, if he left it till after eight, they'd be able to sit together and talk.

'Yours must be the best tended ulcer ever,' she remarked one day with a smile, sitting opposite him at a wooden table in the corner of the hospital wing. 'I must have changed the bandage every day since we met.'

'And I hope you'll tend to me daily for as long as we both are here,' he said warmly. 'I would never have believed that I'd be thankful to have an ulcer, but I am. It's led me to you, Dorothy, and I shall always be grateful to it for that.'

'Me, too.' She heard a trace of awkwardness in her voice, and she gave a slight cough.

'With the one pound a week we're allowed to spend,' he went on, 'I'd like to buy you something to show how much I appreciate the care you've given me, but I think you would not like what the canteen calls luxuries—cigarettes, horse meat, ink and socks. These are not for you,' he said in mock gravity.

She laughed. 'No, I don't think they are.'

'And as I enjoy music very much, I would like to take you to one of our weekly concerts, which are of a pleasingly high standard, but this would not be allowed, I feel sure. You'd be seen as consorting with the enemy, and they'd send you away. And this I would hate. Seeing you every day is the one thing that makes this place bearable for me.'

Her heart leapt, and she stared at him, her dark brown eyes opening wide, a tentative smile on her lips. 'Is it really, Franz?'

He nodded. 'Yes, it is,' he said quietly.

A wave of pleasure swept through her.

'No one's ever before told me that I made something bearable for them,' she said, and she could feel herself colouring with embarrassment.

'You are the sun that lights up the darkness of this place. You've become very special to me, Dorothy.'

'I have?' Her voice was almost a whisper.

'Yes, you have.'

Their eyes met, and held. Neither said a word.

Dorothy cleared her throat. 'So you go to the concerts here, then?' she asked, breaking the silence. 'I pass the theatre when I go to Administration, but I've never actually been inside.'

He shrugged. 'Yes, sometimes. I used to go to concerts in Morbach, and I miss them. But I never go to the theatricals. There is no talent for acting here and the productions are commonplace. But as with everyone else, I like best the cinema, which we now have twice a week.'

'You call the cinema *Kino*, don't you? I've heard other internees talking. I realised what it meant as it's almost the same as the English.'

'Ah, you are learning German!' he exclaimed in delight.

Because if she refused to give up the German, that's exactly what she'd be doing.

It would be insanity.

He raised his eyes and looked at Charles and Sarah, who were sitting across the table from each other. They must be as appalled as he and Maud at Dorothy's news.

Especially Sarah.

His brother was less judgmental as a person, being temperamentally inclined towards laziness and inertia, but Charles's assertive, opinionated wife, Sarah, must be utterly horrified at the idea of a German becoming a part of the family.

Well, it wasn't going to happen, and that was that.

Pushing back his uncomfortable awareness that he'd recently said the same thing about the unsuitable woman with whom his son, Robert, was infatuated, and that he appeared to be a long way from separating Robert's affections from Lily, he cleared his throat.

'Given the news that Dorothy broke to her mother and me yesterday, and which we promptly passed on to you,' he began, 'you won't have been surprised, I'm sure, that Maud and I asked you to dinner at what is, I recognise, very short notice.'

'No, we weren't,' Sarah said with a slight smile.

'But we were both delighted, I'm sure, that you allowed us to enjoy the excellent meal before you raised the subject,' Charles cut in.

Sarah nodded. 'Most definitely. It's commendable that your cook can turn out such a meal with so little warning, given that we're still constrained by rationing. It would have been a shame to have spoiled it.'

Maud wiped her lips with her napkin. 'We're extremely lucky that Cook has never shown any desire to go off and work in any of the factories or companies now employing women.'

'We're both very lucky about that,' Sarah agreed.

'I know. We'd have hated to lose her after so many years. I can't imagine another cook coping in the way she does. But with luck, she soon won't have to contend with rationing. Food no longer has to be sent to the fighting soldiers, and German U-boats won't be stopping any more supply ships from getting through, so things should get easier.'

Joseph shifted his position in his chair. 'Indeed. But to go back to Dorothy's news. No doubt you'll have been as shocked as we were at the idea of her marrying a German. A German, I ask you! Can you believe it! Marrying the enemy! My own daughter! It beggars belief. Well, I won't let it happen!'

He thumped the table.

The clattering of silver and tinkling of glass resounded the length of the table.

Maud leaned across and put her hand on his arm. 'You must try to relax, darling. Getting into a state won't achieve anything. All it'll do is stop you from thinking clearly.'

'I *am* thinking clearly,' Joseph snapped, pushing her hand away. 'It's Dorothy who isn't. Even if she'd thought herself in love, from the moment we heard that Thomas, her own uncle, had lost his leg and most of his hand because of the Germans, she should've withdrawn her affections. And by God, that's what she'll do, no matter what she said yesterday. I promise you, when Thomas gets home, there'll not be a single German for miles around. You agree, don't you, Charles?'

Charles nodded. 'Both of us do. We're as horrified at the idea as you, Joseph. But I think it unlikely that Dorothy will continue with the engagement.'

nancy that had occurred in the three years between her birth and that of Robert.

As soon as Franz had heard that, he'd become even more anxious that she didn't take any unnecessary risks, and from the moment that they'd woken up at the end of October and seen that the ground was sheened with frost and the leaden grey sky threatened snow, going outside, he'd told her, would be an unnecessary risk, both for her and for their unborn child.

From that time on, he went across to the shops first thing every morning, bought whatever he could from the limited choice on the shelves, and took everything back to the house before leaving for the school where he taught.

The care he took of her made her feel deeply loved, and she was grateful for that. But at the same time, she couldn't help feeling frustrated by the limitations placed on her movement.

Having worked hard for most of the war years, she was used to being busy from morning till night, and to find herself restricted to the house was difficult to get used to.

And it wasn't as if she was ill—she was only pregnant, a point she'd made hesitantly on the only occasion since the onset of winter on which she'd suggested going outside.

It had been early in January, and as the fall of snow in the night had been unusually light, it hadn't taken Franz long to clear a path through the snow from their house to the road, and then with the other men in the village, to sweep the snow from the area in front of the shops.

After that, he'd come back into the house to exchange his shovel for the enamel blue can in which they daily collected a litre of goat's milk from the produce shop.

He'd left the front door open for a moment or two, and

she'd felt a gust of crisp morning air on her face. She'd felt revitalised.

Perhaps she could be the one to take the can across the road for the milk that morning, she'd suggested, staring through the doorway with longing. She'd be extremely careful, she assured him.

But he'd refused to allow this. She had only to fall once, he'd told her, just once, and he'd left her to complete the sentence.

In her heart, she'd known he was right, but it had been all she could do not to cry at the thought of yet another day confined to the house. But the loving concern she'd seen on his face stayed with her in the weeks that followed, and she'd never again asked to go outside.

Fortunately, she'd soon have her freedom back, she thought, glancing through the wood-framed window to the crossroads on her right.

In just over two months, the winter would have passed, the baby would have arrived, and once more she'd be able to visit her neighbours. She especially looked forward to being able to go across to Herta's for coffee and cake, so that Herta didn't always to have to come over to her.

How lucky they were to live across the track from Karl and Herta, whom they liked so much, and with whom they'd become such good friends in the relatively short space of time that she and Franz had lived in Rundheim.

Her gaze settled on Karl and Herta's half-timbered house, its dark wood outer beams stark against the ivory pallor of walls that were melting into the whiteness of the world around them, and she felt a wave of gratitude towards Karl. It was thanks to Karl that she and Franz now lived in Rundheim.

A couple of months after Franz had started teaching at

scenery that now surrounded her was different from that into which she'd been born.

She rubbed her eyes to erase the memory of her childhood days, and looked back at the window, but the glass in front of her nose and her mouth had misted up, and she couldn't see through to the street.

Raising her forearm, she wiped away the milky screen.

Then, flattening her left cheek against the cold window-frame, she pressed as close to the glass as she could and stared again down the hill that ran to the south, following it until it had left the town and was lost in the world that lay beyond, a seamless vista of undulating whiteness backed by a threatening grey sky.

The sole patch of colour came from the thick cluster of pines that soared up from a distant hollow, a spiky band of vivid dark green set against a backcloth of pristine white.

That was the road she would take if she were to go back to England.

Not that she could ever go back.

She'd never forget her father's anger when he'd realised that she'd no intention of giving up Franz.

Apoplectic, he'd accused her of betraying both her family and her country, not to mention her uncle Thomas, who'd suffered devastating injuries in the war.

It didn't matter to him that Franz hadn't in any way been involved in the fighting—it was enough that he came from their enemy's homeland.

Her father had flatly refused to meet Franz, and had made it crystal clear that if she went ahead and married him, he'd sever all contact with her. They all would. She'd no longer be considered a member of the Linford family.

Since she'd never for one minute entertain the idea of

leaving Franz—she loved him far too much for that—she'd turned to appeal to her mother.

'Your mother will agree with me,' her father had snapped, forestalling her.

'Your father and I are of the same opinion,' her mother had said quietly. 'You need to listen to what your father says and think very seriously about this, Dorothy.'

Later, the few friends in whom she'd confided had been equally appalled at what she was proposing to do.

It would be impossible to live comfortably in such a hostile atmosphere, she and Franz had concluded.

And with Franz confident that Dorothy would be accepted in Germany in a way that he wouldn't in England, they'd moved to Germany.

Germany was her home now and always would be. She would probably never go back to England, and she didn't know why she'd suddenly started thinking so wistfully about what she'd left behind.

She took a step back from the window.

That wasn't strictly true. She *did* know.

6

D orothy knew that her nostalgia hadn't been fuelled by the difference in climate—it had been triggered by the letter she'd received from her father the day before, telling her of her grandfather's death.

She turned and stared across the room at the tall dark-oak kitchen cupboard that stood against the wall, and at the envelope lying on the shelf beneath the cupboard's glass-fronted upper half.

A lump came to her throat. If she'd been able to walk out of the house for a moment or two, the ice-cold morning air might have frozen her grief and stopped it from hurting so.

But she hadn't. And deep within her, she was still crying.

Standing with her back to the window, and her eyes on the envelope, she reached behind her and tightened the strap of the pinafore apron that was wrapped around her distended stomach.

Having done so, she stood for a moment or two, biting her lower lip, her gaze never leaving the letter. Then she walked across to the cupboard, picked up the travel-scuffed envelope and looked down at the stamp in its corner.

A smudged circle of black surrounded the date of posting, and all but obscured the profile of George V. Slowly, she ran her finger across the king's face.

For all of the weeks that the letter had been journeying towards her, Arthur Joseph Linford, her much-loved grandfather, had been dead.

And she hadn't known that. Not till the day before.

Her relief that she'd sent her Rundheim address to her father was overwhelming.

In her every thought about England since she'd left her home, her grandfather had been at its centre, and it would have been unbearably sad to have continued imagining him at the heart of the family, when he no longer was.

His death would have left a gaping hole at the core of the family. But while the loss of the wonderful person he was would ever live with them all, the effect on the structure of the business would have been negligible.

Her father had taken over as chairman of the company a few years earlier, and he would've slipped just as easily into the role of head of the family, for that was what he now was, being the oldest son.

And he had the dominant character needed in a leader, unlike her uncle Charles, who liked an easy life, and Uncle Thomas, who'd have returned to the family by now, an injured man, in need of all of his energy to adjust to the unenviable situation into which he'd been placed.

She took the letter from her father out of the envelope, and looked at it again.

He'd told her in stilted terms that her grandfather had died in December, had been buried in the churchyard near

Chorton House, and that, to everyone's surprise, Robert had been left their grandfather's house in Hampstead.

Robert being given his grandfather's house would probably have irritated her father, she thought, who'd failed to stop Robert from marrying Lily, just as he'd failed to stop her from marrying Franz.

But it would also have shocked them all.

It wasn't difficult to imagine their faces as they sat in the solicitor's office, listening to the terms of the will.

Although her father and Uncle Charles had been born in Kentish Town, in the house attached to Linford & Sons' building yard, they'd moved into the lovely house in Hampstead in the year before Uncle Thomas was born.

The three boys had effectively grown up in that house, close to the Heath, and the family had always assumed that the house would be left to them.

Instead, Robert was the beneficiary. He, his wife, Lily, and their baby son, James, would be the ones who lived there.

She wondered what Joseph thought about Robert being favoured over Nellie, and how Nellie would react.

Nellie invariably had an opinion about everything, and this was unlikely to be an exception. And what would Uncle Charles and Aunt Sarah think about Louisa and Christopher being overlooked? To favour one grandchild in such a way over the others could cause a rift within a family.

And there'd been one further surprise in her father's letter.

Knowing what the family felt about her marriage, she hadn't expected to be mentioned in her grandfather's will, but everyone had been left a share in Chorton House, for which the cost of the staff and its maintenance would be met by the company for as long as the family wished to own it, and to her delight, she'd been included.

It wasn't the share in the house that had brought tears to her eyes, it was knowing that her grandfather must still have had some feelings for her.

Her father had given her to understand in his letter that her grandfather, although thoroughly disgusted with her, had refused to remove her name from his will. The tone of her father's letter told her, though, that she'd never be welcome at Chorton House.

And he'd made it clear that he'd never be writing to her again.

Tears brimmed.

Swiftly she wiped them away with the back of her hands, tucked the letter carefully back into the envelope and slipped it into her pinafore pocket.

Reaching up to the cupboard, she opened the glazed doors, took a step back and stared up at the set of bone china on the top shelf and the crystal wine glasses, all of which she'd brought with her from England. They'd been given to her by her grandparents some years before.

She was old enough to start thinking about her bottom drawer, they'd told her long before her nursing days had begun, and they'd given her a few things to start her off.

'Who knows whom you'll meet,' they'd teased when she'd started at the hospital in Highgate.

But by the time she'd met the man she loved, her grandfather had been the only grandparent left, and there'd been no teasing from him, and no more presents.

Rising up on her toes, she took the willow-patterned sugar bowl from the shelf, sank back on to her heels and ran her fingers lovingly around the rim.

The front door opened and she glanced around as Franz

came into the living room, bringing with him a blast of freezing air.

As he kicked the door hastily shut behind him, she thrust the bowl back into the cupboard and turned to greet him.

'It's nice and warm in here,' he said, with a broad smile, and he pulled off his gloves and blew into his hands. 'I've an hour before my classes begin, and I thought I'd come and sit with you. I can read my lesson notes here just as easily as I can at school, and it gives me that little bit longer in the day to be with you.'

He tucked his gloves into the pocket of his thick brown jacket, took off his hat and jacket, hung them over the wooden hooks to the right of the front door, and went across to her.

She turned back to the cupboard and closed the glass doors.

'You didn't have to put the bowl back, you know,' he said, coming to stand behind her.

Sliding his hands around her stomach, he hugged her gently to him and kissed the nape of her neck.

'You'll obviously have been thinking about your grandfather,' he went on, 'and grieving for him—it's only natural— and if holding the china he gave you makes you feel better, then that's what you must do. I haven't forgotten how homesick I was in England, and I know how much you must miss your family, especially at such a time.'

She turned in his arms, looked up at his face and attempted a smile. 'You're right, I *was* thinking about Grandfather. Home won't seem the same without him.'

He loosened his hold on her. 'Rundheim is your home now, *Liebling*,' he said quietly. 'And it'll be the home of our children, too. Not England.'

'I'm so sorry, Franz.' She put her arms around him and pulled him close to her again. 'I spoke without thinking. Of course, I think of Rundheim as home. Wherever you are, that's my home, and it always will be.'

He kissed her forehead. 'And I'm sorry for speaking like that. It's just that while we were clearing the snow, we were talking about what's going on in the country, and saying how worried we were. I really don't understand people. None of us do.'

'Don't fret so, darling Franz.'

'It's hard not to. The Kaiser's now gone, and under the Weimar Constitution, we've got a democratically elected President, a Bill of Rights and a system of proportional representation. If you're over twenty-one, you can vote for the *Reichstag*, and the *Reichstag* makes the laws. You'd think everyone would be delighted.'

'From what you're saying, I'm assuming they're not.'

'No, they're not! They're attacking the Government from both sides. On the left, the Communists don't want democracy—they want a dictatorship of workers. And the right-wing politicians hate the Government even more.'

'And you think there'll be trouble because of that?'

'A man called Wolfgang Kapp is trying hard to make it so. He and others blame the government for signing the Treaty of Versailles, saying its terms are so bad for Germany, and so humiliating. They say it wasn't the German Army that surrendered, but the German Government. I can see trouble ahead, just when we need peace.'

'You're frightening me, Franz.' She put her hand protectively on her stomach.

He hugged her. 'Oh, I'm so sorry, *mein Liebling*. I shouldn't have been talking about this, not now, not when you're so full of grief. And when I'm sure there's no real need to worry. Forgive me.'

Smiling reassuringly, he ran his fingers down her cheek.

'Rundheim's a long way from any large towns, which is where any trouble would be. And as you've so often said about our lovely village, this is a place where everyone cares about everyone else.'

'And it's true.'

'Yes, it is. And that will never change.'

7

K nightsbridge,
April, 1920

HER FACE SET in an expression of acute boredom, Louisa let her reading book fall on to the mahogany occasional table at the end of the sofa, and started to swing her legs backwards and forwards under the seat of the elegant pink plush-velvet sofa that faced the two armchairs in which her parents sat.

Sarah looked up from her book. 'Stop doing that, Louisa, please,' she said. 'You're making it quite difficult to concentrate.'

Louisa gave the sofa two sharp kicks, and stopped. She sighed noisily.

Charles smiled at her. 'You're ten, Lou. You're not a baby any longer, so I suggest you stop behaving like one. You've had your tea, and you've been down here for an hour. Don't you think it's now time that you went back upstairs and asked Nanny to help you get ready for bed?'

'Since you ask, no, I don't think it is. Like you said, I'm not a baby. I'm old enough to decide when to go to bed.'

'That's enough, Louisa!' Sarah said sharply. 'You'll apologise at once for your rudeness.'

'I'm sorry,' Louisa said, and she scowled.

'You need to work on the expression on your face as well as on the words,' Charles said, a hint of amusement in his voice. 'You look anything but sorry.'

Louisa glanced at her father and giggled.

'Rudeness isn't funny, Charles. As your father said, Louisa, it's time you prepared for bed. Nanny will have finished with Christopher by now and she'll be waiting for you.'

'I *really* am sorry, Mummy. Please, let me stay up a little longer? You said you'd tell me what Cousin Nellie said when you went out to tea with her today, and you haven't. Why did she want to see you? Was it about Walter?'

'If Nellie and I had wanted to share our thoughts with you, we would've invited you to join us, wouldn't we?'

'*Was* it about Walter?' Louisa persisted.

Sarah hesitated. 'She did mention him, yes.'

Louisa clasped her knees to her in excitement, and bounced up and down. 'What did she say?'

Sarah stared at her in surprise. 'Of what possible interest can this be to you?'

'Because if Cousin Nellie marries Walter, I'm sure she'll ask me to be her bridesmaid. I've never been a bridesmaid before. Cousin Dorothy was mean and didn't ask me.'

'Even if she had, you wouldn't have gone. No one in the family went to Dorothy's wedding. It was shameful of her, marrying a German.'

Louisa gave another bounce. 'So what did Cousin Nellie say?'

'Just that she's hoping your uncle Joseph will start making an effort to get to know Walter. As yet, he's hardly spent any time with him.'

Charles nodded. 'I'm inclined to say, I agree with Nellie. After what's happened with Robert and Lily, and with Dorothy, it's time that one of Joseph's children married a suitable person. Nellie's his last hope. If Joseph got to know Walter, he'd like him. He's a pleasant lad, and he's both clever and shrewd. He's going to make an excellent solicitor.'

'Nellie seems to think so, too.'

'And what's more, he seems temperamentally perfect for Nellie. As soon as I met him, I could see that, and that's why I invited him to Chorton that weekend. I was certain that he and Nellie would get on well, and they did.'

'I'm sure you're right, Charles, but—'

'Good gracious!' Charles sat upright, and stared at Sarah in mock amazement. 'You don't mean that I might actually have got something right for a change?'

Sarah laughed. 'I'm not that bad, am I?'

Louisa nodded vigorously. 'You *are*, Mummy. You're always telling Daddy off.'

'Don't worry, Lou. As the saying goes, your mother's words are like water off a duck's back.'

'What does that mean?'

'Next time you go to a pond,' he said, 'watch how although ducks dive under the water, they come up looking dry. That's because they've a kind of oil on their feathers that stops the water from sticking to them.'

'I see. At least I think I do.'

'If you really want to know, Louisa, Nellie thinks her father's avoiding Walter because he doesn't approve of the

be a nurse to spend much time with him. He was frequently at Chorton, anyway.' She took hold of his hand with her free hand. 'And while I was falling in love with you, he was falling in love with Lily.'

'Is that your reason to write to him?'

She released his hand and pulled the shawl more tightly around Elke. 'No, it's because, like me, he married someone Father disapproved of. It means that he might be less hostile than Father. Although, I don't know—they work together so they might have made up their differences despite Robert's marriage. Perhaps it would be better to write to Father, after all.'

He shrugged. 'If you think there's any point in persisting. But I hate the thought of seeing you so disappointed again when day after day, there's no letter in reply.'

'I *do* want to give it another try—they're my family. I want Elke to know she's got English relatives. I'm glad we've agreed that I'll speak English to her, and you'll speak German. It's right that she'll know both languages.'

'You must be prepared, *mein Liebling*, that she may not want to speak English as she gets older. At some point, she'll begin to understand what's happening in Germany today, and she might feel that much of the fault lies with England and France.'

'I know that.'

'After all, first, they saddle us with a huge war debt that's going to be really difficult to repay. And then, just to make it even harder, they take away our coal and steel industries, which would've been our means of paying. This hardly gives our new democracy a chance.'

'I do understand it's a difficult time, dearest Franz.' She hesitated a moment. 'Whatever happens, I'll always be English, you know, and will always feel English, even though Rundheim is now my home.' She paused, and gazed anxiously up at him. 'You won't turn our child against England, will you?'

He smiled warmly at her. 'Of course, I won't. I very much enjoyed my time in England. Until I was interned, that is. That was somewhat humiliating.'

'Please, Franz.'

'England gave me you, *geliebte* Dorothy, and I'll always be grateful for that. I promise you that our Elke will know the affection I have for your country, and always will have— provided, of course, that England doesn't act against Germany any more than it's already done.'

'Thank you, dearest.'

He stood up. 'I must go, I'm afraid. Herta will be here before too long,' he said, straightening the feather quilt. 'She'll look after you until I get back. I know she can't wait to see the baby. She'll be even more keen for the next four months to speed by so that you and she will be able to walk your babies together.'

'For Elke's sake, I hope she has a girl, although I know that Karl, like you, would prefer a boy.'

'They will be happy with either,' he said, moving across to the bedroom door. 'I shall come straight home at the end of school, and will do my preparation for tomorrow's classes here. I shall be longing to see little Elke and her mother again.'

THE BEDROOM DOOR OPENED SLIGHTLY, and Dorothy saw Herta's face appear in the gap.

'Come in, Herta,' she called. 'I'm awake.' She glanced down at the wooden crib on the floor next to the bed. 'Elke's asleep, though.'

Herta pushed the door wider open and came further into the room.

'How are you?' she asked. 'Or is that a very silly question after all you've been through? Can I see her?' Not waiting for an answer, she went eagerly round the bed to the crib, and bent over the baby. 'When Franz called for Karl, he said she's the most beautiful baby ever,' she said, gazing at Elke, her voice breaking.

Dorothy laughed. 'And of course he didn't exaggerate.'

'No, he didn't.' Herta's voice was full of wonder. 'She's really lovely, Dorothy.' She looked up at Dorothy, her eyes glistening. 'She truly is.'

'And your baby will be as lovely, too.'

'Of course, she will.' She smiled happily at Dorothy, and then looked back at Elke. 'I'm sure I'm having a girl, but I haven't told Karl. I might be wrong, and in case I am, there's no point in saying something I know will disappoint him.'

'Franz, too, wanted a son, but look at him now! He's besotted with Elke. Karl will be the same if it's a girl.' She changed her position in the bed. 'Before you sit down, which I hope you'll do, will you get yourself a coffee?' she said. 'Franz told me he'd ground some beans this morning, so all you need do is boil the water.'

'I had a coffee at home, so I'm fine, thank you. But can I get you a drink?' Herta asked.

'Franz brought me something.'

Herta pulled a high-backed wooden chair to the side of the bed, and sat down. 'I asked how you were, but I didn't wait for an answer, I was so anxious to see little Elke.'

'I'm tired, which is to be expected,' Dorothy said. 'And I'm very grateful that you're using English today. I don't think I could have coped with German quite this soon after the birth.'

'You speak German brilliantly, Dorothy, and you can even pick up any nuances. You don't yet speak it quite like a German, but you're getting close. And Franz said you're now able to read the newspaper.'

'He's exaggerating a bit, but I *am* getting better, I can tell,' she said with a smile. 'But any improvement is thanks to you as well as to Franz.'

'I've been glad to help. But you know I'm always happy to practise my English, and so is Karl, so whenever you want to switch languages, you must say. Now, is there anything I can do for you or do in the house?'

'I don't think so, thank you. *Frau* Arnstein was very organised yesterday, and very kind. She knew what she was doing, ordered Franz to stay downstairs, and brought Elke safely into the world. And she tidied everything before she left. I'm very grateful to her.'

Herta smiled. 'We're lucky; the Armsteins are very good neighbours.'

'And today, Franz has looked after me very well. I'm so lucky. And I'm so lucky also that you and Karl have helped with the shopping and chores in the last week or so. We couldn't have had better friends.'

'We all feel lucky, then. Franz's arrival came at exactly the right time for Karl. I can tell you now that I'd been worried before you moved here that maybe Karl was restless, and not completely happy, and then you and Franz were here and all was well again.'

Dorothy stared at her in surprise. 'Why would he be restless? You and he are perfect together.'

'I think we are. But you know, I sometimes wondered if that was enough.'

Dorothy frowned in puzzlement. 'I don't understand.'

Herta looked up at the wooden rafters supporting the

ceiling, and then back at Dorothy. 'Nor do I really.' She smiled at Dorothy. 'But you're tired, and I should be letting you sleep, or we should be talking about your sweet little Elke.'

'I'm not too tired, Herta, for you to tell me what you mean. And we'll have a lot of time in the years to come to talk about Elke, and about your children, too.'

She manoeuvred herself into a sitting position, pulled her quilt higher, re-arranged the woollen shawl around her shoulders, and stared at Herta. 'Now I'm ready to listen.'

Herta shrugged. 'It's sounds a little silly,' she began, smoothing down her pinafore, 'but it was so easy for Karl and me. Perhaps too easy, I think, and not very exciting. At least, not for him.'

'What do you mean?' Dorothy asked.

'We went to the local schools in our neighbouring villages, and we met when we trained to be teachers. We fell in love and got married. When the war came, Karl had no choice but to go into the army.'

'I understand that.'

'He was seen to be good with writing and to be good with ideas, so he was kept in Germany to help with the administration of the General Staff's internal affairs. After the war, we settled here, near where we grew up, and Karl teaches in the Gymnasium here.'

'And isn't that good?'

'I don't know if it is. Every day, he teaches literature to his students, literature written in different parts of the world, that tells of the different histories of those places, of their different customs, of the different scenery that surrounds those people.'

'Franz said he's a brilliant teacher.'

'But all he's known for himself is life in a village, and for a short time, in a small town, always surrounded by people, most of whom, like him, have never been far from the place where they were born. Everything he knows about the world outside has come from books. By marrying me when he did, he missed the chance to explore some of those places he's read about. And this is a source of regret, I'm sure.'

Dorothy nodded. 'I can see how this might worry you.'

'It did until you and Franz came along. But no longer. You come from London, a large town we've heard so much about, and from a family very different from the families who live here in Rundheim.'

Dorothy smiled. 'That's an understatement.'

'And Franz is a man who did something that I think in his heart, Karl wishes he'd done—he went to live in another country. He had new experiences, and was able to talk with people who had different backgrounds and ideas from his.'

'I see,' Dorothy said slowly.

'But now it is all right,' Herta said happily. 'Now you and Franz are living here, Karl has someone he can talk with, who can discuss from experience and a wider knowledge, not just from the pages of a book, and this has been wonderful for him. He's a different man now. So it is us, Karl and me, who are the lucky ones.'

Dorothy reached out her hand to Herta. 'Then we're all lucky, and nothing at all, I'm sure, will ever change our luck.'

K nightsbridge,
  Sunday afternoon, late June, 1920

HER FACE SULLEN, Louisa stood in the reception room and stared out of the window at the row of houses on the opposite side of the road.

The late afternoon sun had brought warmth to the grey-brown bricks of the row of three storeyed houses, and coated with gloss the black wrought-iron railings that fronted the narrow balconies outside the first floor windows and the iron railings on either side of the few stone steps leading up to the front door of each house.

Hearing a sound behind her, she turned and saw her mother coming into the room.

'It's still really nice outside,' Louisa said angrily, and sat heavily on the window seat, glaring at Sarah. 'I keep on asking, but you haven't told me why we had to leave Chorton so early.'

'We'd had a lovely weekend, and it was time for it to end,' Sarah snapped, sitting in the armchair.

'But you promised we could stay at Chorton till tomorrow morning as it was Cousin Nellie's birthday weekend. You said Daddy wouldn't have to go to the bank tomorrow, even though it was Monday.'

'I realise that.'

'Weekend means staying till Monday. And Christopher, too, said you promised. So why did we have to leave as soon as we got back from the picnic by the river? It's not fair.'

'We were there for the most important part of the weekend,' Sarah told her firmly. 'The birthday party for Nellie last night was lovely. Mrs Spencer did herself proud with that delicious buffet, and we let you and Christopher stay up late and join in with the first few games. You enjoyed the evening, didn't you?'

'Only until you made Lily take us up when she went upstairs to check on baby James,' Louisa said sulkily. 'I'm not six like Christopher. I should've been allowed to stay up longer.'

'At the moment, you sound considerably younger than six. What a disappointment that is after you looked so very grown up last night.'

'I'm not a baby, you know.'

'Indeed, your appearance was rather too grown up, I suspect, for your aunt Maud. She hinted very pointedly that she didn't think a ten-year-old should be wearing a miniature version of her mother's dress.'

'But my dress had pink lace over the cream taffeta, and your lace was black. And you wouldn't let me wear black beads like you did, so we weren't dressed the same.'

'Be that as it may. I could tell it was what Aunt Maud was

thinking. And she obviously disapproved also of Christopher wearing long trousers with his dark-blue velveteen jacket.'

'I really liked Lily's scarlet dress,' Louisa said. 'I'd like one like that, too. And in silk like hers.'

'I can just imagine what Aunt Maud would say if she saw you in anything like that!' Sarah exclaimed with a laugh. 'You're at least ten years too young for such a style.'

'And the sparkling bands she wore over her long scarlet gloves were made of the same beads that were on her dress. Did you notice that? I'd like some glittering bands like that, too, and the same sort of gloves.'

Louisa held up her arms and made as if rolling long gloves down to her elbows.

'Can I have gloves like them, please?'

'Yes, in a few years' time.'

She lowered her arms and glared at her mother.

'Come on, Louisa,' Sarah said briskly. 'You've had an excellent weekend—don't spoil it now. And it wasn't only last night that was enjoyable, was it? You and Christopher had a lovely time this morning, too, playing hide and seek in the thickets and gardens with Nellie, Walter and Robert. And Lily let you carry little James for a while, didn't she?'

'I suppose so.'

'And we had a delicious lunch on the terrace with all the large terracotta pots of flowers around us. And you enjoyed the wagon ride to the river for our picnic. You were even allowed to take the reins for a while. You've had a wonderful weekend, darling, and it doesn't really matter that we've come home a little early, does it?'

'But Robert was going to teach me to play draughts this evening.'

'He'll teach you another time, I'm sure. And you're forgetting, the party had already started to break up. Aunt Maud took Uncle Thomas and Aunt Alice back to London immediately after our lovely Sunday lunch. They didn't stay for the picnic. So we weren't the first to leave, by any means.'

'Aunt Alice looked very pretty, didn't she? I liked the white dress she was wearing. I want one like that, too. Uncle Thomas is always so bad-tempered, though.'

'Don't forget, he's frequently in pain.'

'That's no excuse. If it wasn't for Daddy teaching her how to play charades and do those paper games, Aunt Alice would have hated the party. You'd think Uncle Thomas would've been pleased that Aunt Alice was being looked after by Daddy, but he wasn't—he was scowling.'

'It can't be easy for Uncle Thomas,' Sarah said firmly. 'You should remember that. And if you ever notice him struggling with anything, you should immediately offer to help. Don't wait to be asked.'

Louisa frowned. 'I'm not going to let you change the subject, you know. Why *did* we come home early, Mummy? And why didn't Daddy come back with us? Why did Uncle Joseph drive us back?'

Sarah hesitated. 'It's nothing for you to worry about, Louisa. But when we got back from the picnic, we found that Lily wasn't there. Daddy and Walter went out to look for her. And so did Cousin Robert.'

'Where was she?'

Sarah gave her a slight smile. 'If anyone knew that, they wouldn't have needed to spread out and look for her, would they? She probably just went out for a breath of fresh air. But we were somewhat surprised that she'd left the baby upstairs on his own. He's only just turned one, after all, and his nanny had been given the weekend off.'

'But being a baby, he wasn't going to go for a walk, was he?'

Sarah smiled. 'True. But Joseph had wondered if James might be coming down with a cold, and that was why Lily hadn't joined us on the picnic. It just seemed strange that she'd leave him for any time at all, let alone for so long.'

'When we were in the cart, waiting for her to climb in, I heard Uncle Joseph tell her he'd send for a doctor if he thought it necessary.'

'That's right. We all find Lily a tremendous bore, the way she's always going on about James, but one has to admit that she's a very caring mother. She can't have intended to leave him for long, so we were worried that she might've had an accident. Since they were all out trying to find her, it seemed more sensible that we come home.'

Louisa kicked the base of the window seat. 'When will Daddy get back?'

'Tomorrow, I expect. I doubt it'll be this evening. Unless they found her fairly soon after we left, of course. If they did, he'll be back before long.'

There was a soft tap on the reception room door.

'Come in,' Sarah called.

The door opened and their nanny stood in the doorway, holding Christopher's hand.

He was ready for bed, and was shifting his weight backwards and forwards from one slippered foot to the other. Over his pyjamas, he wore a plaid dressing gown tied around his waist by a tasselled cord.

'I beg your pardon for interrupting you, Mrs Sarah, but Christopher was anxious to see his father before he went to bed. Coming home earlier than planned seems to have unsettled him. Also that Mr Charles didn't return with you.'

'Given the circumstances, you were right to bring

Christopher downstairs, Nanny. You can leave him here with us, and I'll take him up in a little while. Louisa can go up at the same time. Thank you.'

The nanny released Christopher's hand, and left the room.

He ran across to the sofa where Sarah was sitting, and sat down next to her.

'You *are* a baby, Christopher,' Louisa said.

Sarah stared at her in displeasure. 'He's understandably upset, Louisa. You, too, asked for an explanation for our hasty departure, if you recall.'

She looked down at Christopher, and smiled. 'Daddy isn't back yet, darling, but there's nothing to worry about. I was just explaining to Louisa that Lily went for a walk and might have hurt herself, so Daddy and the others are looking for her.'

He looked up at her. 'Uncle Joseph will be pleased that Aunt Lily's gone. He hates her,' he said solemnly.

Sarah looked at him in surprise. 'What makes you say such a strange thing, darling?'

'Because he does. He's always giving her horrible looks.'

She gave a little laugh. 'I'm sure you're mistaken.'

'He won't be,' Louisa cut in. 'Christopher notices everything. When we went up to bed last night, he told me that Uncle Thomas was looking very angry with Daddy and Aunt Alice when we were playing charades. He didn't like it when they were laughing. I hadn't noticed that, but when I thought about it, I realised he was right.'

'Good gracious, Christopher! What a lot of hostility you seem to have found during what I thought was a lovely evening. I think we all know that Uncle Joseph would have preferred Robert to marry someone more suitable, but to say that he hates Lily is a little strong, I rather think.'

'He does,' Christopher insisted.

'And as for Uncle Thomas's attitude, in all probability, it was frustration and wistfulness that you saw on his face, not anger. And possibly a little envy, too. He'll have wanted to be able to move around easily with Aunt Alice himself, and join in with the games. But given his disability, neither of those was really possible. It won't have been anything more than that.'

'I like Lily, and I don't like Uncle Joseph,' Christopher said bluntly. 'Lily read Louisa and me a story when she took us upstairs last night. She's nice. But Uncle Joseph frightens me.'

Sarah turned slightly towards him. 'Now you listen to me, Christopher. Uncle Joseph is not just head of the family, he's also the chairman of Linford & Sons. One day you'll need a good job. Daddy's a banker, and we'd rather hoped you'd join him in the bank. But from what your tutor has said, and from what we've seen for ourselves, you've no interest at all in numbers.'

Christopher pulled a face.

'So I'm right, then—you're unlikely to want to follow in Daddy's footsteps. It might be, though, that construction would interest you—there are many different aspects to it. If so, because you're family, Uncle Joseph would see that you were taught everything you needed to know, as he did with Robert, and he'd give you a good position in the company.'

'Would I be the boss?'

She smiled. 'No. Cousin Robert will take over as chairman when your uncle retires, but there are other important posts to be had. Make no mistake, Linford & Sons is an extremely successful firm, and will continue to be so as your uncle's a shrewd businessman. You would do well to make sure that you stay on the right side of him.'

'I don't want to build houses. That'd be boring. And I don't want to work in a bank. That'd be boring, too. I want to do what Lily used to do.'

'I think not, Christopher.'

'She told me that when she met Robert, she was working on a farm, and she used to milk cows, and plough up fields, and mend fences. She said she could do just about any job that needed doing on a farm. I like being out in the country-side, so that's what I want to do.'

'All I can say is, there's plenty of time for you to change your mind. Now, it's quite late enough—both of you must go up to bed. Daddy obviously won't be back tonight, so there's no point in you waiting up. But I'm sure that everything's fine in Chorton, and that Lily's been found by now, so there's no need for you to worry.'

Neither Christopher nor Louisa moved. They stared at Sarah, their faces anxious.

'Well, then,' Sarah said with a smile. 'To give you some-thing nice to think about when you go to bed—and this is a big secret, so you're not to tell Daddy—but you've probably got a new baby cousin by now.'

Louisa screwed up her forehead. 'Whose is it?'

'Nellie told me a while ago that she'd seen a letter written by her sister—your cousin Dorothy—to Uncle Joseph. In it, Dorothy told him she was expecting a baby in the spring. I imagine the baby's been born now.'

'When can we see it?' Christopher asked.

'I'm afraid we'll never see it as Cousin Dorothy made a completely unacceptable marriage. But you now know that you've another cousin.'

'Why is it a secret from Daddy?' Christopher asked.

'Because Uncle Joseph doesn't know that Nellie read his

letter, and in a moment of carelessness, your father might tell Uncle Joseph that she did. You shouldn't really read a letter addressed to someone else, should you?'

'Yes, you should,' said Louisa. 'How else would you know what's in it?'

10

R*undheim,*
August, 1920

DOROTHY ROSE FROM THE TABLE, still clutching her letter, and went across the room to the large black pram in which lay three-month-old Elke.

Bending low over the pram, she gazed down at the baby. Then she straightened up and turned towards the table, her eyes filled with tears.

Franz dropped his newspaper and stood up, concern on his face.

'What's wrong?' he asked, hurrying across the room to her. He hugged her tightly, and then, with his arm around her, he led her back to the table, dragged his chair next to hers, and they sat down together, his arm still around her shoulders.

She glanced at the letter again. 'Nellie told me about her birthday party at Chorton, and how it ended in disarray.'

suppose we can add that the war is behind us and we've learned our lesson the hard way. As we've been ordered to get rid of the air force, end conscription, and hand over our weapons, we'll never be able to go to war again.'

11

J oseph's Club, London,
   October, 1920

NODDING from time to time at fellow members he passed, Joseph made his way across the Club's library, inhaling with pleasure as he walked the aroma from oak-panelled walls that had long been engrained with the mingled scents of beeswax and tobacco.

When he reached his favourite leather armchair, one of the two that flanked the marble fireplace, he sat down, loosened the lower two buttons of his waistcoat, indicated to the waiter who'd appeared at his elbow to come back later, and settled comfortably into the seat.

He took his pipe from one of the pockets in his jacket, and a tin of Three Nuns tobacco and a gold lighter from another.

Putting a wad of tobacco into the palm of his hand, he

rolled the bowl of his pipe around his palm, letting the pipe fill itself. Then he tapped down the tobacco and added a few short strands of tobacco to the bowl. He breathed in through the stem of the pipe to check its draw, tamped the tobacco again, and then lit it with the flame from his lighter.

Leaning back, he drew deeply on the pipe as he sat there, surrounded by the soothing low buzz of men's voices, waiting for Charles to arrive.

A short time later, he heard footsteps. Looking up, he saw that Charles was approaching. Straightening up, he beamed at him.

'You look like the cat who got the cream,' Charles said, sitting down opposite Joseph. 'And I'm not surprised— congratulations on Nellie's engagement. You won't be sorry you gave your consent, and more to the point, Nellie won't be, either.'

'Thanks, Charles,' Joseph said, and he raised his finger to the hovering waiter. 'We had champagne at Robert's yesterday, so if you agree, we'll toast Nellie and Walter today with our customary cognac. It feels apt now that the upset with Lily is some months in the past, and we've cause for celebration today.'

'Agreed. So tell me about yesterday. You and Walter disappeared into the garden after the excellent lunch that Robert had laid on, and the next thing we knew, Walter and Nellie were announcing their engagement. I take it Walter didn't go down on one knee on the grass, not in that suit!'

Joseph laughed. 'You're right, he didn't. Well, there's not really much to say. He asked for my consent and I was delighted to give it.'

'Congratulations again.'

'As you've always said, he's a fine young man with the makings of an excellent lawyer, and we both know how much help and support he's given the family in recent months. What's more, I'm confident that he's capable of keeping our Nellie in check. And not many men could do that!'

Charles smiled. 'She's a great girl. If Louisa turns out to be as delightful as Nellie, Sarah and I would be thrilled.'

Joseph nodded. 'It's kind of you to say so. She certainly knows what she wants. Walter chose yesterday to ask for my consent because he was under orders from Nellie to do so, you know,' he added in amusement. 'She figured, quite correctly, that I'd be in such a good mood, seeing that things were so much better at Robert's, that this would be a good time for Walter to pounce.'

Both laughed.

He paused while the waiter placed a snifter of cognac on the low mahogany table next to each armchair, and then left.

'Having said that, I was ready a long time ago to give my consent,' Joseph went on, as he picked up his glass. 'We invited Walter for dinner last night and discussed possible dates, and also the wording for the newspaper announcement.'

'You do move quickly!'

'You would, too, if Nellie was behind you, pushing you along!'

Both laughed again.

'Not surprisingly, like so many young girls today, she wants a June wedding, so it'll be June next year. She wants Louisa to be her bridesmaid, and Christopher to be a pageboy. James will be able to walk by then, and I think she's going to ask Christopher to hold James's hand and walk him down the aisle so that James, too, can be part of the procession. But let her ask them herself.'

'I will. Louisa will be ecstatic. And so will Sarah. She knows that she'd never have heard the end of it if Louisa hadn't been asked. Lou's been discussing what to wear ever since we saw the proprietorial look in Nellie's eye whenever she gazed at Walter.'

'If that's the case, I'm delighted we'll be lightening the load on Sarah,' Joseph said. 'Nellie owes her a lot.'

'She does?' Charles raised his eyebrows questioningly.

'As I understand it, Sarah responded to Nellie's anguished plea for help when she thought I wasn't making any effort to get to know Walter. And I must admit, I wasn't. I know you sang his praises, but at first, I was reticent—his background and lack of personal finances, you know.'

Charles grinned at him. 'We all know the way you think, Joseph.'

Joseph smiled. 'It seems that Sarah reminded Nellie that I'm always interested in anything to do with property, and she suggested that although Walter was articled in a general practice, it might be worth him keeping an eye on what was happening in the field of Property Law. She thought that if he waylaid me with what he'd found, I'd be sure to notice him. Clever Sarah—it worked.'

'Well, I couldn't be more pleased.' Charles picked up his snifter. 'Did you know that Walter's asked me to be Best Man?'

'I didn't, but I'm not surprised. You introduced them, after all.'

They each took a sip of their cognac.

'Do you realise, Joseph,' Charles began, putting his glass back on the table, 'we've been sitting here for almost thirty minutes, and you haven't yet mentioned the housing market? I trust that it's going well, and that your failure to bring up your favourite subject within minutes of my arrival doesn't bode ill.'

'Fear not, Charles. My silence on the matter merely indicates my degree of pleasure in knowing that in less than a year, Nellie will be marrying a highly suitable man, who clearly adores her. But since you've mentioned the housing market—'

Charles gave a theatrical yawn.

'—we're doing as we were doing back in February when you came to the site and saw the estate houses that we're building in pairs, rather than in lines as we used to. We've built a great many more like that since then, and all on that same model—three bedrooms upstairs and an internal bathroom, all for family use as servants' quarters are no longer needed.'

'Indeed.'

'There's a plumbed-in kitchen and an internal water closet, and in everything we've done, we've rigorously followed the new regulations about drainage and sewage, and making sure that there's separate clean running water for drinking.'

'I must admit, I did think the houses were impressive.'

'And so, I'm happy to say, do the buyers. Not surprisingly, given the demand for houses and the reasonableness of the price and attractiveness of both the houses and the location, they're selling very well, and that's why we're still building them in great numbers.'

'Do you expect the demand to last?'

'In a word, yes. Especially from people at the managerial and administrative levels. It's good news for the future.'

'And what about the demand from those not at that level? Manual workers, for example.'

'Admittedly, that's falling. But as we're still building

property for rent, we're meeting the need for both kinds of housing, and I'm sure we'll be landlords as well as builders for some time to come. Our decision a few years ago to use some of the profit from our wartime contracts to buy up land along the main routes into the city has really paid off.'

'I'll say this for you, Joseph, you've a good eye for the housing market. You're always ahead of the rest by a step or two.'

'And that's the way it's going to stay, Charles, whether it's me in the chair, or Robert. Robert, too, has a real feel for the the business. Linford & Sons will be in safe hands when that time comes.'

'It's a long way off, I'm sure.'

'I certainly hope so. And it's more likely to be so now that Nellie, who's supremely gifted in finding ways to separate me from the contents of my wallet, which has a somewhat ageing effect, will be Walter's responsibility in a year's time. It'll be poor Walter who's taking the knock. Let's drink to that.'

They raised their glasses.

'How's Thomas doing with the interiors?' Charles asked. 'It's very different from the life of excitement and adventure that he'd always hoped to have.'

'Losing a leg and a hand makes a difference to anyone's life. I'm sure that dealing with house interiors isn't what he would've chosen—he was clearly bored stiff in the short amount of time that he worked for the company before the war—but he's had to accept his limitations.'

Charles swirled the cognac in his glass. 'D'you really think he *has* accepted them? Because I'm not so sure. He invariably declines invitations to join the family for things such as Robert's monthly Sunday lunches.'

'He went to Chorton for Nellie's birthday, didn't he?'

'Because he was virtually forced to go. And he wouldn't want to upset Nellie. He's obviously fond of her. But he's abrupt and surly whenever we do meet, both to us and to his wife. Yet Alice is charming. She's an extremely pretty young woman, and very considerate of his needs, but he seems to delight in belittling her.'

Joseph nodded. 'I often wonder what she saw in him. If she'd seen him before the war, the attraction would be easy to understand—he was a good-looking man who could be excellent company. But when she nursed him in the hospital, he was long past his best. There's no accounting for it.'

'But he's still an attractive man, when he isn't scowling. And on the rare moments when he forgets to resent the fact that you and I stayed at home and contributed to the war effort in a different way from him, and didn't go off to fight, as he did, he can be very amusing.'

'That's generous of you, Charles, since he seems particularly angry with you.'

'I imagine that he's jealous of us all. Severe injuries like his probably take a lot longer to adjust to than we'd realised.'

'Well, for Alice's sake, and for ours, let's hope the process in Thomas's case is speeded up.'

'To go back to Nellie's wedding,' Charles said, glancing at Joseph above the rim of his snifter. 'Are you inviting Dorothy?'

'No,' Joseph said bluntly. 'As I told her when she married the Hun, she's no daughter of mine.' He paused. 'She'll have had her child a few months ago. I'm sure that Nellie's in touch with her, but doesn't want me to know that. She thinks I'll be angry. Knowing Nellie, she'll be struggling with how to let me know which I've got—another grandson or a granddaughter—without disclosing that she's writing to Dorothy.'

'Do you want to know?'

Joseph shrugged. 'Not really. It's nothing to do with me now.' He finished his cognac. 'Maybe I *would* like to know, but that's all.'

R undheim,
  October, 1922

AT THE BEGINNING of what turned out to feel a very long week, for the second time, Dorothy lost a baby in the initial stages of pregnancy.

Having lost one baby in the first few months of a pregnancy about a year after Elke had been born, and aware of her family history of miscarriages, a part of her had been expecting it to happen again.

But another part of her couldn't believe that she might be so unlucky a second time, and at first, when the bleeding had come, and then the pains, she'd flatly refused to accept that she was losing another child.

She couldn't be—not again.

But it had happened.

And she'd been devastated, absolutely devastated, and Franz, too.

Although the baby in her womb had been there for no more than a few weeks, they'd already started talking about their child's future.

But now, forced to confront the cruel realisation that it no longer had a future, both were overwhelmed by their sense of loss, and by the deep pain of having nothing to hold in their arms and grieve over.

They couldn't even kiss their baby and say goodbye, it had been so young.

All they had was the knowledge that for a short amount of time, the son or daughter that they'd both so longed for had lived within Dorothy.

Perhaps she should have done something differently, she'd sobbed to Franz in the early days of their loss. Perhaps it had been the coffee she'd drunk. Maybe she should have stuck to water.

No matter how hard he'd tried to reassure her that she wasn't to blame, that it was an act of nature and nothing she'd done, she'd been fraught with a sense of guilt that intensified her anguish.

Much as he'd wanted to stay at home with Dorothy, Franz had no choice but to go to the school and teach his classes.

In his absence, Dorothy had moved slowly around the house, unable to stop crying, unwilling to go out, ever clinging to Elke as if afraid to let her go.

In the evenings, Franz, suffering, too, could do nothing but stand back helplessly and watch her, not knowing how to comfort her. And greatly in need of comfort himself.

At the end of the week, his lunch finished, sitting at the wooden table, a glass of *schnapps* next to him, the slight odour of boiled cabbage lingering in the air, Franz stared at Dorothy's back as she stood in front of her two kitchen sinks, her head bowed as mechanically she washed their glasses and bowls in the soapy water in one sink, rinsed them in the soda water in the adjacent sink, and put them on the board to drain.

He knew that he had to speak, had to try to lift her from the dejection in which he could see she was mired.

'Just because I can't see your face, Dorothy,' he said gently, 'it doesn't mean that I don't know you're crying.'

She spun round and faced him, the washing-up brush in her hand. 'It's better than sitting there like you, cold and dry-eyed,' she railed at him, her voice breaking. 'We've lost our baby, Franz! It's happened again! And I don't know why.'

She thumped her chest with her free hand, and tried to keep talking, but her words were swallowed in a choking sob, and she put her hand to her mouth.

He looked at her, his face white. 'I feel the same distress as you, my love—of course I do—but I've had to pull myself together and go to work. The pupils must be taught.'

'And it's time I did the same, is it? Pulled myself together? That's what you're saying, is it? Well, I can't, Franz. I can't.'

Water dripped from the bristles of the brush and gathered at her feet in milky-white pools of suds that spread across the floor. 'Herta's just had another baby,' she cried. 'And Nellie had a little girl in March. What's wrong with me?'

With a loud wail, she turned back to the sink.

He got up, moved swiftly across to her, put his arms around her and kissed the back of her head. 'We've got Elke,' he said, hugging her. 'So you know you can have babies, and one day you *will* have another, I'm sure. If you can tell yourself that what has happened may have been for the best, then it might help you feel better. This is what I'm having to do.'

She pushed him back from her with her elbows, dropped the brush into the sink, turned and stared up at him. The ridge of the sink was hard against her spine, her face accusing. 'For the best?' Her voice rose. 'How can my babies dying be for the best?'

One of his colleagues had explained to him, he told her, that if a woman miscarried, it was often because the baby had something wrong with it. No parents would want to give birth to a child that would have a life of suffering, would they? Miscarriage was nature's way of making sure that their babies were perfect.

'I wanted our baby, perfect or not. And you should've done, too.'

'Of course, I did.' He put his arms around her, but she pushed them away. 'I would have loved our child whatever it was like,' he said. 'I expressed myself badly. But surely we wouldn't want any child to have so much wrong that they felt pain and couldn't live a normal, happy life?'

'I suppose not.'

'And when you hold our next baby, and see that it's completely healthy, you'll be glad that things turned out as they did.'

She gave a loud sob. 'I don't know if I can go through this again.'

He pulled her gently to him and put his arms around her again. Relaxing, she leaned against his chest. 'You could if you had to,' he said. 'Any woman who could leave the family she loved, and leave her country, to come and live with a very ordinary man like me, without any of the material comforts she would've had in England, can do anything she puts her mind to.'

'I don't know,' she said through her tears.

'I do. You're stronger than you realise, Dorothy. One day, we will have another child, and in the meantime, we have our Elke. Our serious little Elke, who's a miniature of you, and who's inherited your courage, too, I'm sure.'

'She's certainly serious, but she *is* a joy, isn't she?' Dorothy said, her voice quivering. 'And as we've got her, it wouldn't be too terrible if I couldn't have another baby, would it, even though I know you wanted a son very much, and so did I?'

Tears started trickling down her cheeks again.

He kissed first one wet cheek, and then the other. 'Of course, it wouldn't,' he said, stroking her hair. 'Our Elke has the energy of two children or more, and she's going to keep us on our toes. You see, I haven't forgotten my English expressions.'

'Indeed, you haven't.' She wiped her eyes with her apron and attempted a watery smile. 'I'm glad we use English as well as German at home as both are part of Elke's heritage. And now I must finish the washing-up.'

'Before you do, it's occurred to me that perhaps it would be better for you not to go to Karl's tomorrow evening. You don't need to, you know. They'd understand.'

She kissed him on his cheek. 'I shall be fine, Franz. You mustn't worry about me. I'm not going to cry any more, I promise. You're right that it's time I pulled myself together, even if you didn't put your thought into words. I'm very happy for Herta and Karl, and I want to help them celebrate that little Sofia now has a brother. If they thought it would hurt me too much to see baby Hans, they might start avoiding me, and I would hate that.'

He tightened his arms around her. 'I love you, Dorothy. You have a good heart. That you were sent to Alexandra

Palace was my good fortune. Every day, I feel deep gratitude that you are my wife.'

She put her hand to his cheek. 'And I love you, too, Franz. I really do. And I didn't mean the nasty things I said —I know you're grieving, too.'

'Why don't you leave the rest of the bowls and sit with me for a while?' he suggested. And he took her hand and led her to the table. 'After all, I'll have to do some marking shortly, and then prepare for tomorrow's lessons.'

'There's nothing that can't wait, I suppose,' she said, as they sat down side by side. 'I was going to bottle the apples Ruth Weinberger gave me, but it's a little late to start on them, and I'm not in the mood. I'd much rather sit here with you.'

She attempted another smile.

'Good, because there's something I wanted to talk to you about. I was going to discuss it with you a few days ago, but with what's happened ... well, you know.'

'What is it?'

'I'm thinking of joining the National Socialist German Workers' Party.'

'What?' She straightened up, and wiped the damp from her face with her forearm. 'But you don't like extremism, left or right. You've always argued for moderation. And that's an extreme party. At least, it is if I've understood correctly what you've been saying about it for the past couple of years.'

He coloured. 'I *do* still mistrust extremism, and I *do* still favour moderation. But realistically, we're not going to have a moderate government again, or not for a very long time. And since that's the situation, I think I'd be wise to do what Karl and most of my colleagues have done, and that's join the Party.'

She stared at him in amazement. 'You mean Karl's joined! After everything he's said about them?'

'And still does say, but not publicly. Neither of us agrees with everything Adolf Hitler says. But I do think people need someone to make us feel better about ourselves again after that humiliating Armistice, and Hitler seems to be able to do that.'

'I suppose that makes sense,' she said slowly. 'The Party's name is quite a mouthful, though.'

'Ah, but increasingly people are calling it the Nazi Party for short. It used to be called the Nazi-Sozi Party, from *Nationalist* and *Sozialist*, but with the *Nationalist* element becoming increasingly important, they dropped the *Sozialist* bit.'

'Nazi is certainly easier to say.'

'But the funny thing is, the term Nazi was already in use long before the Party came into being. Personally, I'm amazed they let themselves be called Nazis because it's actually a colloquial, derogatory name for a backward peasant. It comes from Ignaz, a shortened form of Ignatius. You hear it all over Bavaria, where the Party began. It was the people there who were opposed to the Nazis, who first called them by that name.'

'It does seem strange it's allowed,' she said. She shrugged her shoulders. 'Well, if you think it's the best thing to do, then join. After all, it's only one party among many. It can't do any harm, can it?'

There are some issues about the interiors of the new estate houses that I need to discuss with Thomas. What are you planning to do today?' he asked, pushing his chair back and standing up.

'I can assure you, I won't be embroidering or following Mrs Morley throughout the day, checking up on her as she goes from one task to another. I'm having morning coffee with Sarah. Nellie said she might drop in at Sarah's later and bring Emily with her. If she does, I'll leave as soon after that as I can. Emily's a delightful child, but an extremely lively one, and I'll have said what I want to say by then.'

'Which is?'

'That Louisa needs to be disciplined. Her behaviour is appalling. I'm amazed that Sarah and Charles tolerate such rudeness.'

'As I've said before whenever we've had this discussion —she's only seventeen. Our three were spirited, too, at that age. It's easy to forget that. Furthermore, Louisa was twelve at the time of the trouble. We don't know how much she knew about what was going on, but she'll have sensed that something was wrong. We shouldn't underestimate the effect it could have had on her.'

Maud smiled. 'While I'm delighted to hear you speak in support of your niece, Joseph—a pleasure rarely afforded me, I might say—what happened in the past is no excuse for Louisa's behaviour in the present. None of our children was ever rude in the way that she is to Charles and Sarah, and to the rest of the family, too.'

'I'll admit, it *does* seem excessive at times.'

'While her attitude towards Sarah doesn't entirely surprise me—they've never really got on, not in the way that Louisa has always got on with Charles—her rudeness these days to Charles, too, *does* surprise me. At her age, she's old enough to know better.'

'Go easily, Maud, won't you? Mothers can be touchy when it comes to criticism of their children.'

'I assure you, I'll approach the subject with subtlety.'

'Then that, my dear Maud, will be another first time.'

14

R *undheim,*
    End of June, 1927

DOROTHY COULDN'T REMEMBER the heat being so relentless, or so dry, in any previous June.

It was taking every ounce of her energy to push the pram up the steep hill that led back to the centre of the village, and considerably longer than usual.

With the sun beating down on her head and her back, and with clouds of dust billowing up from the ground at each turn of the wheels and sticking to everything, including the baby, she was forced to pause every few minutes to wipe the dirt from her sweat-damp face and to clean Dieter's face and hands.

It had already been hot when she'd gone out earlier on her own to do her shopping. And later, when she'd left the house with the baby, and had realised that the sun had grown even stronger, she'd hesitated about whether she should be taking Dieter for a walk.

But just like Elke when she, too, had been a year old, Dieter was suffering considerable pain from teething, and knowing that the motion of the pram would settle him, she'd overcome her reservations.

The moment she reached the halfway point up the hill, a loud explosion of jazz erupted with force from a nearby building. Startled, she stopped abruptly and stared at the half-timbered *Kaiserhalle* on her right.

The musicians must be practising for the evening's entertainment, she thought. And since she felt in need of a short break, she wheeled the pram to the pile of wooden planks stacked next to the track, sat down on the top plank, and rocking the pram to and fro, listened to the music.

When the music stopped, and it was clear that the rehearsal had finished, she glanced from the hall to the pub next to it.

It was where Franz and his friends went after the Party meetings. She knew how much he liked the hard-boiled eggs they sold, pickled in a mixture of vinegar and pepper, and since she'd never been able to do them as well herself, she decided to buy him a couple.

Standing up, she brushed the dust from her dark blue cotton dress as best she could, and then wheeled the pram to the pub doorway, put on its brake, and went into the dim interior.

In addition to buying two of the eggs in the large glass jar on the counter, she bought three bread rolls and a plate of *Frickadelle*. She'd come to quite like the flattened balls of minced meat, which they ate cold with mustard or horse-radish, and they would make for a quick and easy meal that evening.

Not that they needed to eat early after all, she thought as she went back outside. She put her shopping into the pram and started pushing the pram up the last stretch of hill that led to the crossroads. Not now that Franz had decided not to go to the meeting.

She'd been very glad when he'd told her that he wouldn't be going that evening, and that he might not go again, both because she'd have his company on what would have been a Party evening, and also because it suggested that he might be pulling slightly back from the Party, and in her view, that would be no bad thing.

When she reached the top of the hill, she paused. Wiping her forehead with the palm of her hand, she turned to look back towards the countryside in which she'd just been walking.

At the place where the track left the town and disappeared from sight behind the undulating hills and fields, stood the church, its square white tower topped by a tapering peak of pale grey stone.

The church marked the edge of the town and the start of a deep green landscape, pinpointed with vibrant colour from the wild flowers that grew in abundance, and with sparks of brilliant blue from the tiny lakes that dotted the area.

She lifted her gaze to the band of dark green pines that rose from the distant valley, and beyond their jagged peaks to the backdrop of lilac-hazed crests that reached towards the azure blue sky.

Standing there with the sun beating down upon her, watching the buzzards soar from the far hills, she drank in the view that she'd come to love.

'And how's little Dieter today, *Frau* Hartmann?' she heard a voice behind her ask.

She turned to see a woman in a mid-calf pale grey dress and a brown cotton headscarf coming towards her.

'Good day, *Frau* Arnstein,' she replied, putting on the brake. 'He's finally stopped crying, thank you. I'm hoping his teeth have come through at last.'

Frau Arnstein peered into the pram, and then looked back at Dorothy, her face creasing into a smile. 'He gets more like his father every day, with that fair hair and those blue eyes. So different from Elke.'

Dorothy nodded. 'I know. He's a miniature of Franz, and Franz says Elke's a little version of me. But tell me, how's *Herr* Arnstein? Is he better now?'

'God be praised, he is. He finds this heat very difficult, though. But don't we all? When he brings your eggs tomorrow, you'll see how much improved he is.'

'That's very kind of you. But you've already given us so many eggs.'

Frau Arnstein waved away Dorothy's gratitude. '*Herr* Hartmann keeps our steps clear of snow in the winter, which my husband can't do because of his back, and you shop for me when my arthritis is bad. It's a pleasure to have a way of thanking you.'

'Well, it's appreciated.'

Frau Arnstein nodded. She tightened the kerchief bow under her chin and wiped the perspiration from her face with one end of the bow.

'I must go,' she said. 'It's my week for helping to clean the synagogue. At least it'll be cool inside. Goodbye, *Frau* Hartmann.' She leaned over the pram. 'Goodbye, little Dieter.'

'He's no longer so little,' Dorothy said with a laugh. 'Like his father, he's got a healthy appetite.'

'That's good,' she said, and she turned, hurried across

the road, and walked up the track at the side of Dorothy's house on her way to the northern part of the village.

Dorothy released the brake and started to wheel the pram to the edge of the road, when again she heard someone calling to her. Glancing sideways, she saw Herta, with Sofia and Hans at her heels. All three had their arms full.

Angling the pram in their direction, she smiled at them. 'You've been busy, I see,' she said.

Herta gave a theatrical sigh. 'Karl wanted me to get some freshly pressed linseed oil from the mill. In this heat, I ask you! But of course, I went up there,' she added with a laugh.

'And I picked up a few ham hocks on the way back, and some goat's milk. I know it's late in the day to be shopping, but I've had a busy morning and couldn't get out earlier.'

'I'm very glad we've bumped into each other. I've been meaning to ask you for coffee, but with Dieter keeping us awake at night—well, you know what it's like.'

'I certainly do. Happily, though, my two are now long past that stage.' Herta gazed affectionately down at Sofia and Hans.

Sofia pulled a face at Hans. Hans giggled, and kicked at the dry ground. Dust drifted upwards, and he coughed.

'Don't do that, Hans,' Herta said sharply.

'We won't talk now, Herta—it's hot and we're both tired, and also we've got the children, but we must do so soon. Look, I'm sure I'll sleep better tonight, why don't you come over tomorrow morning? The girls will be back at school tomorrow, and it's one of Hans's mornings at the new *Kindergarten,* if I remember rightly.'

'That would be lovely. I'll be across at the usual time, then.' Herta started to head towards the entrance to her house, and then stopped. 'By the way, I take it Franz will be calling for Karl at the usual time this evening?' she called back.

'No, he isn't, I'm afraid. He's not going tonight. But he'll have told Karl at school. Right, then, Herta, I'll see you tomorrow. Goodbye, children.'

Two sets of dark brown eyes looked up at her as they chorused goodbye.

She gave the three of them a slight wave, pushed the pram across the road, and dragged it up the couple of steps into the house.

'Dieter's still asleep, thank goodness,' she told Franz, who'd come to the door to help her with the pram.

She left the pram just inside the door, took the shopping from the rack under the body of the pram and carried it over to the kitchen area. Then she went across to Elke, leaned over her daughter's shoulder, and looked down at the picture she was colouring.

'That's lovely, Elke. What a clever little seven-year-old you are.'

'She's been very good all morning,' Franz said, coming to look at Elke's work, too. 'She's done everything the school set, and since then, she's been drawing beautiful pictures while I've been marking. Haven't you, Elke? I've managed to get all the books done.' He ruffled his daughter's hair.

Elke brushed his hand away. 'Don't do that, *Vati*. I'm busy. I think I'll go and work in my room.' She gathered up her paper and crayons, clutched them to her chest, slid down from her chair and headed for the stairs that led up to her bedroom.

'Did I hear you talking to Herta just now?' Franz asked, sitting down and starting to put the exercise books back into his case.

'That's right,' she said, going over to the kitchen area and picking up a stone jug that had been standing in a bowl of cold water.

'She's coming for coffee tomorrow. She asked if you were calling on Karl this evening, but I told her you weren't going.' She held up the jug. 'D'you want some lemonade?'

'Not now, thanks.' He closed his bag, and leaned back in his chair. 'Actually, I *am* going tonight after all.'

She heard a tinge of embarrassment in his voice.

She stood still, the jug in her hand, and stared at him in displeased surprise. 'But I thought you'd decided against it.'

'With my marking done, there's no real reason not to go.'

She filled a glass with lemonade, returned the jug to the bowl and went and sat opposite him. She took a sip of her drink and looked at him, her forehead creased in a frown.

'About the meeting, Franz. You said it was about the parade next weekend, and making sure that every house had a swastika flag to hang from the windows.'

He nodded. 'It is. Another parade! Can you believe it?' He laughed in derision.

'I thought that's why you were thinking about not going to the meetings any more, starting with the meeting tonight. It wasn't about having books to mark—it was because Party meetings these days are all about parading. Parading's quite a militaristic sort of thing to do, and that isn't you. At least, I thought it wasn't.'

'You're right, it isn't.' He hesitated. 'Karl thinks I should keep on participating. All the other teachers go, so I'm likely to stand out if I don't.' He gave an awkward laugh. 'I'm not sure how much that matters, but Karl seems to think it might be better not to draw such attention to myself.'

'I understand,' she said quietly.

And she *had* understood, but she hadn't liked it.

. . .

MUCH LATER, sitting alone at the table, with Franz at the meeting and the children asleep in their rooms, Dorothy thought back to the sense of unease she'd felt earlier that evening and that she had, in fact, been feeling increasingly for some time.

It was difficult to articulate something, even to herself, that was a vague apprehension rather than anything concrete. It was rather a series of small incidents, which weren't particularly significant in themselves, but which cumulatively began to paint a picture with larger implications.

The parades were harmless in themselves. She'd read in the newspaper that it was just Goebbels following Hitler's order that he shake up the Party as things had gone rather quiet.

Everything Goebbels did—all the meetings across the country, the posters everywhere, the speeches he made, the numerous parades—had borne fruit, and the Party membership was growing.

What alarmed her was an unpleasant element that was creeping into the Party, that appeared to be going unchecked.

When Nazi stormtroopers had beaten up an old pastor who'd been heckling Goebbels during a Nazi rally, the punishment given them had been derisory, and that had clearly encouraged other like-minded people to indulge in similar violent actions.

And again, the failure to punish a gang of youths who'd thrown stones at the windows of a store above which a Jewish man lived had resulted in other such incidents.

She was inclined to agree with Franz, though, that Hitler couldn't be blamed for the violence. There was evidence that he used persuasion to resolve ideological differences and to quell infighting between different factions of the Party.

As Franz had pointed out, Hitler was a man of the people, and despite being socially awkward, which people claimed he was, he obviously had an amazing charisma, and an ability to settle difficult issues without resorting to despicable acts. So while violence was perpetrated in his name, he couldn't be held responsible for it.

But one thing she couldn't accept was his claim that he cared about *all* Germans, no matter how often he said it. And this growing feeling in particular had been preying upon her mind.

She and Franz had been critical of how, when Hitler took over the ownership of the *Völkischer Beobachter*, he'd allowed the newspaper to continue publishing openly anti-Semitic articles.

The newspaper had been suspended for its anti-Jewish attacks on at least three occasions before Hitler had bought it, and while it wasn't as blatant as *Der Stürmer*, whose anti-Semitic caricatures depicted Jews as ugly, with exaggerated facial features and misshapen bodies, it had nevertheless been very anti-Jewish in tone.

But disappointingly, the only change that Hitler had made after acquiring the paper was to fill it with Nazi propaganda.

The anti-Semitism stayed, and was relentless.

So, it wasn't true that he cared about *all* Germans— Jewish people, like the Weinbergers and the Arnsteins, were Germans, too.

She'd relaxed somewhat after the national elections in May as despite their increased membership, the Nazis hadn't performed particularly well.

Both Karl and Franz had accounted for that by saying

that with the country's economy getting much stronger, and with inflation under control and employment on the rise— and she'd read for herself that both were true—no one would vote for a change of government.

So she'd been comforted by the fact that with the economy improving, the Nazis would do even worse in the next elections.

But not very long after that, her hopes had been dashed. She'd heard Franz tell Karl that he didn't think the current economic situation would last.

And if Franz was right and the economy got worse again, the Nazis were likely to increase their share of the vote at the next election, and the idea of them becoming more powerful frightened her.

After brooding on the subject for several days, she'd raised her concern with Franz one evening after the children had gone to bed.

She was worrying needlessly, he'd said cheerfully. He was beginning to think he'd been wrong about the economy. It was looking as if the improvement would be sustained, and that would be bad news for the Nazis.

And then he'd taken her to the door of their house, opened it and led her outside.

As they'd stood in the warmth and peacefulness of the evening, he'd pointed out that what happened in large towns was far away from their little world.

Rundheim was a friendly, welcoming community, where everyone helped each other, irrespective of religion, he'd reminded her. Just as they helped the Arnsteins, for example, the Arnsteins helped them. And her friends included the Weinbergers as well as the Schmidts.

He'd convinced her, she'd told him with a reassuring smile.

And until she'd seen him leave to go a Party meeting that evening that he hadn't really wanted to attend because he feared—yes, it was fear that had governed his decision, fear about what might happen if he didn't go—she'd believed that he had.

But left alone with her thoughts, she knew that deep down within her, that kernel of anxiety was still very much alive, and was growing.

15

C horton House
Late August, 1927

LOUISA STOOD in the middle of the drawing room at Chorton House and glared at Charles and Sarah. Hovering in the doorway behind her, Christopher held a basket of blackberries in one hand, and gardening gloves in the other, his face nervous.

'I've done what you asked, haven't I?' Louisa accused. 'I took Christopher berry-picking, didn't I?'

She scowled over her shoulders at Christopher, and then turned back to her parents.

'He's thirteen, and that's more than old enough to stay on his own. If he's a scaredy-baby, Nanny can sit with him. It's what nannies are for, after all.'

Charles put his diary down on his lap. 'Must you always be quite so rude, Louisa? It's wearying. And it's tedious. You know that Nanny stayed in London to visit a family keen to engage her services.'

'You shouldn't have let her, then.'

'Your mother and I have been invited to the vicarage for dinner this evening,' he said firmly, 'and feel obliged to go, even though we're not particularly keen, so you must stay here with Christopher.'

Louisa thrust out her lower jaw. 'It's not fair. I wanted to go for a drive this evening. I thought that's why we've come for the weekend, so I could practise. What's the point of having a car if I'm not allowed to use it? Some birthday present that is!'

'You're being ridiculous,' Sarah said angrily. 'There'll be plenty of other occasions to practise.'

'Since I've had to be your unpaid nanny all afternoon, I should be allowed to choose what I do this evening. Mrs Spencer can keep an eye on Christopher, can't she?'

'No, she can't,' Sarah snapped. 'That's not the housekeeper's job. It's hard enough to get help, let alone good help, and I wouldn't dream of attempting to take advantage of Mrs Spencer's kindness so that you can have your own spoilt way. You'll do as you're told and stay at home with Christopher.'

'I don't mind being on my own,' Christopher volunteered.

'You're too young to be left alone, Christopher,' Sarah said firmly. 'And apart from anything else, Louisa, you're not experienced enough to go out in the car by yourself.'

'And I never *will* be if I don't get the chance to practise. You're just being mean for the sake of it.'

Charles stood up. 'Apologise to your mother at once, Louisa!'

'No, I won't. She's mean.'

'Apologise!' he thundered.

Louisa stared at her feet.

'Apologise to your mother,' he repeated icily.

'Sorry.'

Sarah glanced at Charles, shrugged her shoulders and turned back to Louisa. 'I've heard more sincere apologies,' she said, 'but I suppose that'll have to do. I look forward to the day you outgrow this continual belligerence and start behaving like a civilised young lady—you may be seventeen, but you act more like a two-year-old.'

Louisa stared with mock incredulity at Charles. 'How can you stand her? Oops, you can't really, can you? You found someone else.'

'How dare you!' Charles exclaimed, his face red with anger. 'You've no idea what you're talking about. And anything that happens between your mother and me is *our* business, not yours.'

He took a step towards her, his face cold.

'I hate to say this but the only person in the house whom it's hard to stand is you, Louisa. Your insolence can no longer be excused by your youth, if it ever could have been. It's high time you took a long hard look at yourself and decided if this is the sort of person you really want to be.'

He turned towards Sarah and smiled. 'I think it's time to start dressing for dinner, darling, don't you?' he said, his voice affectionate.

Sarah rose to her feet. 'I agree. Mrs Spencer will serve your food in thirty minutes, Louisa. You'll sit and eat it with Christopher, and with any luck, some of his gentle disposition will rub off on you. You're definitely not to take your dinner up to your room and leave Christopher by himself, and you'll sit with him after you've eaten until it's time for him to go to bed. I hope that's clear.'

. . .

'IT'S SO BORING, having to stay in all evening,' Louisa grumbled. She dropped her spoon and fork into her empty pudding bowl and pushed it away from her. 'Mother and Father are so unfair.'

'I think they're all right,' Christopher muttered.

'You would! That's because you're such a goody-goody. I don't know how anyone at your school can want to be your friend.'

'I don't know how anyone at your school can want to be *your* friend, either,' Christopher retorted. 'You're always in a bad temper. *And* you lie.'

'No, I don't. *You're* lying if you say that I'm a liar.'

'So, it was just a drive, was it? You weren't planning to go and see that horrid Maisie this evening, then? Sorry. My mistake.'

She leaned across the table and pinched his arm. 'Shut up, you idiot! If Mrs Spencer hears you, she might say something.' She sat back, her eyes narrowing. 'How did you know I was going to Maisie's?'

'I'm not stupid. Or deaf. I heard you talking to her on the other side of the wall. I was in the thicket, looking for blackberries.'

'Well, you can't blame me wanting to see her. She's the only friend I've got here. Some of the village girls are going up to her house tonight, and I wanted to meet them. Since we're always coming to Chorton, I thought I might as well get to know some people here.'

Christopher drew in his breath with a horrified gasp. 'Mummy would have been really angry if you'd gone to someone's house without an adult. And after she'd said you're not to drive by yourself. Suppose something had gone wrong?'

'Nothing's going to go wrong, is it?'

He sat up straight. 'You're not still going, are you? You're not to, Mummy said.'

Louisa threw her napkin on to the floor, and stood up. 'All right, then, I won't. You're such a cowardly baby,' she said with a sneer. 'It's no wonder you need someone to sit with you.' She glanced at the clock on the mantelpiece. 'It's eight o'clock. It'll soon be your bedtime, baby, so you might as well go upstairs now.'

Christopher got up, put his napkin next to his pudding bowl and started to move away from the table. Then he stopped suddenly, turned and stared at Louisa, his face anxious. 'You won't go, will you, Lou? Promise me you won't.'

She smiled at him. 'I promise, silly. I'll sit down here and read for a bit, and then I'll go up. I might as well have an early night as there's nothing else to do.'

SHE CLOSED her book and listened hard. There was still no sound coming from Christopher's room, making it about fifteen minutes or so since she'd last heard any movement upstairs.

She put her book down, went across to the door and opened it. For a moment or two, she stood there listening, but there was no sound in Mrs Spencer's quarters, either. Not that she'd expected any—the housekeeper had to be up early every morning to supervise the housemaid, and she'd certainly have long been asleep.

She glanced at her watch, and smiled. Although she was later than she'd wanted to be, there was still time to get to

Maisie's, meet her friends, and be back at home before there was any likelihood of her parents returning.

Being as quiet as possible, and avoiding the stairs that she knew would creak, she crept up to her room, and changed swiftly into a lilac long-sleeved day dress with a mid-calf hemline and a dropped waistline. She chose neutral-coloured stockings to go with it, and finished the outfit with a large brooch and a long string of pearls.

A quick glance in the mirror told her that she'd got the look she wanted. It was attractive, but not so dressy that Maisie and her friends would be faced with the difference between her family's money and theirs.

She pinched her cheeks to give herself some colour, picked up her small lilac-beaded bag, and crept back down the stairs. Having checked her bag for the door key, she quietly opened the front door, slipped through the gap, and closed it carefully behind her.

Ahead of her, the gravelled drive glistened pale in the light of the watery moon.

She hesitated. Despite the moon, it was darker than she'd expected. She must've taken a little longer getting ready than she'd realised.

She looked up at the sky.

The purple-grey dusk had melded into a blackness that was fast absorbing the hills and the trees. It was a blackness that was somehow so much deeper, so much denser, than the night sky that hung above London.

A sudden nervousness ran through her. She glanced back at the closed door, and bit her lip.

Her parents were right that she hadn't had much experience of driving, and she'd never before driven in the dark. If she went to Maisie's, it would be the first time she hadn't had anyone at all in the car with her.

Perhaps she should abandon her plan and go to bed. After all, if she didn't go to Maisie's, it wouldn't really matter —Maisie would have company whether or not she was there.

She shook herself.

What was the matter with her? It would take her just over five minutes to drive there, and that was nothing at all. And it would give her some much-needed experience of starting the car and of driving at night.

She'd be on quiet country lanes, and there wouldn't be any farm carts or tractors or horses, and probably no other cars, either, at such an hour. It couldn't be safer.

All in all, it was the ideal time and place for her to get in some practice.

She took a deep breath and walked resolutely down the drive to her car.

SHE WAS GOING TOO FAST down the hill, she thought in a white flash of panic. She must slow down.

Her headlights picked up a sharp bend looming in front of her. Gripping the steering wheel tightly, she swung into the bend, her knuckles white, her foot searching wildly for the brake pedal. She found the pedal and pressed down hard.

The car spun to the right.

And kept on spinning.

Frantic, she turned the wheel sharply to the left, but the car wouldn't stop spinning.

It just wouldn't stop!

She pounded up and down on the brake. But still it spun.

A bright light filled the windscreen.

In sudden blindness, she released the wheel. Her hands flew to her face and, covering her eyes, she screamed.

There was an almighty jolt. Her head was thrown sharply back. She saw the steering wheel race towards her.

Silence.

Then nothing.

16

The metal-framed bed was hard beneath her pain-wracked body. Muted sounds came from the area around her. An occasional metallic clink. The hum of people talking. The rustle of paper. A door closing.

Her throat felt dry.

Her head pounded.

She opened her eyes. Hazy dark-blue and white shapes drifted in front of her, and then drifted away again. She closed her eyes. Lights flickered on and off in the ebony-red world behind her eyelids.

She opened her eyes again. and blinked a few times. A smiling woman in a dark-blue dress, wearing a large white pinafore apron, swam into focus.

She closed her eyes, and opened them again.

The woman was still there.

She put a hand to her forehead, and felt a thick bandage.

'What happened?' she whispered.

'You've been in a car accident,' the nurse told her. 'But you're not to worry. You're a very lucky girl—you've walked away with some cuts and bruises, and a bump on the back of your head, but nothing serious. Your forehead needed a few stitches, but at the most, you'll have a very small scar.'

'I'm in hospital?'

'That's right, in the Horton General. We're south of Banbury. Your family insisted on you being brought here because of our reputation. We're one of the few places with a resident house surgeon, which is important as you can't be too careful with head injuries. So there's no need for you to worry.'

Louisa put her hand to her head again. 'I was in a car crash, you say?'

'That's right. You were driving.'

'But I don't remember it.'

'That's not at all unusual, Louisa. You may find that your memory of what happened gradually returns, but it may not. The important thing now is to relax. Your body has had a great shock, and it'll take time to get over it.'

'When can I go home?'

'That'll be up to the doctors.'

'Where're my parents? I want to see them.'

The nurse hesitated. 'I'm afraid they're not here at the moment.'

She turned her head slightly towards the nurse, and winced. 'Ouch. It hurts.' She rubbed her forehead gingerly. 'Will you ask them to come and see me, please?'

'Of course, dear. But I suggest you try to get some sleep now. Sleep is the best healer of all.'

She pulled her bedsheet up to her chin. 'I don't want to sleep. I want to see my mother and father.'

The nurse bent down at the end of the bed and tightened each of the folded corners. 'Visiting hours are in the afternoon. Go to sleep now, dear. You'll feel better later on if you do.'

. . .

LOUISA OPENED her eyes and stared at the ceiling. Her head still hurt, but not quite as much as it had done earlier.

Some memories were starting to return. She remembered going out in her car, and she remembered having been told not to.

She'd felt a bit scared, she recalled, but had ignored her fear and had driven away from Chorton House. But after that, her mind was blank.

How stupid she'd been, going out in the car, despite being anxious about doing so, given her lack of experience.

Her parents must be so angry with her. And they'd a right to be—she should never have disobeyed them in the way she had. She couldn't wait for the visiting hours so that she could tell them how truly sorry she was.

And she really was.

She turned her head to the left, and saw that her uncle and aunt were sitting at the side of her bed next to each other.

'Uncle Joseph!' she exclaimed, her voice a croak. 'Is it visiting time? I thought Father and Mother were coming.'

'Well, you've got us instead,' Maud said. She looked around the ward. 'This seems a pleasant room, light and airy. And the nurses are very friendly. They were kind enough to give us a cup of tea. I'm sure that they'll bring you one, too, when they know you're awake.'

She paused, glanced quickly at Joseph, who sat in silence, staring down at his clasped hands, and then turned back to Louisa.

'We've brought you a bottle of Kia-Ora,' she told her. 'And some new biscuits called Jaffa Cakes. We thought you

might like them. The nurse is looking after them for you.'
She fell silent, and glanced again at Joseph.

Louisa's gaze moved from her aunt to her uncle.

'Mummy and Daddy must be furious with me. And I'm
furious with me, too. I deserve whatever you're going to say,
Uncle. I should never have gone out when I'd been told not
to. I desperately wish I hadn't. If I could live through the
evening again, I'd stay in without question.'

'Unfortunately, that's not possible,' Maud said quietly.

'I know,' she said, and she turned her head to her right
and looked towards the entrance to the ward. 'I hope they
get here soon. I can't wait to tell them how sorry I am. They
must've had such a shock when they heard what happened.'

She turned back to her aunt and uncle, her eyes filling
with tears. 'I'm not just saying it—I really *am* sorry that I
disobeyed them. And that I left Christopher alone. I know
he gets scared. I deserve much worse injuries than I got. And
I must've done so much damage to the car. Did I?'

Tears rolled diagonally down her cheeks and slid on to
the pillow.

'We haven't yet been to see the car,' Maud said. 'But I'm
told you did. It was only to be expected—you hit another
car, after all.'

'Another car? So that's what the bright light was. I
remember seeing a light, but not what happened after that.'
She tried to sit up, but fell back. 'I'm aching all over,' she
said, breathing heavily. 'What about the people in the other
car? Are they all right? I need to say sorry to them, too.'

Joseph stood up and walked round the bed and out of
the ward.

A wave of alarm swept through Louisa. She stared at
Maud's face, her mouth suddenly dry. 'Auntie Maud, you're
frightening me. What is it?'

Maud leaned closer to Louisa, and took her hand.

'There's something you have to know, Louisa, and your uncle is too angry at the moment to tell you himself. It was your parents' car you hit.'

She shook her head. Pain bounced from side to side. 'No, I couldn't have done,' she cried. 'They were at the vicarage.'

'They left halfway through dinner as the vicar came over unwell.'

Her breath seemed to leave her body.

'Oh, no. Oh, please, no.' She pulled the sheet up to her mouth and bit it hard.

'Your car went into the driver's side—your mother was driving. It seems your door swung open and you were thrown clear. Your father was able to walk away, but your mother wasn't. She was knocked unconscious, and she lost a lot of blood. They think she's broken her hip and her leg. Hopefully, nothing more than that.'

Maud tightened her fingers around Louisa's hand. 'She was brought here, too. For a while, we didn't think she'd pull through. But it now looks as if she will. But if you'd hit the car door just a little more centrally ... Well, it doesn't bear thinking about. As it is, she's very ill, but the doctor thinks she's probably going to live.'

As if from far away, Louisa heard a scream.

Her world went black.

SHE OPENED her eyes and smelled boiled cabbage in the air. And cleaning fluids.

For a moment, she wondered where she was, and then she remembered. And she remembered, too, why she was there. And what she had done.

Numb inside, she lay still.

Footsteps approached. She didn't move.

'You fainted,' the nurse told Louisa, when she reached her bed. 'When you came around, you were somewhat distressed, and Doctor gave you a mild sedative to calm you down. Your aunt and uncle have left.'

She smoothed Louisa's pillow. 'But you've another visitor. He was waiting for you to wake up.' She paused. 'The police want to talk to you, but we've told them they'll have to wait till tomorrow morning.'

'Who's my visitor?' she asked.

'Why don't I get you something to drink, and maybe a sandwich, and then you can find out for yourself?'

HER SANDWICH UNTOUCHED, Louisa lay with her face turned towards the entrance, waiting.

The swing doors opened and her father walked in. He was moving stiffly, she noticed. As if in pain. Guilt rose in her throat, and threatened to choke her.

Followed by acute remorse.

He went and sat on one of the two empty chairs next to her bed.

Her eyes filled with tears.

His face drawn, he looked at her and tried to speak. But he failed, and gazed back down at his hands, knotting and unknotting his fingers.

'Your mother's going to live, the doctors have told me,' he said at last, staring into his lap.

She opened her mouth to say she was sorry, but her words were washed away by her tears.

He raised his eyes again to look at her face. 'All I'm going to ask,' he said, a tremor in his voice, 'is that when the police come and interview you tomorrow, you say that you were driving carefully, and went into the bend on the correct side of the road. You'll tell them that a car crashed into you, and you don't remember anything after that.' He paused. 'Is that clear?'

'I don't understand,' she said, her voice shaking. 'I was skidding, and I crashed into your car. It was my fault. I must be punished.' A loud sob escaped her.

'If you take the blame for the accident, it could ruin your life. I'm going to tell the police that an animal ran out in front of our car, and Sarah swerved to avoid it. It'll be recorded as an accident, with no fault on either side. Whatever I feel—' He choked on his words, and coughed.

'Whatever I feel about your behaviour,' he began again, 'we mustn't make things worse than they already are. Joseph and Maud know the truth, but they're the only ones. And of course, Walter—all of us are being guided by him. And that's the way it must stay.'

'What about Christopher?' she whispered.

'He mustn't be told. He knows you left the house when you shouldn't have done, but he believes the explanation that I've given him for the crash.'

'But it doesn't seem right.'

He gave a cry of despair, looked up at the ceiling and then back at her. 'Nothing about it is right, Louisa. Nothing. Your mother may never completely get over this. She's been very badly injured. The doctors think she'll recover, but it could affect her health in the long term.'

He put his face in his hands.

'I'm so sorry, Father,' she sobbed.

He nodded, his hands still shrouding his face. 'Despite the pain she's in, your mother's managed to make it clear that she doesn't want you punished,' he said, his voice muffled. 'I don't know if I could have been as generous as she has. But we must respect her wishes.'

Tears trickled between his fingers and disappeared into the cuffs of his shirt.

He pulled out a handkerchief and blew his nose.

'Your uncle Joseph spoke to Walter as soon as he heard what had happened. According to Walter,' he continued, trying to steady his voice, 'if we told the truth, you might be prosecuted. You're old enough for that to happen. And he said that it was possible, depending upon the charge, that you'd be found guilty of an Offence Against the Person. Your mother doesn't want that.'

'But I want it, Father,' she cried. 'I deserve to be punished. I don't want Mummy to take the blame. And I promise you, I'll never drive again. It's the only way I can punish myself.'

'Nevertheless, your mother is going to take the blame. What you want is irrelevant. She's giving you another chance, and you'll take it. And if her kindness adds to your feeling of guilt, then I'm glad.'

He stood up. 'I've said what I came to say. We're both so very disappointed in you, Louisa. At some point, you'll be allowed to visit your mother, but not for a while. When they tell me you can leave the hospital, I'll come and collect you and take you back home.'

'Thank you,' she whispered.

'I'd much rather send you somewhere far away and out of my sight, but it would give the lie to our statements, and I'm not prepared to go against your mother's wishes. In no way does it mean that I've forgiven you, though. I don't know if I'll ever be able to do so. Is that clear?'

She nodded.

'One last thing,' he added. 'Christopher's in a terrible

state about what's happened to Mummy. You can start to show him some love. It's the very least you can do, since your selfishness and disobedience means that he won't have his mother at home for a while.'

His face wet with tears, he turned from her and walked away.

As she watched him cross the ward to the exit, she knew deep in her heart that she'd lost something she'd valued greatly, but hadn't ever realised it.

17

K nightsbridge,
December, 1927

BENEATH A SOMBRE DECEMBER SKY, the Linford family gathered in Charles and Sarah's Knightsbridge house for an afternoon tea to welcome Sarah home.

Sitting in her favourite armchair, surrounded by a profusion of winter roses and anemones, with a dark-blue tartan rug over her knees, and tea in a bone china cup at her side, she looked pale, but was smiling.

'I'm so pleased to be home, Maud darling,' she told her sister-in-law, who sat at her side, a flute of champagne in her hand. 'I never want to see the inside of a hospital again—beyond the inevitable check-ups, that is. That awful smell of antiseptic. I still can't shake it, not even here. It's completely drowning my favourite Arpège.'

Maud smiled at her. 'I can assure you that no one near you is going to smell anything other than your heavenly scent.' She paused. 'How have things been with Louisa? I know she was worrying that the thought of you both being under the same roof again might cause you to relapse.'

Sarah gave a slight shake of her head. 'If she was, then that was Charles's doing. As far as I'm concerned, there's no point in harbouring resentment, especially not towards my own daughter. It wouldn't change a thing, would it?'

'No, I doubt it would.'

'She keeps telling me how sorry she is, and I have to believe that she is. For the moment, anyway. I've no idea how long the new Louisa will prevail.'

'I rather think it might be here to stay, Sarah. I'm sure her remorse is genuine, and so is Joseph. The fact that she so nearly lost you has made her aware of how much she loves both you and Charles. I suspect that we'll see a very different Louisa in the future.'

'I'd like to think you're right. And maybe you are. Charles said that she's stuck to her vow of not driving again and keeps refusing another car. While I'm sure it's partly because she's now too scared to get behind the wheel, it could also be her way of showing us the genuineness of her regret.'

Maud nodded. 'I agree.'

Sarah looked across the room at Louisa, who was sitting in a corner next to a couple of empty chairs, and then back at Maud.

'I never thought I'd say this, but I actually feel quite sorry for her. Guilt isn't an easy thing to live with. You only have to ask Robert. He won't have forgotten.'

'So you're usurping my place as the family misfit, are you, Louisa?' Thomas said, coming up to her. He carefully balanced his cane against the side of the empty chair next to her, and then sat down beside her.

She glanced at him in surprise. 'And what does that mean?'

'That I'm the one who usually goes out of the way to avoid people. But today, *you've* assumed that mantle. Not that I blame you.'

'And what does that mean?'

'That you've been so obnoxious to everyone over the past few years that they're bound to want to give you wide berth. It's a much better idea that *you* shun *them* before they shun you. As a matter of self-respect, if you like.'

She glared at him. 'No one's shunning me—I'm sitting here out of choice. Your faculty of correct deduction must be missing, Uncle, as well as your leg. Oh, my goodness!' Her hand flew to her mouth. 'That was so thoughtless of me. I'm sorry.'

Thomas laughed. 'I'm glad to see that you haven't completely drowned your former spark in a sickening flood of remorse. Potentially tedious family gatherings used to be enlivened by your contributions. You were quite the rudest Linford, and invariably went to great pains to prove it. The rudest after me, that is. Rudeness is something we have in common.'

'Not any longer we haven't. I've changed.'

He smiled at her. 'It's a bit early to say that, don't you think? What's it now, about three months since the accident? Why, that's no time at all. Anyway, what I actually came across to say is that if you wanted to call on me at any time, I daresay Mrs Carmichael could rustle up a cake from somewhere.'

'Since you admit that you're the rudest Linford—even

worse than I used to be, and that was pretty bad—why would I want to visit you?'

'Loneliness, dear Louisa, out of loneliness. I know what it is to be lonely, and I suspect you soon will, too. And when you do, that'll be another thing we have in common.'

'Is this a guessing game? Am I now meant to ask you what you're talking about?'

'Christopher let it out of the bag that your parents had expressly forbidden you to leave Chorton that evening, but you disobeyed them and went ahead.'

Thomas looked reprovingly at her.

'You took the car out in the dark,' he said, 'inexperienced as you were, and an accident resulted. Maybe Sarah *did* swerve to avoid an animal. But maybe the truth was that you lost control of your car and drove into Sarah.'

She gave an awkward laugh. 'You should be a fiction author, Uncle Thomas, with that imagination of yours. Mother told you what happened, and she's more likely to know than anyone else.'

'I'm merely surmising that at some point, it might occur to the family that Sarah, who's known to be the most careful of drivers, and who'd be even more careful when driving up a hill at night in the dark, would be in complete control of her car at all times. Whereas you...'

He shrugged. 'Reasoning thus, they might just come to the conclusion that the person responsible for the accident was you, Louisa.'

'You don't know what you're talking about,' she snapped, her face white.

'No matter what you might wish to believe, I'm inclined to think that most of the family will eventually come to feel that the blame lies at *your* door. But whether or not they do, they'll know for certain that if you hadn't disobeyed your parents in the first place, there wouldn't have been an accident.'

'Rubbish!'

'Sarah's injuries are a direct result of your wilfulness,' he continued, ignoring her, 'and that alone is enough to make you the family's least favourite person. Don't think they'll make allowances for your youth, because they won't—not for a girl who's been relentlessly unpleasant for years.'

'You don't know what you're talking about,' she said, her voice unsteady.

'As I say, Louisa, you know where to find me.' He stood up. 'I'll leave you now as I can see that Nellie's on her way over here.'

Resting heavily on his cane, he moved away.

'Oh, Lou,' Nellie said. She bent down and hugged Louisa, and then settled into the chair where Thomas had been sitting.

'It's awful to see your mother looking so weak, isn't it? She's always been more than an aunt to me—she's a real friend, and I can't bear seeing her suffer so. And it must be so much worse for you as her daughter. What a thing to happen. I'm just so relieved that you and Uncle Charles weren't seriously hurt as well.'

'Thank you, Nellie. It's been so dreadful.' Louisa's eyes filled with tears.

Nellie caught hold of her hand, and squeezed it. 'Now you're to stop all that. Aunt Sarah's home, and she's getting stronger all the time. Before long, she'll be back to her old self. You'll see.'

'I do hope so.'

'Anyway, it's a really bad idea for you to sit here on your

own, so we're going to go over to Walter as soon as he's finished talking to Robert. In the meantime, you must have something to eat. And a drink.'

'I don't want anything, thank you.'

'You need to eat,' Nellie said firmly. 'You love cucumber sandwiches, and you love scones with clotted cream and strawberry jam. And there are some delicious-looking little cakes and pastries. Your Mrs Morris is a marvel in the kitchen.'

'I'm not hungry.'

'When you see the food, you will be. We'll go to the buffet and each get a selection, and then we'll join Walter. He'll have had long enough to talk to Robert by then.'

Louisa glanced towards Robert and Walter, who were deep in conversation.

'I don't think we should interrupt them.'

'Of course we should,' Nellie said brightly. 'I'm sure that Walter's only telling Robert about an Act that'll probably come in next year. It's going to give women the same voting rights as men. He was full of it in the car on the way here. All women over twenty-one will be able to vote, and not just those over thirty who've got property. Watch out, men, is what I say.' She laughed.

Louisa managed a smile. 'So you'll be able to vote, Nellie. That's exciting.'

'Yes, it is. I like the idea of my voice being heard. Come on! Let's go and get something to eat.'

'I really don't feel like eating anything. You go.'

'I'm not leaving you alone. If you stay here by yourself, you'll just get sad all over again.'

'I've not stopped being sad,' Louisa said, a break in her voice. 'Not for one minute since I learned that Mother had been hurt.'

Nellie put her arms around her again. 'Dear Louisa, it wasn't your fault. Keep reminding yourself of that. No one blames you, least of all your lovely mother. So you mustn't, either.'

'But I've been so horrible to her and Father over the years, Nellie. I feel so bad about that. But I can't undo it, can I?'

'We've all been a trial to our parents at some time or other—it's part of growing up,' Nellie said dismissively. 'We all need to see how far we can go. That's normal.'

'I think I rather overdid it.' She paused. 'The family must hate me, and I wouldn't blame them.'

Nellie leaned across and hugged her again. 'Of course they don't, Lou. Whatever gave you that idea?'

'NELLIE'S BEEN TREMENDOUSLY upset about Sarah, as indeed we all have,' Joseph said, glancing across the room at Nellie and Louisa. He turned back to Charles. 'You must be very relieved to have Sarah home again. How's it going with her and Louisa?'

Charles shrugged. 'Louisa's trying hard. I think she's genuinely sorry about what happened. I'm still struggling to forgive her, though. I keep having to remind myself that she's very young, and we were all young once and did things we shouldn't.'

'And some of us, too, when we weren't so young,' Joseph remarked drily. 'And some of us carried on doing them, confident of never being found out.'

Charles straightened imperceptibly. He stared hard at Joseph.

Joseph stared back.

'That's all in the past,' Charles said, dropping his gaze. 'If it wasn't true before the accident, you can be sure it is now. Coming so close to losing Sarah taught me a lot about what I held most dear. I'm a different person from the man I used to be. You can believe that.'

'I certainly hope you're right, Charles. Secrets have an unpleasant habit of being found out. We both know that.'

Charles coloured slightly. He cleared his throat. 'To go back to Sarah. Although she's still obviously nowhere near right, the doctor's confident she'll eventually be as good as new, or almost as good. To be honest,' he added with a half-smile, 'and I never thought I'd say this, I can't wait for her to start nagging me again.'

Joseph nodded. 'I can understand that.'

'And as for Louisa, in a way, if I'm honest with myself, what she became is partly our fault. Sarah and I saw ourselves as compromised by what happened in the past, and we felt powerless to control Louisa, and ended up being too lax.'

Joseph nodded. 'I must say, I have to agree. But it's the future that matters, Charles. You've needed your family's forgiveness in the past. Take my advice, and forgive Louisa. As you say, you had a role in what she became.'

'You make a good point, and I'll try.'

Joseph clapped Charles on the shoulder. 'Good man. Listen, I've an idea! Why don't you come out to our latest development next week and let Robert and me show you around? Christopher and Louisa, too. I'd suggest Sarah as well, but it might be too much for her. Her leg is unlikely to be strong enough yet.'

'You're right; that'd be beyond her at the moment. I'd enjoy it, though.'

'The weather's set to be dry, so we can carry on building for a little longer. It's some years since you've been to an estate under construction, and I think you'd find it interesting. And so might Christopher. He told Maud that he didn't want to be a banker, so maybe he'll think about joining Linford & Sons when he's older. If he never sees what we do, he won't know if he'd like it.'

'I take it from your cheerful manner that the demand for houses is still high.'

Joseph stared at him in surprise. 'Why wouldn't it be?'

Charles shrugged. 'Just that the birth rate's steadily dropping, and families are getting smaller. Couples seem to be limiting the number of children they have, now that they can do so more easily. And that's true of manual workers as well as those in the managerial class. When we were little, five or six children was common, and you often saw families with as many as ten. But not any longer.'

'That's true. Nevertheless, more families than ever before are in need of housing. One of the reasons is that an increasing number of people are getting married these days, and at a younger age, so the number of separate households is on the increase.'

'I wouldn't have thought of that.'

Joseph smiled. 'Well, it's happening, and there's now a growing demand for units particularly suited to those who're newly married, and also for smaller families.'

'Obviously, that's good news for the company.'

'Also, people are living longer. We're frequently hearing from retired couples who need a smaller home now that their children have married and moved away. And it's not just the demand for houses that's rising.'

'Don't tell me you're talking about the company again,' Thomas said, coming up to them.

'Indeed, we are, Thomas,' Joseph said smoothly. 'I was about to tell Charles that the demand these days isn't limited to the size of the house—it's also for a specific interior. But since that's your area, and you're here now, you can tell him.'

'Joseph means that buyers today expect their homes to be brighter, cleaner, and more comfortable than the homes they'd grown up in, and they've become more precise about what they want. After the war, it used to be a bathroom with a fixed bath, but now the bath must be enclosed, the walls half-tiled and the taps chromium-plated.'

'Good gracious!'

'And as servants are hard to get, more housewives are having to do their own cooking, and are spending quite an amount of time in the kitchen, so kitchen fittings have assumed a tremendous importance. It's no longer enough to have hot and cold running water in the kitchen, kitchens must now be partly tiled, and fitted with a sink, draining board, cabinet, larder and two gas points.'

'Well, you do surprise me,' Charles remarked.

Thomas shrugged. 'It doesn't stop there. It's the same with the rest of the house. Buyers want electric power points in the hall and on the landing, for example, and gas and electric power points at the fireplaces.'

'That must keep you on your toes,' Charles said. 'I'd no idea that customers today were quite so prescriptive.'

'They certainly are,' Thomas said. 'They're getting their ideas from periodicals. Now that more people are buying their homes, magazines are featuring countless articles about furnishings and design, so I suppose it's not surprising that there's now an interest in every aspect of the home.'

'It means that the interiors' department will have to be expanded before too long,' Joseph said. 'When Christopher's a little older, it might be something he'd be interested in. Robert will obviously run the company when I step down, but that's a long way off, I hope. And Thomas will continue to head the interiors' department. But there are other important positions to be had.'

'It's certainly food for thought. Sarah and I would be very happy to see him join the company. We told him so not long ago.'

'To come back to the present,' Thomas said, leaning heavily on his cane. 'I've stood for long enough. The only reason I came across, Joseph, was to find out when we're leaving.'

'Set up a visit for us, will you, then, Joseph?' Charles said. 'We'll work round whatever date suits you. Now, if you'll both excuse me, I must go back to Sarah.'

Joseph turned to Thomas as Charles left. 'I'll ask Maud if she's ready. If she is, we can leave now. But I'd like to say a quick goodbye to Robert first. Have you seen him recently?'

'He was in the garden with Walter and Christopher a few minutes ago. They'd taken James and Emily outside as they were getting restless, as any sensible children would be in a tedious family gathering.'

'That's more like it, Thomas,' Joseph said cheerfully, clapping him on the shoulder. 'I kept wondering where the old Thomas had gone.'

'At least I came today,' Thomas snapped. 'I was strongly tempted not to. I came for Sarah, and for no other reason. She's had a raw deal.'

'I think we'd all agree with that. Ah, here's Robert!' Joseph exclaimed as Robert and Walter approached them, followed by James and Emily. 'Thomas tells me you've been in the garden. What have you been up to?'

'We've been picking holly for Uncle Charles and Aunt Sarah, haven't we, children?' Robert said, smiling down at them. 'Christopher's taken everything they picked to Mrs Morris. She can use it to decorate the house, if she wants.' He turned back to his father. 'I think we'll get off now.'

'And so will Nellie and I,' Walter cut in. 'Emily's clearly tired. And as for Sarah, she looks exhausted.'

All three glanced across at Sarah, whose face was ashen.

'Sarah looks as if she ought to be in bed,' Joseph said. 'We're going to head off, too.'

'If you'd like to come with us, Thomas,' Walter suggested, 'Nellie and I can easily go via Kentish Town and drop you off.'

'I think I'll take you up on that. Thanks, Walter.'

'I'll just get Nellie. We'll say goodbye to Sarah, and be back,' Walter added, and he moved away.

'It's good to see Sarah back at home, isn't it,' Robert said, taking James's hand. 'And Louisa must be relieved. She's very quiet, which is so unlike her. But it must have shaken her badly to have been involved in a crash that so seriously hurt her mother, no matter how innocent her involvement.'

Joseph coughed.

His eyes met Thomas's.

Thomas gave him a knowing smile, and went across the room to Walter.

18

L ouisa stood at the window, staring at the blackness outside. Her face, pale and unhappy, was thrown cruelly back at her by the dark of night.

She stepped forward, pressed close to the glass, and peered through her reflection to the world outside. Her breath misted the window, clouding her vision, and she leaned slightly back, wiped the window with the sleeve of her cardigan, and again moved close to the cold glass.

Gazing to the left, she stared up the road towards the bright lights of Upper Sloane Street and the cluster of fashionable shops at the top of their road.

Shopping for clothes was never going to be the same again.

Everything had changed in that one terrible moment of impact.

Her mother was so much weaker now, and although everyone said she'd get stronger with the passage of time, she was unlikely ever again to have sufficient energy to battle over what Louisa should or shouldn't be wearing, and would probably not have the least interest in doing so.

And for her part, she would never again want to override her mother's wishes.

As she'd surreptitiously watched her mother throughout the day, she'd witnessed the effort she was making to conceal the pain she was still in, and seeing her mother in agony, looking so weak, so fragile and so lost in the house she used to dominate, had brought home the enormity of what she'd done.

No matter how much progress she made in the coming weeks, there were bound to be inevitable consequences to severely breaking her hip and her leg, and her mother was going to have to live with them for the rest of her life.

And so was she.

She deserved to feel as awful as she felt, and would always feel, but her mother didn't. And she was never going to be able to make amends to her mother for that.

And her relationship with her father and Christopher may have been irreparably damaged, too.

As soon as the last of the family and friends had left, her mother had gone up to bed, assisted by the nurse her father had engaged to ease her first few weeks at home, and Louisa had been left with her father and Christopher.

They'd eaten their supper in silence, and when she and her father had moved to the sitting room, Christopher had said goodnight and gone up to his room.

He, too, had obviously seen their mother's struggle that day and had been visibly upset throughout the supper.

Not long after he'd gone upstairs, Louisa had heard him crying in his room, and she'd hurried up to comfort him. But he'd refused to open the door, and had shouted to her to go away.

In the end, she'd had to give up and go back downstairs. Her father had glanced across at her, but had said nothing.

It was no wonder her brother wouldn't allow her to comfort him, she thought in despair.

Even though he was ignorant of the role she'd played in the accident, for most of the thirteen years of his life, she'd never made the slightest attempt to get to know him, nor had she gone out of her way to be kind to him.

Quite the opposite.

And despite the efforts she'd made with him in the past three months, it was much too soon for her to expect him to look to her to help him through his misery.

When his sobbing had finally stopped, she'd gone up again to see if he wanted her to sit with him for a while, but the silence that had slid from beneath his door had told her that he'd cried himself to sleep at last, and she'd turned away and gone back down to her father.

Despite looking worn out and drained, he'd sat with her for a little longer, his newspaper raised in front of him.

She'd desperately wanted to introduce the sort of conversation they used to have in the evenings, but she hadn't known how to begin.

The only words that sprang to her mind were words of apology and deep regret, but she'd already used those words so many times over. So she'd sat there in silence, staring at her book with unseeing eyes.

Her father had been the one to break the weighty silence that had lain between them.

He'd put down his paper, and told her, his voice very quiet, that all their differences needed to be relegated to the past.

He and her mother accepted that she genuinely regretted the accident, and the behaviour that had led to it, and it was time now, with her mother back home and getting better every day, that they looked only to the future and tried to become friends again.

Then he'd got up, bid her goodnight, and he, too, had gone upstairs.

Left alone with her thoughts, memories of the past few years flooded into her mind, accusing her.

She'd taken some difficulty between her parents some years earlier, and made it all about herself. Having done that, she'd taken it upon herself to punish them daily with her insolence and surliness.

Sensing deep within her that whatever had happened between them had rendered them powerless to rein her in, her defiance and hostility had been unbridled. The more they let her get away with, the worse her behaviour.

Over the years, she'd become a monster.

But she didn't blame her parents for failing to check her behaviour—she now understood the paralysing effect of guilt.

From the moment she'd learned that she was responsible for her mother's injuries, she'd understood what it was to feel a prisoner of the past, and utterly helpless.

And it wasn't just her parents she'd targeted with her rudeness, but the rest of her family, too!

Perhaps she'd been trying to show off to the family the power she held over her parents. She didn't know. But whatever it was, she will have made them all intensely dislike her. Uncle Thomas had been right, and Nellie had been wrong.

And why wouldn't they hate her? After all, she hated herself.

But if only it hadn't taken something like this—something so irreversible—to show her how much she loved her mother! How much she loved both of her parents and her brother.

She'd told her father that she'd never drive again, and she wouldn't. And she'd be tireless in trying to make her family believe how much she loved them. If she tried hard enough, maybe one day they'd see for themselves that the old Louisa was truly dead, and then they might like her again.

For a long moment, she stared at the spectral face that confronted her from the windowpane.

Then she stepped back, took hold of the gold tasselled cord at the side of the window, and tugged it firmly downwards. Motionless, she watched as the curtains closed over the Louisa that was gone forever.

19

K nightsbridge,
March, 1928

'YOU LOOK VERY NICE,' Nellie said, smiling at Louisa across their table in The Georgian in Harrods. Light streamed down on them through a skylight decorated with ornamental wrought ironwork and a plasterwork frieze of stylised ferns and fountains. 'That colour green really suits you.'

Louisa glanced down at her long-sleeved sage green drop-waisted dress, and adjusted the lie of the pleats in her skirt.

Looking back at Nellie, she beamed. 'Thank you,' she said. 'This is actually the first time since the accident that I've given any thought about what to wear. But knowing I was seeing you today, and remembering how Mother invariably returned from meeting you, full of how attractive you'd looked, I thought I'd better make an effort.'

Nellie laughed. 'That's praise indeed, though I'm not sure that it was entirely deserved. Your mother has an excellent eye for clothes, and I used to try to dress as she did. Mother was always complaining that my clothes were far too grown up, but I wanted to look as stylish as Aunt Sarah, and I ignored Mother.'

She took a small coconut and lime *gâteau* from the silver stand in the centre of the table. 'Help yourself, Lou, won't you? But you don't need to worry about making an effort. You'd look attractive in whatever you wore—you're a naturally very pretty girl.'

Louisa blushed.

'While I was delighted when you suggested that we meet for tea,' Nellie said, wiping the sides of her mouth with her starched white napkin, 'I was also intrigued.'

'I didn't want anyone to hear what I wanted to ask,' Louisa said. She took a salmon and cucumber sandwich and bit into it.

'Now I'm even more intrigued.' Nellie smiled encouragingly.

Louisa swallowed the sandwich, and took a deep breath. 'I hate asking you this as I know Uncle Joseph would be furious if you said yes, so I'm putting you in a difficult position. But something Mother said some time ago made me think you were writing to Cousin Dorothy. If you are, could I have her address, please? I'd like to write to her, too.'

Nellie sat back in her chair and stared at Louisa. 'Well, you *do* surprise me, Lou! I'd run through one or two things in my mind that you might be wanting to ask, or to tell me, but that wasn't even on the list. Do you mind if I ask why you want to contact Dottie?'

Louisa gave an awkward laugh. 'This is going to sound so silly.'

'I'm sure it isn't.'

'It's just that I've felt very alone since the accident, and not really a part of the family any longer. And I think Cousin Dorothy might understand. She's been cast off, too, you see.'

Nellie leaned forward. 'But you haven't been cast off, Lou, as you put it,' she said gently. 'Is this because you're still blaming yourself for the accident, and you believe we're blaming you, too? If you believe that, you're wrong.'

'I'm blaming myself for a whole lot more than that. Before the accident, I'd been ghastly to everyone for years. I don't blame them for not liking me. I wouldn't like me, either. Uncle Thomas has made me see things very clearly.'

'I wouldn't think he's the best person to listen to, Lou.'

Louisa shrugged. 'I've started visiting him, you know. He's so bad tempered that I thought that by going to see him regularly, I'd be showing the family how sorry I am.'

Nellie looked at her in amusement. 'And what does Uncle Thomas feel about you adopting surly old him as your road to redemption?'

Louisa bit her lip. 'I don't really know. He usually grunts at everything I say.'

They looked at each other, and burst out laughing.

'Of course, I'll give you Dottie's address. I'm sure she'll be delighted to hear from someone other than me. I suggest, though, that you ask her to write to you at my address. I know what your mother thought of Dorothy's marriage, and this isn't the time to upset her.'

'I'll definitely do that. Thank you, Nellie. I hadn't thought of that.'

'Now tell me what you've been doing to amuse yourself. I imagine you won't be including your visits to Uncle Thomas in your list of enjoyable activities.'

. . .

IT WAS funny how merely writing a letter could make a person feel so different, Louisa thought as she made her way back home from the post office the following morning, a lightness in her step that had long been absent.

The evening before, the minute she'd finished her letter to Dorothy, she'd stopped feeling quite as alone.

It was true that Nellie had been dismissive of her certainty that the family blamed her for the accident, and would have shunned her if they could.

And it could well be that if her uncle Thomas hadn't put the thought into her mind, she'd never have assumed that those who didn't know the truth about what had happened would work it out for themselves, and secretly hold her responsible.

But he had. And once the seed had been planted, the belief had grown.

Until now.

Until she'd unburdened herself to Dorothy.

The mere act of writing everything down, and sharing it with someone who didn't know her, who wouldn't be blinded by having already judged her, had made her feel so much better.

She'd found herself smiling all the way to the post office, and by the time she got back to her house after posting the letter, she'd still been smiling.

What would Dorothy think when she received the letter, she thought, walking up the few stone steps to the glossy front door. Maybe she'd reply; maybe she wouldn't.

It didn't really matter either way as something good had already come out of writing the letter, but it would be lovely if she did.

20

R undheim,
Three weeks later

DOROTHY SAT on her wooden chair and stared at the letter she held in one hand and at the envelope in the other.

Louisa had written an address in the top left-hand corner of the envelope, but it wasn't her Knightsbridge address—it was the address of Nellie and Walter's house in Camden Town.

She obviously didn't intend to tell her parents that she'd written to Dorothy, but that wasn't really surprising when she thought about it.

When Nellie had first started writing, she'd indicated that their aunt Sarah intensely disapproved of her action in marrying a German. Their aunt's attitude had been that she should have refused to marry Franz, even if she thought she loved him.

That attitude had been understandable, especially in

view of what had happened to her uncle Thomas. And it might also be the way that her uncle Charles felt.

Uncle Charles and her father had the closeness of being brothers, and although they were very different in temperament, her uncle might agree with her father in this. And he was bound to be loyal to his wife. Clearly, though, it was an attitude that their daughter didn't share.

She read through Louisa's letter again, lingering on the section about the accident the year before.

It wasn't the first time she'd heard about the accident as Nellie had written to her about it. But Nellie hadn't known all the facts, and from what Louisa had said, still didn't.

Louisa had told her the whole truth, adding that apart from Uncle Joseph, Aunt Maud and her parents, and now Dorothy, no one knew that she was responsible for her mother's injuries.

Her uncle Thomas had guessed, but she'd never confirmed to him that he was right. Christopher didn't know. Nor did Nellie.

The accident may have happened some months before, but it was still clearly very much alive in Louisa's mind, Dorothy realised, and she hadn't yet come to terms with the part she'd played. Misery seeped from every line of her letter.

Frowning slightly, she tried hard to remember what Louisa looked like.

She vaguely remembered a pretty little girl with dark hair. But as Louisa couldn't have been more than five or six when she'd last seen her, and she hadn't seen her for long as she'd been so busy at that time with her voluntary work at the hospital, she had no clearer recollection than that. And anyway, at eighteen Louisa would look very different.

She glanced down at the letter again, and felt a sudden rush of warmth.

It was as if the letter had brought her closer to London and to her family—closer to home, in fact—than she'd felt for a very long time.

She caught her breath. She shouldn't be thinking like that. Rundheim was her home. She loved Franz with all her heart, and as she'd told him in the past, wherever he was, that would always be her true home.

But if you could love more than one person at a time, and you obviously could, there was really no reason why you couldn't look upon more than one town as home.

And it wasn't as if her feelings for London were in any way a reflection upon how she felt about Rundheim, because they weren't. She loved her life in Rundheim.

Nevertheless, she decided, folding the letter and returning it to the envelope, that wasn't an observation she intended to make to Franz.

There was a risk that he'd jump to the conclusion that no matter what she said, her feelings for Rundheim had been affected by what had been happening in Germany over the past few years, and not in a good way.

But they hadn't.

Or perhaps they had. Just a little.

If she were truly honest with herself, she recognised that there was a nub of fear that now resided deep within her, and that she'd been consciously trying to prevent from swelling up and overwhelming her.

Louisa's letter would help with that. With another line of contact with England, she felt a little less cut off, and that made her feel stronger.

She started to stand up, and stopped. Less cut off were the words she'd used in her mind.

She frowned.

She'd known from the moment she married Franz that she'd been cast out from the family. But perhaps, unaware, she'd blocked it from her mind to protect herself from feeling the full force of pain caused by such an action.

By refusing to let herself recognise her real sense of loss, she hadn't truly faced it. But that sense of loss had ever lain deep within her, unacknowledged.

Until now.

Until the letter from Louisa.

Feeling, erroneously or not, that she'd been rejected by her family, Louisa had reached out across land and sea in a gesture of friendship towards someone she'd felt sure would understand, and with whom she thought there could be a bond, despite a difference in age of about thirteen years.

With someone she thought must feel equally cut off, as she'd described it, from the rest of the family.

Well, she must let Louisa know as soon as humanly possible that her friendly overtures hadn't fallen on barren ground.

Standing up, she tucked the envelope into the pocket of her pinafore, went across to the kitchen cupboard, opened one of the drawers and took out several sheets of paper and a pen.

21

R undheim,
    April, 1933

LEAVING the pine forest down in the depths behind them, and also Herta and Karl, who were climbing more slowly, Dorothy and Franz made their way up the slope that led out of the valley.

When they reached the top, they put their wicker baskets on to the ground and catching their breath, stood and stared across the wide expanse of grass that lay between them and the edge of the village.

To their far left, a tiny lake glistened in the afternoon sun, a glittering speck of blue in a carpet of brilliant green. In the distance ahead of them, the square white tower and tapering peak of Rundheim's church were pristine in the sunlight.

To the right of the church, beyond a smattering of wild cherry trees that were veiled in white flowers, a line of half-timbered houses straggled up the hill, their criss-crossing beams a stark dark brown against the off-white walls.

Beyond the houses lay the Gymnasium where Franz and Karl taught, and behind that the elementary school.

The eyes of both were drawn to the windows of the half-timbered houses, to the flickering flashes of black, red and white from the swastika flags that hung over windowsills, flapping in the breeze.

Both turned swiftly away from the sight.

'Shall we start walking again?' Franz asked.

'Perhaps we ought to wait for Karl and Herta,' Dorothy said.

She picked up her basket, and looked back down the valley.

'Come on, you slowcoaches!' she called.

From halfway up the slope, Karl and Herta raised their baskets in acknowledgement, and then made a great show of walking even more slowly.

She laughed and turned back to Franz. 'Now that the weather's started to improve, we should do this more often, just the four of us. I've really enjoyed it. And Sofia and Elke were thrilled to be left in charge of Dieter and Hans. At thirteen, and surrounded by friendly neighbours, they're certainly old enough.'

'I'm not sure how overjoyed Hans was to be left in the care of his sister—she's not that much older than he is,' Franz said drily. 'And they'll have their work cut out with Dieter! He'll be telling them all what to do. It's rather gone to his head, I'm afraid, being allowed to join the *Jungvolk* before he's even eight.'

'Hitler Youth or not, I'm sure the girls won't stand any nonsense from him.'

She drew in a deep breath of the flower-scented air. 'Oh,

this is glorious. How I wish some of my family would visit us! They'd love it here. I know James is a little older than Elke, but from what Nellie's told me about him, I'm sure they'd be good friends. And Nellie's Emily has just turned eleven, like Hans, so she'd get on with Sofia and Dieter.'

She gave a sudden laugh. 'Did I tell you that Nellie told me how to get from the underground station to her house in Camden Town in case I ever wanted to go and see them? She thinks I should go back for a visit.'

He nodded. 'You did.'

'I think I'll tell her how to get to our house from Morbach, as that's the closest town. Perhaps she'll come to us one day.'

Franz nodded. 'I'd like that, too, *Liebling*—and it may still happen. It's not impossible that Nellie might come. After all, she's continued writing to you over the years. And Louisa, too, now writes regularly. She might visit us, too.'

'I'd love it if either came, or both.'

'Here we are.' Karl's voice came from just behind them.

And he and Herta came and stood alongside them. Panting heavily, they put down their baskets, and joined Franz and Dorothy in staring at the view.

'We heard you talking about Dieter,' Herta said when she'd could speak more easily. 'He's certainly grown up in the last few months. That's probably down to school as much as anything else. He seems very happy there.'

Dorothy nodded. 'He is. He likes his teacher, so I'm delighted that he's going to have her next year as well. And twenty-three in a class is a good number. His first morning there, when they'd taken down the details of my family and Franz's, and then our parents' details, they let me stay for the first half hour, and I could see how quickly he was settling.'

'I was certain he would.'

'I was so relieved that he didn't seem remotely bothered when I had to leave. But that's as it should be. It's good also that he'll be meeting children from other villages, too.'

'Hans was the same about school,' Herta said.

She paused and stared hard at the village.

'People don't seem in any hurry to take down the flags they put up for Hitler's birthday, do they?' Herta said slowly. 'It was five months ago! It's making me wonder if we shouldn't hang out our flags again—our two houses rather stand out from the others.'

Dorothy glanced sideways at her. 'I doubt you'll find many Nazi flags to the north of the crossroads.'

'But where we live, nearly every house has a flag,' Herta said, her voice anxious. 'It's only when you look at the village as we're doing now, that you realise how many flags there are.'

'I hate to say it, but Herta may be right,' Karl remarked. 'As teachers, we're supposed to set an example. And actually, more than one colleague has told me that we should be visibly supporting the government.'

Franz nodded. 'I've had that said to me, too. I suppose that because we're a long way from Berlin, we've become a little complacent, but that may not be wise. After all, the Brownshirts travel around, and from what the papers report, they appear to beat up anyone they consider to be against Hitler.'

'But they're not likely to come to Rundheim, are they?' Dorothy said in concern. 'And we're not against Hitler, as I'm sure our neighbours know.'

'Nevertheless, it might be sensible to blend in with the other houses,' Franz said slowly. 'I think I'll hang out our flag again when we get back, Dorothy.'

Karl nodded. 'And we will, too. After all, we support the government. It's thanks to Hitler that things are finally looking up. We were saying only yesterday that everything's getting cheaper—rents, postal charges, insurance premiums. People seem happier and are smiling again. And are going on picnics,' he added with a laugh.

They picked up their baskets, and started walking again.

'Things aren't so rosy for the Jews, though, are they?' Dorothy remarked with a touch of bitterness as they went along.

'Ask *Herr* Weinberger how many people have stopped going to him, even though he's an excellent dentist. An excellent *Jewish* dentist. And ask the Jewish doctor, too, how many patients he's lost. And that's here in Rundheim, not in Berlin. The newspapers are full of anti-Jewish tirades, and there are people who actually believe what they read. Even here.'

As they passed the church, a gust of wind blew a cloud of dust and rice into the air. Pausing, they looked up and watched it swirl around, fall and settle at their feet.

Herta bent down, picked up a handful of rice and held it out to Dorothy.

'If you think so badly of the Brownshirts,' she said, 'why did you allow Dieter to be a pageboy at the Schmidt girl's wedding yesterday? And why did you make him a Brownshirt uniform to wear? And let him walk behind the groom, who was dressed in *his* Brownshirt uniform? And follow the bridal couple beneath the brown-uniformed guard of honour, whose arms were outstretched in Hitler's salute?'

Dorothy coloured. 'The honest answer is that I was afraid to say no when Olga Schmidt asked me if Dieter could do it. Brownshirts are thugs, and no one wants to upset thugs. And Franz likes Peter. Don't you, Franz?'

'Yes, I do.'

'It's Olga we're not so keen on,' Dorothy said. 'But the uniform was just for the wedding. He won't be wearing it again.'

'That aside, I thought Dieter did very well,' Franz said, as they started walking again. 'Holding his head up high like that, with his shoulders back and staring straight ahead. That's not bad for a boy of his age. I was very proud of him. Mind you, I'm sure it's down to the *Jungvolk*. We're grateful to Hans for persuading the group to accept young Dieter.'

'I'm glad he's now a member, too,' Herta said. 'It's nicer for Hans to have a friend to go with. But I'm still a little surprised that you gave in, Dorothy.'

Dorothy shrugged. 'It would've been difficult not to. Boys like wearing a uniform, don't they? From the minute he saw Hans in his black shorts and brown shirt, with the area's triangle on his left sleeve, he wanted the same. And the group's activities seem to be excellent. What boys of their age don't want to go camping, ride their bikes across the countryside, take part in plays, collect a badges for each achievement?'

Herta beamed. 'Exactly!'

'As far as I can see,' Dorothy went on, 'it's mainly about physical education, and yes, there are some militaristic elements thrown in, but it all seems harmless enough. And Franz was all for it. He thought that Dieter's membership might bring him advantages in school and on every level.'

'That's what Karl said. And if young people are going to make an idol of someone, as they tend to do, there are worse idols than Hitler. You should see the children when he's on the people's radio, which he often is as there are so many national holidays these days. They're fascinated and sit listening to him in silence.'

'Ours are the same.'

'For that, if for no other reason, getting the radio was worth the sixty marks we paid,' Herta added with a laugh.

'Does Sofia like the *Jungmädel*?' Dorothy asked as they went past the wild cherry trees, turned left and started up the hill towards the crossroads in the centre of the village.

Herta smiled. 'She loves it. Is Elke going to join? I know she went to a meeting.'

'She doesn't seem to want to. I thought she might see it as a way of meeting boys, if nothing else, since the girls' group sometimes joins up with the *Jungvolk,* but she said that she didn't like it there. She knows her own mind, and doesn't really like group games and team sports. I was the same at her age,' she added.

'Watch out, girls!' Franz warned, turning back to them, and indicating with his hand that they move aside as two women approached, each with a large tray of pies and cakes on her shoulders. When the women had passed them, they resumed walking.

'Seeing those cakes reminds me—I was going to ask why you didn't go to the wedding meal yesterday,' Herta said. 'We didn't see you at all after the church.'

'Elke was upset that she hadn't been asked to be a bridesmaid, and I could just see her confronting Olga Schmidt, and very firmly ticking her off for the omission.'

Herta laughed. 'Me, too. She's a quiet little thing, but she's brave enough to say it.'

'So after the church, I suggested she went up to the Weinbergers to show Leah the dress I'd made her. They weren't at the wedding so Leah wouldn't have seen it. Suddenly, she was all smiles, and off she sped.'

Herta exaggerated a mournful face. 'Sofia will be moaning later that we should've let her go with Elke—I can just hear her now. Oh, look at the men! Trust them! Have you seen where they are?'

Dorothy looked up from the path and saw that Karl and Franz had stopped in front of the pub. 'Hm. I wonder what excuse they'll come up with,' she said in amusement.

'Karl and I need to talk about what we'll be teaching next year,' Franz said as she and Herta approached them. 'We thought we might do so over a drink.'

'Then you'd better get started at once—you've only got four months to go,' Dorothy said with mock gravity.

Laughing, she and Herta took their husband's baskets from them, and the two men disappeared into the dark interior of the pub.

'But you could've gone to the meal after the wedding without Elke,' Herta said as she and Dorothy continued up the hill. She waved her baskets at a couple of chickens that were running across the path in front of them. 'So, what was the real reason?'

Dorothy hesitated. 'Actually, Franz and I had a bit of an argument on the way back from the church after Elke had left, and by the time we got home, neither of us was in the mood to go. It was probably my fault.'

'But you and Franz never seem to argue,' Herta remarked in surprise. 'Obviously I wouldn't presume to ask what it was about.'

She glanced at Dorothy, a smile hovering on her lips.

Dorothy laughed. 'Of course you wouldn't! But you don't have to—I'll tell you. It was about something that happened the evening before the wedding, or, rather, something I think happened. But Franz insisted that I was mistaken.'

Herta frowned. 'You mean at the Schmidts' *Polterabend*?'

She nodded. 'That's right. I don't know if you noticed, but the Arnsteins didn't go to the *Polterabend* at all, and the

Weinbergers left almost as soon as they'd got there. They didn't even stay for the breaking of the porcelain, and they didn't have a thing to eat or drink.'

'But that was their choice, wasn't it? Everyone can come and go as they please. It was an invitation to everyone, as they always are.'

'That's just it. I'm wondering if it really *was* to everyone. If it was, why didn't the Arnsteins go and why did the Weinbergers leave so swiftly?'

'I'm sure they had a reason.'

'But Leah was wearing her best dress, so they'd clearly intended to stay. I saw *Frau* Schmidt say something to them as soon as they got there, and then they left. They weren't even there long enough to say hello to anyone.'

Herta shrugged. 'Maybe one of them suddenly felt ill.'

'Or maybe they were made to feel they should leave. And don't you think it's odd that they didn't go to the wedding yesterday? The Jewish townsfolk always go to our weddings, and we go to theirs. But if you think about it, there wasn't a single Jew inside or outside the church yesterday morning. You must admit that's unusual.'

Herta nodded slowly. 'Thinking about it, yes, I *do* agree. But the Schmidts aren't to everyone's taste. We're polite to them, but although Franz like Peter, we don't really like them as a family. Others might feel the same. Maybe the Weinbergers looked in to pay their respects, but had no intention of staying, despite Leah's dress.'

'That's what Franz said. He was annoyed with me and said I was reading too much into it. He accused me of taking one or two isolated incidents—or rather, one or two suspicions—and building them into something they weren't.'

Herta frowned. 'I'm sure he's right, Dorothy. Everyone in

Rundheim is friendly with everyone else, whether they're Jewish, Christian or heathen.'

'I used to believe that, but now I'm not so sure.'

As they neared the crossroads, the familiar smell of the stables and warm cow dung drifted towards them. A large wooden-wheeled trailer drawn by two cows was passing along the road in front of them, and a man leading a wagon and two horses was approaching them from the opposite direction.

A solitary pig was meandering slowly down the centre of the road, pausing every few minutes to sniff the ground. Behind him trailed two thin cats, which stopped and started in time with the pig.

'I do hope you're right, Herta,' Dorothy added quietly, as they stood in front of Karl and Herta's house. 'This has always been such a peaceful and harmonious place in which to live. I'd hate anything to change that.'

22

L *ater that day*

'WELL DONE, DOROTHY,' Franz said when Elke and Dieter had finished helping Dorothy to wash and dry the supper dishes, and had gone to their rooms to read, and she was making a pot of coffee.

'Well done for what?' she asked, pouring boiling water on top of the grounds in the pot.

'For softening your opinions. Herta and Karl are inclined to view Hitler in a more positive light than we do, and you were sensitive enough to our friendship to avoid being too critical in anything you said.'

'I admit, I *did* have to bite my tongue on a few occasions,' she said, carrying the pot across to the table and sitting down opposite him.

'One thing Karl and I talked about and decided to do—if you agree, that is—is that we'll join them when they go to

Karl's uncle's next month for his asparagus day. He's the uncle who's got a restaurant in the countryside. Apparently, it's got a large garden with tables and chairs, and his uncle is used to feeding a number of people at any one time.'

'That sounds fun.'

'I think so, too. Karl said that the folk from the surrounding farms always go on asparagus day, and musicians, too. There'll be lots of young people for Elke and Dieter to play with, and they can swim in the lake. They'll enjoy it, and so will we.'

She beamed. 'I'd love to go. Herta suggested us going with them last year, but I thought it too far for Dieter to cycle, even though the ground's supposed to be fairly flat. But he's been cycling a lot recently in his determined attempt to get the cycling badge, so he'd easily manage it. Will it be all right with Karl's uncle if we go, too?'

'It was his uncle's idea, I believe.'

'Then I'm already looking forward to it,' she said happily. She picked up the coffee pot and poured the coffee. 'Did you and Karl get round to planning your lessons as well as the asparagus trip?'

'We made a start on it.' He hesitated. 'We rather went off at a tangent, I'm afraid. I was trying to dissuade him from something he's planning to teach, but he thinks I'm worrying needlessly.' He shrugged. 'He's probably right.

'What is it he wants to teach?'

'A poet he's always taught in the past. I thought it might be wiser to pick a different one for the coming year.' He leaned towards her. 'But I'm not the only one who's worried about something, am I? You've been looking quite anxious recently.' He paused. 'I think that seeing Dieter in the brown shirt yesterday was a shock, wasn't it?'

She bit her lip. 'I suppose it was.'

'And I suspect you don't like it that he keeps on singing *Horst Wessel Lied*, that Nazi song he learnt at *Jungvolk*, and rather tunelessly, too.'

She gave him a half-smile. 'It's not that easy on the ear, is it?' She hesitated. 'I suppose it's that, but it's also more than that. Basically, I don't like living in a dictatorship, because that's what we've got now.'

'Surely that's an exaggeration!'

'Is it? Since March, everyone has had to become a member of the Party. They don't have a choice. The Nazis have wiped out all political opposition with their strong-armed tactics. Look at the way they've arrested all of Hitler's opponents, and banned from the *Reichstag* those he considers his enemies. It makes me very uneasy, Franz.'

'But to call it a dictatorship!' He attempted a laugh.

'Think about it. As recently as January, Germany had fair elections. But now, only a few months later, Hitler can do what he wants for the next four years—he no longer needs the approval of the *Reichstag*. How else would you describe it?'

'I admit that those are sweeping powers for anyone to have.'

'But for a man so associated with violence to have them, a man so strongly anti-Semitic in his views—it makes me very fearful.' She sat back and stared at him. 'I don't understand why you aren't more concerned about the situation. You've always been moderate in your beliefs.'

'I think you're worrying unnecessarily. Yes, Hitler's now very powerful, but if the economy's thriving, and at last it is, does it really matter? As for the Jews, Göring declared only last month that they weren't in any danger.'

She laughed in derision. 'And you believe that, do you? Despite Nazi soldiers sticking posters on the windows of

Jewish-owned businesses, saying "Germans, protect your-self. Do not buy from Jews"? And despite the boycott at the start of April of Jewish shops, banks, offices and large stores? Admittedly not so obviously so in Rundheim, but the news-papers showed us what was happening elsewhere.'

'It was called off after three days, wasn't it? Everyone in the country ignored it.'

'Nevertheless, the intention had been there. And what about all the recent anti-Jewish laws? And look at the attacks on communists! How can it be right for policemen to go into the houses of communists on the pretext of inspecting them, and then take them away in open trucks?'

'But they're being sent to concentration camps, and they'll be fed well, and able to do sporting activities.'

'No one's got the right to do that to someone else,' she insisted.

'Communists are subversive. It's no bad thing to re-educate them.'

'And that couldn't have been done while they were still in their homes? Of course it could. Our freedom's gone, and we're now living under a shadow of fear, Franz.'

He opened his mouth to speak.

'No, don't deny it. You joined the Party when you didn't want to. You're going to Party meetings you'd rather not attend. We've hung out our Hitler flag again so that we'd merge in with everyone else. We dressed Dieter as a Brown-shirt because we were scared to say no to our neighbours. And this doesn't concern you?' She sat back and stared at him. 'Sometimes I think I don't know you at all.'

They sat for a few minutes in silence, drinking their coffee.

'As a teacher, of course I believe in freedom of thought,' he said at last. 'And I can see that on occasions recently I've gone against what I believe, and haven't spoken up for what I think should be happening.'

'This is what I mean, dear Franz.'

'The things you mentioned *are* a concern, and if they continued, it would really alarm me.' He reached across the table, and took her hand. 'But I truly believe that you're making too much of this, *mein Liebling*.'

'I'm not sure that I am.'

He smiled reassuringly. 'History has taught us that every new government starts its term in office by trying to make its mark. As soon as that's done that, though, it settles down and life continues as before. That will happen in Germany, too. You'll see.'

'I do hope you're right, Franz. I really do.'

23

R undheim,
May, 1933

WHILE HERTA WAS busy talking across the wooden table to Franz and Karl, Dorothy stared happily around the large garden behind the restaurant belonging to Karl's uncle.

Various-sized groups of people, all of them clearly enjoying themselves, were sitting at the many wooden tables, in the centre of each of which stood a jar of colourful wildflowers and several bowls of white asparagus.

Beyond the tables, a large grass-covered open space stretched away to a small lake in which there were already children swimming. Others were running around the water's edge. All of them were laughing and shouting loudly to each other.

Elke, Sofia, Dieter and Hans, she noticed, were gazing longingly at the water, and at the fun the children were clearly having.

A cacophony of discordant musical notes suddenly blasted out from the side of the garden, and everyone turned sharply towards the sound.

It had come from a number of local musicians, who had sat down on wooden chairs grouped in a semicircle, and had begun to tune their instruments while they waited to play.

Karl had told them that a band would be playing throughout the afternoon, and that people would go up voluntarily to lead a general sing-song, or to perform a solo.

The children looked back at the lake, but Dorothy continued to watch the musicians until they started playing. Then she twisted round to look at the opposite side of the garden.

Smoke curled upwards from two wood fires. Above each of the fires hung a spit with a whole pig on it, and several of the men standing near the fires were taking it in turns to rotate the spit, while chatting to friends, a beer in their hand.

Karl followed Dorothy's gaze. 'My uncle's a keen hunter,' he told her. 'In winter particularly, he goes out daily with his friends, usually looking for wild pigs. He's never happier than when he's got a gun in his hand. He and his hunting friends practise on clay pigeons tossed up from a machine.'

'Have you ever been hunting with him?'

Karl shook his head. 'Not me. I've absolutely no interest in it. He used to ask me to go with him, but he's now given up. I could never go—I couldn't bring myself to see an animal killed. I'd be down on my knees, pleading with them to spare the animal's life,' he added with a laugh.

Franz paused, a piece of white asparagus in his hand, and raised his eyebrows. 'But you'll be having some cutlets, won't you? The pigs had to be killed, didn't they?'

'Ah!' said Karl. 'But I didn't take part in the slaughter, and nor did I see it. That makes all the difference.'

Sofia and Elke exchanged glances. 'That doesn't make sense, *Vati*,' Sofia said. 'If you refused to eat it, they wouldn't have to kill the poor pig.'

'It isn't just *Onkel* Karl who eats the pork, though—it's other people, too,' Dieter said.

Hans looked admiringly at Dieter and nodded.

Herta smiled at the children. 'But your father has to eat, don't you think, Sofia?'

'He can just eat the asparagus,' Sofia said, indicating the bowls in the centre of the table, which were full of thick white asparagus chunks that had been lightly boiled in hot water, smothered in melted butter, and then covered with a sprinkling of breadcrumbs. 'It's really nice.'

'Sofia's right,' Elke said, and they smiled at each other.

'But Karl needs to eat something substantial, and so do I,' Franz said, his expression very serious. 'After all, if we're going to be leading the singing later on, we must build up our strength. Eating a hearty meal now is the way to do so. Wouldn't you agree, children?' he asked.

The four children stared at him, open-mouthed.

'You're not going to sing in front of everyone, are you?' Elke croaked. She and Sofia exchanged a look of anguish, and then turned back to Franz in wide-eyed horror. 'Not with your voice.'

Dorothy looked quizzically at Franz. 'Are you seriously thinking of going up and singing?'

'Why ever not?' he asked cheerfully. 'And I might even do a solo. Karl said he could be persuaded, too. It would be good for us to be known for singing, as well as for teaching. In fact, we should all go up there and sing together. You, me, Elke, Dieter, Karl, Herta, Sofia and Hans. Just two big happy families, singing enthusiastically for the enjoyment of all.'

'That's an inspired idea, Franz,' Karl said, clapping him on the back. 'We're having a lovely day, and performing for everyone would be the perfect way of showing our appreciation.' He smiled broadly around the table.

'Why are you looking at us like that, children?' Franz asked, his eyes wide in bewilderment. 'Such horrified faces. Surely you don't mind us singing in public? After all, it isn't about hitting every note correctly, which obviously we won't, it's about the pleasure of performing.'

'You'd empty the garden of everyone, *Vati*! At your first attempt at a high note, they'd all run off screaming.' Elke looked at Sofia, and both of them burst out laughing.

'Wait till you hear the noise my father makes,' Sofia said, and she groaned loudly. 'I bet his voice is even worse than your father's. You can't sing in front of everyone, *Vati*. It'd ruin their day. And I'd die of embarrassment if anyone I knew heard you.' She turned to Herta. 'Tell him not to go up there, *Mutti*,' she begged.

'No, I won't. I think it's a very good idea that our families add to the entertainment this afternoon. As Franz said, I think we should all go up there. You children, too,' Herta added. She cleared her throat and tried out a high note above her range.

'Whatever note you were aiming for, *Mutti*, you missed it,' Sofia said pulling a face. 'It was flat.'

'I feel quite hurt that you don't want to sing with us, Sofia, and worse still, that you don't even want your parents to sing at all,' Karl said, his voice laden with sorrow.

Elke caught her mother's arm. '*Mutti*, please tell *Vati* not to think of doing this,' she said with urgency. 'We promise to be as good as gold all week if no one sings.'

'Please!' she and Sofia wailed.

'You can't do it, *Vati*,' Hans and Dieter chorused together.

'What a noise!' Dorothy said, laughing. 'Your fathers certainly know how to get a reaction from you. If you stopped and thought for a moment, you'd realise that on a hot afternoon after a large meal, and with a few beers inside them, the only reason they'd move from the bench would be to get another beer. Isn't that so, Herta?'

'Your mother's right, Elke. The four of you are safe to assume that no one will be performing in public.'

Visibly relaxing, the children looked at each other in relief, and giggled.

Franz stood up. 'Just to prove that your mothers have predicted correctly, children, Karl and I will go and have a few words with Karl's uncle, and get another beer at the same time. Can I bring you anything, Dorothy?'

'Not for me,' she said.

'Herta?'

Herta shook her head. 'No, thank you.'

'Can we go and watch the musicians, *Vati*? But not to sing,' Elke added hastily, clambering up from the bench. The other children scrambled to their feet after her. 'And then go to the lake?'

'That's fine, Elke,' Franz said, 'but you must let your meal go down before you go into the water. And you must stay close to the water's edge at all times.'

'We will,' Elke said, and the four of them ran off towards the band.

Karl and Franz made their way across to the group of men surrounding Karl's uncle.

'Karl's aunt and uncle play in the band at the park café where a number of his family usually go for coffee on

Sunday afternoons,' Herta said. 'The whole family's musical, apart from Karl.'

Dorothy watched the children form a line in front of the musicians and start to clap their hands in time with the music, and then she turned back to Sarah.

'Actually, talking of swimming, it wouldn't be a bad idea if the two of us went for an occasional swim. There are several lakes near Rundheim. We could go there when the children were in school. It'd be a good way to thin out a little.'

'You're not fat, Herta,' Dorothy said. 'But,' she added, and she felt herself blushing, 'it's reminded me of something I wanted to ask you.'

'Ask away.'

'It's not something one normally talks about.' She laughed in embarrassment.

Herta stared at her curiously. 'You know you can ask me anything.'

'It's just that you stopped having children after Sofia and Hans. Hans is eleven, so I imagine you must have done something to make sure there wouldn't be any more. Apart from the fact that I've had several miscarriages and I'd hate to have another, with Elke and Dieter the ages they are, and being thirty-six now, I don't really want to start all over again, no matter how much Hitler wants us to have more children.'

Herta pulled a face. 'I don't want any more, either.'

'So far, I've been lucky,' Dorothy continued. 'But I'm always worrying that my luck will run out.' She cleared her throat. 'So how do you stop yourself getting pregnant?'

'Karl does it. He puts on an *Überzieher*.'

'An overcoat!' Dorothy exclaimed.

Herta giggled. 'Not exactly. Just think for a minute, Dorothy.'

Dorothy frowned, and then her brow cleared. 'Oh, I see,' she said. 'But I thought they were difficult to get, with the Nazi Party so against contraception. And they're very expensive, aren't they? And how would you get them in Rundheim without everyone knowing what you were doing?'

'You don't need many—they can be washed and used over and over again. They're made of rubber, you see. You'll obviously need to talk to Franz about this. If he agrees, Karl will tell him where to get one.'

'We'd be really grateful.'

'It's better than what we used to have to do. My grandmother told me that the best thing to do was to use a little piece of soft natural sponge soaked in a solution of water and vinegar.' She pulled a face. 'But it was so messy.'

'It sounds it! I'll talk to Franz, then. I'm sure he'll feel as I do. Many thanks, Herta. That's a huge weight off my mind.'

Herta sighed heavily. 'I wish I could get rid of the weight on my mind as easily as that.'

'What're you worrying about? Perhaps I can help.'

Herta shook her head. 'You can't, I'm afraid. It's Karl and what he's teaching. But you can't make him listen, he's so stubborn. I'm sure Franz has told you what Karl's doing.'

'Franz said he'd tried to dissuade Karl about something, but he didn't go into details. It struck me as unusual as they've never before disagreed about their teaching material.'

'Karl insists on teaching Heinrich Heine's poetry, and I think that's very unwise.'

'But he teaches Heine every year. He's his favourite poet, isn't he? I've heard that Karl brings Heine's poems alive for the pupils. It's good that he teaches a poet he loves and understands so well, isn't it?'

'Of course, it is. It's just that—and I hate myself for even thinking like this, let alone saying it, Dorothy—but it could be risky. Heine is Jewish.'

Dorothy smiled with incredulity. 'But that doesn't make his poems or novels any less excellent. That's the sort of literature young people *should* read, isn't it, but might need guidance with?'

Herta nodded. 'That's what Karl said, and he doesn't heed me any more than he heeds Franz. He can't see that there's a risk in what he's doing. Not here in Rundheim, he says. Not among friends, in a school that he's taught in for years. He loves Heine's poetry and sees no reason not to teach it as he's done every year since he started at the school.'

Dorothy nodded slowly. 'I suppose the trouble is, Karl is a good man, and trusting of others. But not everyone is as good. Would you like me to ask Franz to speak to him again? From what he said before, I know he's worried, too.'

'That would be so helpful. Thank you. You and Franz are good friends.'

'It's the least we can do, especially when you've been so kind as to invite us to join you today.'

'And you must come again next year, too. Even though the white asparagus season lasts until the end of June, Karl's uncle always holds his celebration on the third Saturday in May, so you know now the date to save.'

'We'd love to,' Dorothy said.

'Right, then,' Herta said, standing up. 'Enough of being serious. Let's go and watch the children and see that they're not doing anything stupid. And I'm going to stop worrying about Karl as it's pointless to do so,' she added.

24

C horton House,
Saturday evening, July, 1933

LOUISA PICKED up her glass of white wine, settled back in the large comfortable sofa and looked around the sitting room while she waited for Nellie to finish pouring herself a glass of her favourite Chateau Mossé, and come and join her.

The stone flags were covered by rugs that had faded over the years. Their former colours were reflected in the jugs of dried flowers that stood on the tables and windowsill, and in a large display in the hearth, which would be replaced in winter by a blazing fire. It was a quiet, understated room, she thought, one in which it was easy to hide from the outside world, and relax.

It was a sign of the person she used to be that she'd never properly seen the house until after the accident—she'd always been too busy finding fault with her parents or

Christopher, or carping about what she'd like, but didn't have.

But in the years since her eyes had been opened to the unpleasant truth about how badly she'd behaved, she'd increasingly come to appreciate the quiet beauty of Chorton, and to realise that in having been able to spend so much of her childhood in such a house, she'd been given a unique experience to treasure.

She glanced up as Nellie came across to her.

'A penny for them,' Nellie said, sitting down in the armchair closest to Louisa.

'I was just thinking what a lovely warm and friendly room this is, and I was wondering what an outsider would think the first time they saw it. That's all.'

Nellie glanced over the rim of her glass at Louisa. 'So, what do you think of our guest, then?' she asked. 'Or rather your father's guest. He was the one who invited Mr McAllister for the weekend.'

Louisa took a sip of her wine. 'I was talking generally. But as far as Mr McAllister goes, I've hardly seen him. He and Father talked about business for the whole of the journey from London—that's how they met, you know. Mr McAllister's put his money into the bank and Father's overseeing everything. And after they got here, they disappeared into the Library with Uncle Joseph. I walked to the village to get some fresh air, so I missed lunch.'

'You may not have talked to him much, but you've certainly seen him. So, what do you think of his appearance?'

Louisa's eyes narrowed. 'I know that about twelve years ago, my father invited Walter here for the weekend, certain that the two of you would get on, and he was right. But that doesn't mean he's doing it again, this time for my benefit, if that's what you're thinking.'

Nellie's eyes opened wide in mock surprise. 'Nothing could have been further from my mind. But now that you've brought up the subject,' she added with a giggle. 'D'you think he's good looking?'

Louisa shrugged. 'He's got a nice back of the head, which is just about all I've seen of him. What d'you think?'

'I wouldn't call him handsome, as such. In the sort of books I read, he'd be described as craggy. Craggy is better than handsome. Take a good look at him this evening, Lou. I think you might like what you see.'

HIS FACE A SCOWL, Joseph stood fidgeting while Maud adjusted his bow tie. 'Is a suit really necessary?' he grumbled. 'He seems a casual sort of person, and we're only nine of us this evening.'

'We've dispensed with a dinner suit, but wearing a suit is a requirement. We don't know Mr McAllister well, and it's a matter of respect.'

'He doesn't seem the sort of person who'd mind if I appeared in nothing but Mrs Spencer's pinafore. If I did, I'd feel much more relaxed.'

'Well, for the sake of everyone present this evening, especially the ladies, I sincerely hope that you'd have chosen the wrap-around pinafore, and not the one that's open at the back!'

Joseph grinned at her. 'The latter would certainly have started a lively conversation, wouldn't it? So, what do you think of the man, Maud?'

She stepped back and surveyed the tie. 'You'll do,' she said. 'I haven't really given him any thought. Should I?'

'Charles has obviously got his eye on him for Louisa. He wants to repeat for Louisa what he did for Nellie, so he must think Mr McAllister a possible match for Louisa. I'm glad that Charles and Louisa seem to be closer these days. Charles, too, has behaved pretty badly in the past, and more than once, and it's only right that he's given Louisa the same chance of redemption that he had.'

'I completely agree.'

'A positive outcome of the accident is that it showed Charles how much he cares for Sarah, and it's improved him as a person. Just as it's improved Louisa.'

Maud picked up a light stole for the evening. 'I'm sure you're right about Charles's intentions. Charles would know that Mr McAllister is financially sound, being his banker, but while he'll have come with references, I doubt that they commented on his suitability as a son-in-law. I imagine that's what this weekend's about.'

Joseph nodded. 'We'll listen to the man with that in mind. It'll be easier to get the measure of him as we aren't a large group. I'm sorry that Sarah couldn't join us, but the way that she's thrown herself into the organisation of the latest charity dinner shows that she's back to her former self, and that's something to celebrate.'

'It's unfortunate that Charles mistook the dates and Sarah's dinner clashed with his weekend invitation to Mr McAllister, but if his plans work out, there'll be plenty of other occasions for Sarah to meet him,' she said, slipping the stole around her shoulders. 'I'd rather thought Thomas might join us,' she added.

Joseph shook his head. 'I knew he wouldn't. He sees Louisa just about every day now that she's in his section, and she's still tirelessly over-solicitous about trying to help him. I can understand him not wanting that all weekend as well as throughout the week.'

'She obviously sees being pleasant to someone so frequently grumpy as a way of atoning for her past,' Maud said.

'I realise that. And so does Thomas. Fortunately, he can joke about it. I'm sorry that Robert couldn't make it, though. It's a pity that he agreed a while ago to take James and his friend to Whipsnade Zoo for James's birthday treat.'

'I'm certain they'll enjoy that as much as a meeting with Mr McAllister, if not more so.'

'I expect they will. The boys were really keen to see the brown bears, and also to see the animals that were bought last year from a defunct travelling menagerie. James saw the pictures in the newspapers of the larger animals walking from Dunstable Station to the zoo, and he's wanted to go there ever since.'

'I'm sure they'll have a lovely time, darling. And if Mr McAllister shows any interest in Louisa, and it's reciprocated, then, as with Sarah, they're certain to meet him on a future occasion. Shall we go down, then?'

'So what are your impressions of Oxfordshire, Mr McAllister?' Joseph asked, indicating that the maid start pouring the port. 'By the way, you'll note that the ladies aren't leaving us this evening. Since we're smaller in number this weekend— and we're usually less formal when we're among friends, anyway—we decided to ignore tradition this evening. And, in fact, I understand that more and more people regularly ignore it these days. So, what about Oxfordshire?'

'It's a lovely county, and one I'd like to know better, sir. Oxford is a good place for someone like me who's an interest in cars, and I should definitely like to talk to you about getting a property in the area. Somewhere in the country-side, but probably a little closer to Oxford itself than we are at present.'

'You've a place in London, too, haven't you, Mr McAllis-ter?' Nellie said.

'It's Philip, Nellie,' he told her with a smile. 'You're right, I have. I'm renting a small flat that's not far from the under-ground station in Belsize Park.'

'A flat!' Maud exclaimed in surprise.

Philip smiled at her. 'Yours is a typical reaction, Mrs Linford. Unfortunately, flats are the victims of widespread prejudice. Unreasonably so, I'd say. People tend to associate them with Victorian tenements and working-class housing. I've even seen them lampooned in popular publications. But if any of those who deride flats took the time to visit one, I think they'd be amazed at what can be done with a small space.'

'How small a space?' Walter asked.

'Most, like mine, have one bedroom, and there's a living room, a tiny kitchen, and a small bathroom. We've central heating and a shared communal space, which includes a laundry. And because I overlook the back, I have a balcony. It's all I need.'

Nellie frowned. 'It doesn't sound an awful lot of room.'

'Nellie's wondering what she'd do with the rest of her wardrobe, once she'd filled all the rooms with her clothes,' Walter remarked.

They all laughed.

'I'll have a home outside London, so a small space in London is all I need or want. I believe that's true of an increasing number of people. It's well situated for getting to my office in London, which is important. Charles tells me that Belsize Park is fairly near your headquarters in Kentish Town, sir.'

Joseph nodded. 'It is. But Kentish Town is considerably less desirable as a residential area. It's why my father bought there. You could get much more property for your money, and there were a lot of potential workers living in the streets around the premises.'

'I can heartily endorse what Philip says about the use of space,' Charles said, taking a sip of port. 'He was kind enough to invite me to the flat one evening, and I was pleasantly surprised by what I saw. Linford & Sons would do well to look into building flats, Joseph. There's going to be a growing demand in cities, I strongly suspect.'

'It's certainly an interesting thought,' Joseph mused. 'We're very much focused on bungalows now, and on our estate houses, too, of course. But there's no reason not to look into this as a possible area for future expansion. I'll have a word with Robert, Charles. My son, Robert, recently took over from me as Chairman of Linford & Sons, Mr McAllister, and I try not to interfere too much.'

'What?' Maud and Charles exclaimed simultaneously.

They all laughed again.

'Did the flat come with furniture, Mr McAllister?' Louisa asked when their laughter had died down.

'I don't know if I told you, but Louisa's recently started working for the family firm, Philip,' Charles cut in. 'She's a member of the house interiors' department. My brother, Thomas, is in charge of that.'

Philip smiled at Louisa. 'Yes, it did, Louisa—it's included in the price. The furniture's made of plywood, and most of it is built in. There's an easy chair, an electric fire, a wireless and a cocktail cabinet.'

'It sounds ideal,' Maud murmured, sounding less than

convinced.

'It is, Mrs Linford. I intend to spend my weekends at the place I get near Oxford, and I'll also stay there when I have to go up to Coventry or Birmingham, for example. The flat will be ample for my needs when I'm in London. And if nothing else, a flat is a useful lesson in managing with less.'

'What's the advantage of managing with less?' Nellie asked.

'The architect who designed the flats believes that we shouldn't be weighed down by our tangible possessions, but should be free to enjoy our other possessions, too, such as the ability to travel. There's a lot to be said for that.'

'I hope you're listening, Nellie,' Walter said, with feigned severity.

Nellie laughed.

'Have you visited many interesting places, Mr McAllister?' Louisa asked.

'I've been to America, and also to France, Italy and Germany. It looks as if I'll be going to Germany again in a year or so. This time to Cologne.'

'To Germany!' Nellie sat up. 'My sister, Dorothy, lives in Germany.'

'Whereabouts?'

Nellie looked swiftly at Joseph, and then back at Philip. She shrugged. 'I've no idea. Father cut her off when she married a German. We're not in touch with her.'

'I don't think we need to maintain this fiction any longer, Nellie, do we?' Joseph said drily. 'You know perfectly well where your sister lives—you've been writing to her for years.'

Nellie opened her mouth to protest, but Joseph raised his finger to silence her.

'She lives in a place called Rundheim, Mr McAllister. I

don't know any more about it than that. But if you want to know more, I'm sure that Nellie will be happy to oblige.'

Nellie glanced at her father, and giggled.

She turned back to Philip. 'It's just as well that Uncle Thomas isn't here. If he heard you say you were going to Germany, he'd probably have got up and walked out. And possibly Aunt Sarah, too. Why are you going?'

'For work. When General Motors purchased a controlling eighty per cent holding in Opel about four years ago, Henry Ford decided to build a complete Ford auto-factory in Cologne. Two years ago, the first Cologne-produced Ford rolled off the production line. I've been invited to visit their research and development department. That's my field of interest.'

Charles stared at him with a degree of concern. 'Do you think it's entirely safe to go there at present? In the newspaper last week, they listed the series of anti-Jewish laws that have been passed since Hitler came to power.'

Philip nodded. 'Yes, I saw that.'

'And there's the book burning in Berlin in May, and the book burnings in other parts of Germany, too. Each was done as if it was something to celebrate—bands were playing, people were marching, songs were sung, and there were loud proclamations that they were cleansing the German culture of the un-German spirit. What on earth does that mean?'

Philip nodded. 'I've been following that, too. It was quite shocking, and definitely anti-Jewish. Nearly all the authors of those so-called degenerate works, such as Thomas Mann, Marcel Proust and Karl Marx, happened to be Jewish. If I were Jewish, I wouldn't be going anywhere near Germany. But I'm not, and I've no reason to think I'll be at risk.'

'A climate of violence affects everyone,' Charles said.

'And there's no doubt that since Hitler came to power, there's been an increasing amount of violent activity in Germany.'

Maud nodded. 'Charles is right, Mr McAllister. I share his concern. Is your trip really necessary?'

'The violence was against books, rather than people,' Philip said, turning slightly to Maud. 'If I felt I'd be putting myself at risk, I wouldn't go. Indeed, if that were so, there'd be no question of me being sent there.'

Walter nodded. 'You're probably right, Philip. The burnings were a horrific display of power, and of disrespect to the country's culture and history, but there's no reason for you to fear coming under attack.'

'Do you like reading, Mr McAllister?' Louisa asked

Philip made a tutting noise. 'Unless you want me to call you Miss Linford every time I speak to you, Louisa, you're going to have to call me Philip you know.'

She blushed. 'Do you read much, Philip?'

'I do, but not the sort of reading you mean. I read car manuals, and *The Times* and *Financial Times*.'

'I'm curious to know what a car expert drives,' Walter remarked. 'As Charles drove you here today, enlightenment was impossible.'

'At the moment, a Morris Cowley. The Cowley's had a major redesign, and has been fitted with innovations. It's now got a rear-mounted petrol tank, hydraulic brakes and Magna-type wire wheels. And the body and radiator design are also new. Unsurprisingly, it was the best-selling Morris last year, and I've enjoyed driving it. But I'll be changing it for a Riley Nine Kestrel next year, which is a fastback low-built sporting saloon.'

'Sarah and I have been trying to persuade Louisa to let

us get her another car,' Charles said. 'What car might tempt her, do you think?'

Philip glanced at Louisa and gave her a slight smile. She blushed again.

'You know I don't want another car, Father,' she said, a trace of irritation in her voice.

'But if you were to change your mind, Lou, it would be useful to know what to look for. As we know nothing about cars, it's wise to take advantage of someone who does. What would you recommend for Louisa, Philip?'

'There are new models coming out all the time, so don't hold me to this. But if you were looking in the next few months, I'd suggest an Austin 12/6 Harley. It's intended for an owner-driver, and not to be chauffeur-driven like most of the earlier cars, so they've simplified its maintenance and made it easier for the owner to service it.'

Charles grunted in appreciation.

'Also, it's the first Austin to have an all-steel body. The original standard saloon had a three-speed gearbox, but the deluxe model that I'm suggesting has a four-speed gearbox. As it was only introduced last year, it should be around for a while.'

Charles nodded. 'Interesting,' he said. 'Very interesting.'

'And, of, course, there's the Ford Tudor Y, made in Ford's new plant in Dagenham. That's a good little car, too, and half the price that cars used to be a few years ago,' Philip added. 'You don't have to be wealthy to own a car these days.'

Charles nodded again. 'That's very helpful, Philip. Thank you.'

Nellie and Louisa exchanged amused glances.

'Tell the truth, Father, you didn't understand a word of

that, did you?' Christopher said, sitting back in his chair and grinning. 'The bit about something being cheaper might have registered, but nothing else. Go on, admit it. Later, you'll be taking Walter aside and asking him to tell you what Philip was talking about. But you'll be out of luck—Walter won't have understood a word, either! There was nothing legal involved.'

'I'm afraid that Chris is right about me, Philip,' Charles said ruefully. 'But I can't vouch for Walter's understanding, or lack of it.'

Walter laughed. 'I'm on a par with Charles, I'd say.'

'It's my fault, I'm afraid,' Philip said. 'I tend to get carried away when talking about cars. But if I'm not being presumptuous, Charles, if Louisa *does* decide she wants a car, I'd be happy to advise you, and could probably arrange something suitable through friends.'

'That's very good of you, Philip. It's much appreciated.'

Joseph helped himself to another piece of Stilton cheese, and took a sip of his port. 'I, too, might ask for your help at a future date, Philip, when we come to change our car. I trust that Maud and I can drop the formality and call you Philip?'

'I'd be very happy if you did so, sir.'

'It works both ways,' Joseph said with a smile.

Louisa glanced at the clock on the wall. 'I think I'll say goodnight now. We'll be leaving soon after lunch tomorrow, and I want to be up early to make the most of the morning.'

'Why don't you show Philip around the house after breakfast, Lou, and perhaps both of you go for a walk after that?' Charles suggested quickly. 'I need to have a word with Joseph and Walter before lunch, and Philip really should see something of the area while we're here.'

Steely eyed, she stared pointedly at her father. 'Of course,' she said. She turned to Christopher. 'You must come, too, Christopher. You'll know all about the flowers we come across. I don't even know the names of anything.'

'I'd like to, Lou, but unfortunately I can't. I've promised to help on the farm with the harvesting of the winter-sown barley and wheat. One of the workers is unwell and I'm taking his place.'

She threw him a glacial look, and turned to Nellie.

Nellie held up her hands. 'Don't look at me. I've promised to test Emily on her mathematics,' she said, and she stood up. 'I think I'll do as Louisa is doing and go up now, too. Goodnight, everyone.'

'Goodnight,' Louisa said shortly. With a furious glance at her father, which embraced her brother, too, she turned and followed Nellie out of the dining room.

'There's no real reason why you couldn't have come with me tomorrow, Nellie, and you know it,' she said as they crossed the hall on their way to the central staircase. 'Now I'm stuck with him on my own.'

Her hand on the banister and her foot on the first stair, Nellie paused. 'Yes, I could've come with you, Lou, and I'm sure that Christopher could have done so, too, and that Uncle Charles doesn't really need to discuss anything with Walter and Father. But we all want see you happy, and it just might be that Philip is what you need.'

'I *am* happy. I don't need Philip or anyone.'

'But it's obvious that you're not,' Nellie said gently. 'At twenty-three, you should be out nightly with highly unsuitable people, going to all sorts of wildly exciting clubs—you should be a source of constant worry to your parents. But you're not. Or not for those reasons, at least. You go to work, meet the same few people every day, and then go home in the evening and sit and read a book. You're not attempting to make any new friends.'

'That's up to me, isn't it?' she snapped.

'Maybe so, but we're your family, and we love you, Lou, and we're worried about you. It seems as if you're still punishing yourself for what was an accident several years ago, and it's time that you stopped. Aunt Sarah is better now. There's no reason for you not to be happy.'

'She still gets pain at times. How could I not punish myself?'

'But you've done so, and we're now saying that enough's enough. To continue in such a way could start to be seen as self-indulgence. Your feeling of guilt has dominated your life for long enough, and prevented you from doing what you should be doing. If nothing else, it can't be good for your mother to be worrying about you like this. You could even make her start feeling guilty.'

Louisa looked at her. Her brow creased. 'I hadn't thought of that,' she said slowly.

'Uncle Charles has obviously invited Philip as he thinks the two of you might get on. He was right about Walter and me, so he might be right about you and Philip. For both of your parents' sake, at least give Philip a chance.'

Louisa gave a slight shrug. 'I don't have a lot of choice, do I?' she said with a half-smile. 'But I promise to think about what you said.'

25

T*he following morning*

'IT'S VERY KIND OF you to show me around this morning,' Philip said, as he and Louisa walked up the gentle slope at the back of the house. 'When I went to bed last night, I was certain you'd find a way of wriggling out of it.'

She tried to look shocked. 'I wouldn't have dreamed of doing so.'

'Wouldn't you?' he asked, and he glanced at her in amusement.

'Well, only for a minute or two,' she said with a smile. 'It would've looked very rude last night to have said no in front of everyone there, you being a guest, and it would have looked even worse if I'd left you to your own devices this morning, everyone else being so amazingly busy today.' He grinned at her. 'I was pretty annoyed at Father, though,' she added.

'It *was* a bit cack-handed, wasn't it?'

'That's a good way of describing his obviousness. But he's landed you in it, too, not just me. You could hardly refuse to be shown around just as I couldn't refuse to be your guide. In the past, I'd probably have said to hell with politeness, and dug my heels in, but not in the present.'

'Then it's lucky I met you in the present.'

'It most definitely is—the old me was most unpleasant. If you had met the old me, you'd have been the one to wriggle out of this morning.'

He smiled broadly. 'I can certainly agree that the present you is a most attractive proposition, and one I'd like to get to know better.'

She felt herself colouring, and giggled in embarrassment. 'I'm not sure that my words came out quite as I meant them to.'

'But *my* words came out as I intended.'

She went a deeper shade of red. 'You don't have to be polite. We've escaped their surveillance, so if you've a car manual tucked in your pocket for emergencies, you can consider this an emergency and hide in a thicket and read.'

He stretched out his hands, palms up. 'How could I be so ungallant when you've shown yourself to be the perfect lady?'

'We've agreed that I didn't have any choice. Consider yourself at liberty to do what you want.'

'As I've been looking forward to spending the morning with you ever since your father suggested it, a morning with you is what I want. It's infinitely preferable to a few hours with my trusty manual.'

She frowned. 'I thought we were being honest with each other. You don't mean that.'

'Yes, I do,' he said.

The warmth in his voice took her by surprise.

For the first time, she looked at him properly, really looked at him.

A strange feeling crept through her body. She could see what Nellie had meant by craggy rather than good looking. Craggy was the right word. And so was rugged. But there was something else about him, something she couldn't find words to describe.

Her mouth felt dry.

Their eyes met, and for a moment they held.

She coughed. 'All right, then,' she said. Her voice sounded high-pitched to her ears. She coughed again.

Reaching the top of the slope, they turned to look towards the back of the house and the view that lay beyond. 'I brought you up here first of all,' she said, 'as I thought you'd like to see the view of the house set against the countryside of Oxfordshire. And there it is.'

She waved her hand in the direction of the panorama that lay beyond the dry-stone wall surrounding Chorton—a sprawling patchwork of hedges and fields, of trees and rolling foothills, and of small stone houses, the colour of honey, topped by roofs, some thatched, some tiled, some in a cluster of gold, and others a fragment of shining honey that crouched amid the green.

Everything gleamed in the brightness of the morning sun.

'It's beautiful,' he said. 'No wonder you all love it here.' A chorus of birdsong rose from the trees. 'What are those birds?' he asked, looking up.

'You're asking the wrong person,' she said with a laugh. 'You should ask Christopher. He knows the name of every bird you're likely to hear. He loves the countryside, and wants to work on a farm. Every time he comes here, which is often, he goes to the farm over there and asks for work.' She waved her arm to the right. 'You might have gathered as much last night.'

'I remember he said he'd be there today.'

His gaze went beyond the thickets and brightly coloured flowers that formed a dense border between the lawn and the stone wall that ran down the side of the garden, to the roofs of the farm buildings that could be glimpsed in the distance.

'The farmer isn't stupid,' she continued. 'In the face of free labour from a strong and willing helper, he invariably finds something for Christopher to do.'

'Such as the all-important task that's preventing Christopher from joining us this morning.'

They smiled at each other. 'Exactly,' she said.

'Good for him.' He looked back at the view ahead. 'Is that the village of Chorton?' he asked, pointing to a group of houses huddling in a gap between the hills.

She shook her head. 'No, there's no such place. When Grandfather married Bertha Chorton, her father gave them this house as a wedding present. All my great-grandfather asked was that they kept his surname alive by calling it Chorton House. Bertha was an only child, you see.'

'That was some present.'

'It was, and Grandfather was happy to call it Chorton House. He and my great-grandfather were both builders, and got on very well. Of course, the house was much smaller then. Just four bedrooms, a reception room, dining room and the servants' quarters. Some years later, Grandfather, helped by Great-grandfather, built an identical two-storey wing on either side of the central staircase.'

He glanced at sides of the house. 'You wouldn't realise they were later additions.'

'That's because they used stone of the same colour and age. Grandfather took over one of the reception rooms in the left wing, and called it his library. It's now Uncle Joseph's library. The kitchen, scullery, pantry, boiler room and servants' quarters, including a bathroom and water closet, are all in the other wing.'

'How many bedrooms are there?'

'Eight, and there are two bathrooms with an integral water closet. There are actually more bedrooms than that as the attic rooms were converted into servants' bedrooms.'

'What a lovely place for you to have been able to come as children,' he said.

'Yes, it was. I was thinking that yesterday. There was always something to do. Our favourite game was hide and seek, which we'd play among the trees. And if the weather was too bad to go out into the garden, we played indoors. Poor Cook. We were always begging her to make our favourite cakes, and let us scrape the bowl clean when she'd poured the mixture into the tins. It would be lovely to be able to go back to that time,' she said, as they started walking down the slope towards the drive.

He glanced at her. 'You sound wistful.'

She shrugged. 'Life was better then.' And she fell silent.

'Which of them founded Linford & Sons?' he asked after a moment or two.

'Grandfather, but some of the money came from Great-grandfather. Uncle Joseph is the oldest of Grandfather's three sons, and he now runs the company, or he did until recently. His son, Robert, is now in charge. Uncle Thomas, Father's brother, looks after the house interiors' section, and I work for him. Linford & Sons banks with Father's bank, so as you can tell, it's very much a family business.'

'It must be extremely pleasant, all of you working for the

same end,' he said, as they went past the house and on to the gravelled drive that led to large wrought-iron gates set in the dry-stone wall. 'Since we're almost at the road, we could have a look at the surrounding area. If you don't mind, that is.'

She hesitated.

'If we went back indoors now,' he continued, 'they'd be greatly disappointed that we'd spent such a short amount of time together. You don't want to do that to them, do you? And put me at risk of having to talk figures with your father, or houses with your uncle. Take pity on me.' He put his hands together, palm to palm, in an attitude of prayer.

She laughed. 'I thought you'd want to talk about houses. You said last night you were interested in buying one.'

'And I am. And I very much enjoyed the discussion last night, but it doesn't mean that I want to carry it into this morning. Your uncle Joseph's invited me to his Club next week, and that's the place to resume our conversation. On a lovely Sunday morning like this, it's far more pleasant to be outside, particularly when you have an agreeable companion.'

He held open the iron gates for her to pass between them. 'And it's far more interesting to talk to you than them,' he added.

She blushed. 'When you put it like that,' she said, 'I can't do anything but agree to a walk. But there's no need to say nice things about me,' she added awkwardly as she went out on to the lane. 'I don't believe they're genuinely felt, so it makes me feel uncomfortable.'

When he'd shut the gates, they turned to their right and strolled along the lane, the wall surrounding Chorton House on their right, and on their left, a line of roadside hedges that hid from sight the fields behind them.

'The fields over there also belong to the farm,' she said, glancing towards the hedges. 'You can't expect much from a conversation if talking to me is interesting,' she added after a moment or two. 'I'm the least interesting of people.'

'That in itself is interesting.'

Her brow creased. 'What d'you mean?'

'You're beautiful—'

She laughed in derision.

'Yes, you are. But you obviously don't seem to realise it. And when people try to tell you that you're pleasant to be with, you don't believe that either. You have none of the ploys, if that's the right word, of women who know they're beautiful. But you *are*.'

He stopped, and turned to her. 'You have striking eyes, Louisa—they're dark and mysterious. You've features that don't need adornment to look really lovely. Your hair is a wonderful rich brown, and although you've scraped it back from your face without any pretence of style, from the bits that have escaped their restraint, I can see that it's wavy. If you freed it from its confines, I think it would fall in curls around your face. You really are beautiful.'

She felt her heart pounding. 'You're mad.'

He smiled. 'Maybe. But I prefer to describe myself as interested, using both meanings of the word. For a start, I'm interested in why a beautiful woman would try to play down her looks, and not want to be noticed. How old are you?'

'You shouldn't ask a woman such a question, but for your information, I'm twenty-three.'

'So, a beautiful twenty-three-year-old, in the prime of her life, hides from the world, and seems genuinely to have no belief in herself. That's interesting, Louisa.'

'Are you always this blunt?'

'No. My interest has to be engaged before I say what I

think. If I'm not interested, I might comment on the weather, on the thinness of the cucumber in the sandwiches, on the lady's exquisite choice of cardigan, and so on.'

She laughed. 'As I said, you're mad. Up there, by the way,' she said, pointing to the right, 'is a narrow track that runs up the hill between our wall and the farm. Christopher saves time by going over the wall. And so did my cousin Robert years ago when he fell in love with Lily. She was a Land Girl on the farm.'

As they resumed walking along the lane, she told him about what happened between Lily and Robert.

By the time she'd finished the story, they'd reached a bridleway through the fields. They turned left on to it, and began to make their way up a gentle incline.

The hedgerows on either side gradually gave way to low stone walls, and they were able to see into the fields of crops that they were passing, and to glance at sheep grazing on stretches of grass. Every so often, they passed an isolated cottage that glowed in the morning sun.

'What d'you have against cars that you don't want another one?' he asked, breaking the companionable silence. 'Did you have an accident or something?'

She hesitated. 'Yes, I did. I was seventeen at the time. Mother was hurt in the accident. But I don't talk about it. You can tell me, instead, about your Riley Nine Kestrel.'

He stopped walking and stared at her in undisguised pleasure. 'You've remembered the name of the car I'm going to get, Louisa. So you were listening to me just as intently as I was listening to you.'

She gave an embarrassed laugh. 'I've a good memory; that's all. Let's carry on walking, shall we?'

. . .

'IT WAS KIND of your father to let you come out with me this morning,' Philip said, closing the iron gates behind them. 'I've really enjoyed myself.'

Louisa started to walk up the drive. 'It was certainly very unlike him to wave me off on a walk with a man in the way that he did. No chaperone in attendance. No admonition about what might befall a woman who lowered her guard.'

He grinned at her. 'Like I said, it was kind.'

'Or desperate. He's probably hoping that if he pushes me forward, embellished with a car, he might get rid of me. We encourage people to buy our houses by offering extra fixtures and fittings, after all, so someone who wants an Austin, was it, might take me on.'

He laughed.

'Or he might be hoping that I'd be compromised, having being alone with a man in the fields. And in the face of the Linford wrath, the man would have no choice but to do the decent thing.'

He lifted his wrist and glanced very obviously at his watch. 'If you'd like me to compromise you, I'd be happy to oblige. We could go back to that copse we passed—we'd be private there. But we couldn't take too long about it—it's almost time for lunch.'

She stared at him.

Grey eyes that danced with amusement stared back at her.

She burst out laughing. 'Tempting though the thought of rolling around in the dirt, with twigs in my eyes and my ears and in places a lady wouldn't mention, I think I'll give your offer a miss. You're safe. Let's go and have that lunch.'

Both started walking towards the house again.

'On a serious note, Louisa,' Philip said as they reached the front door. 'If I wanted another car, I'd buy one. As for compromising you.' He smiled. 'There's always next time. And I'm very much hoping there'll be a next time. I'll be in touch.'

He held the door open. 'After you,' he said. 'And with that, too, I intend more than one meaning of the word.'

26

J oseph's Club, London,
        the following Wednesday

'I LIKE THE ROOM,' Philip said, looking around the Club's large airy dining room.

The early afternoon sun was bouncing off the crystal wine glasses and silverware set out on the mahogany circular tables, and catching the peaks of the peaked white napkins that stood between the silver knives and forks on the tables as yet unseated.

A mahogany buffet table ran along the length of the back wall, the sheen of its wood agleam in the light of the sun.

His eyes returned to Joseph, who was sitting across from him. 'I'm very grateful to you, Joseph, for inviting me to join the three of you for lunch,' he said, folding his napkin and putting it next to his empty pudding bowl. 'It was an excellent meal.'

'A pleasure, dear boy. It's been a delightful break from our customary routine.' He raised his finger to attract the attention of a waiter. 'Cognac for everyone?' he asked as the waiter approached. Hearing the murmur of assent from Charles, Thomas and Philip, he gave the order.

'Joseph said you were planning to buy a place near Oxford, Philip,' Thomas remarked, as another waiter removed the dirty plates from the table.

Philip nodded. 'That's right. I need somewhere I can easily get to from London, and which is a straightforward run to Coventry and Birmingham, and also to the north of the country. Oxford's the ideal location, and it has the bonus of good rail links as well. It's also an important centre of car production.'

'Will you be looking for an estate house?' Thomas asked.

Philip shook his head. 'I don't think so. I'm sure they're well built and attractive, but I don't want to be near any other house, and I'd like a view. I want a retreat from the world at the end of the week.' He paused, and then added, 'Chorton House isn't for sale by any chance, is it?'

They all laughed.

Joseph took out his pipe and put it on the table next to him. 'You can be sure that we'll do our best to deliver whatever you decide you'd like. We're used to buying an individual plot and building on it from a design approved by the buyer, so we could do that.'

Philip nodded. 'That's good to know.'

'Or we could look for a small country house surrounded by gardens and trees, for example, and make extensive improvements to the interior. We do that on occasions, too.

That's one of the reasons I wanted you to meet Thomas at this early stage. Interiors are his field.'

'Both approaches sound interesting. I'm really grateful, Joseph.'

Thomas grinned at him. 'There's no need to thank Joseph, Philip. You can be sure that he'll be amply thanked in the fullness of time by a form of gratitude that will deplete the funds you've deposited with Charles.'

They laughed again.

The waiter moved around the table, putting a snifter of cognac next to each of them, and then left.

Charles looked at Joseph in amusement 'Forgive me for thinking that you've retired, Joseph. The *we* you keep using is confusing me.'

'There's retirement and retirement, Charles.'

'So it seems.' Charles glanced at Philip. 'It sounds as if you expect to travel a lot, Philip,' he said, picking up his glass and gently swirling the contents.

'Compared with some people, I probably do. I've already been to America—'

Charles, Thomas and Joseph glanced swiftly across the table at each other, and then promptly looked down at their drinks.

'I was there at the time of the Crash and just after,' Philip went on, 'but I don't anticipate going again. Or at least, not for a while. I do expect to be visiting a number of towns across England, though.'

Joseph stared at him in surprise. 'Is this to check out different methods of car production? I believe you said you were in research and development.'

'That's right. You've got to keep learning. We've had more than thirty years of rapid change since Austin produced the first all-British 4-wheel car, and a year later, started Wolseley Motors in Birmingham with the aid of the Vickers brothers, and we must make sure that we continue to progress. My father worked for Wolseley Motors, and that's where I started.'

'So it's an inherited interest, is it?' Charles said with a smile.

'You could say that. I joined my father twelve years ago. It was an exciting time to be an engineer, and it still is. Although the war brought the industry to a standstill, the needs of war production led to the development of new techniques of mass production, and last year, we overtook France to become the largest car producer in Europe. That's a position we want to retain.'

'That's very interesting, Philip,' Charles said, nodding. 'You're clearly excellent at what you do. Your financial status testifies to that.'

'Only in part, I must admit. I also owe a great deal to a generous legacy from my only uncle, and to what my parents left me. Sadly, they're now deceased.'

'Maybe so, but I can see that if I take up your kind offer of help with a car for Louisa, I couldn't be in better hands.'

'I'd do my best.'

Thomas looked at his watch. 'I ought to be going. Work to do,' he said, getting up. He glanced down at Philip. 'I've enjoyed meeting you, Philip. If you feel like stopping by the place in Kentish Town at any time, I'd be happy to show you around.'

'I'll certainly do that.'

'I assume you don't want a lift, Thomas,' Charles said, swiftly finishing his cognac.

'You assume correctly, Charles. George will be downstairs with the car. I'm still enjoying the feeling of independence, having now bought a car and got myself a driver.'

With a nod to his brothers, Thomas left.

Charles sat back and stared after Thomas in exaggerated amazement. 'That must be the first time Thomas has got through a whole meal without accusing us of cowardice for staying at home when he went off to fight, and without mentioning his missing leg. Nor the injury to his hand. What's more, he sounded positively friendly!'

He smiled at Philip. 'Well done, Philip. You've obviously had a salutary effect on him. I'd like to stay longer to work out your secret, but regretfully I must leave, too. I feel it incumbent on me to be seen at the bank at least five minutes before it's time to go home.'

He stood up, paused, and looked down at Philip. 'I believe you're taking Louisa to the zoological gardens in Regent's Park tomorrow,' he said. He hesitated. 'Just you and her.'

'That's right. You've nothing to worry about, Charles. I'll look after her.'

Charles cleared his throat in obvious embarrassment. 'Of course, old man. If I wasn't confident of that, you'd be taking her mother with you.'

Bidding them goodbye, he left the table.

Joseph raised his eyebrows questioningly. 'Another cognac, Philip?' he asked. 'We could ask them to bring it to us in the Library, and relax over it with a pipe or cigar, or whatever your preference is.'

'Another cognac would go down very well, thank you.'

'Good. I've been intrigued since you told me on the telephone that you'd a matter to discuss with me. But as Charles and Thomas had already agreed to join me for lunch today,

I've had to curb my curiosity till they'd gone.' He gave him a wry smile. 'I suspect it wasn't about the number of bath-rooms you'd like in your house.'

Philip laughed. 'You're right; it wasn't.'

Joseph signalled to the waiter, and asked him to bring another cognac to them in the Library. They pushed back their chairs and stood up. Picking up his pipe, Joseph led the way out of the dining room.

'THAT WAS A MOST PLEASANT LUNCH,' Philip said when they'd settled into leather armchairs tucked into a corner of the room. Behind them, the panelled walls were lined with bookshelves. 'I enjoyed meeting Charles again socially, and also being introduced to Thomas for the first time.'

'As Charles said, you saw Thomas on unusually good form. He can be the most infuriating of men. Louisa's about the only one who has any patience with him. You want to hear what Thomas thinks of her ministrations. Or rather, you don't.'

The waiter brought them their drinks, and moved away.

Joseph took out his pipe and tin of tobacco, and looked expectantly at Philip. 'Well?'

Philip leaned slightly forward. 'This isn't top secret, or I wouldn't be discussing it with you. Discretion is required, however. It's one of those things that would be better kept to ourselves.'

Joseph paused in filling the bowl of his pipe, and stared at him with undisguised curiosity. 'If I hadn't been intrigued before, I certainly would be now!'

'I'm exploring the feasibility of an idea, that's all.'

'I see,' Joseph murmured.

'The Government is increasingly of the opinion that there could well be another war. The Treaty of Versailles humiliated Germany, and Hitler seems to be riding on the back of a growing nationalism.'

'I've been watching that develop with some alarm.'

'To take just one point of concern. Under the treaty, Germany was forbidden to have an air force, but we know that German pilots are being trained secretly in the Soviet Union. Knowing of this and other similar breaches in the treaty, the Government feels it would be unwise to underestimate Hitler in the way that we and some German politicians have done in the past.'

'What you say doesn't surprise me. The man's become increasingly powerful after his gains in the March election. And now that they're locking up his opponents in a prison they've opened recently—Dachau, I think it's called—there doesn't seem to be any way of stopping him. I don't mind telling you, Maud and I are alarmed. As Nellie told you, we've a daughter living there.'

'I can understand that. But I wouldn't think you need to be fearful for her, any more than I think I'd be at risk in going to Cologne. But the Government thinks it wise to take a few precautions. They were stung by accusations that they failed to prepare sufficiently in the build-up to the last war, and they're determined not to be caught out another time. If there *is* another time. This is pure speculation.'

Joseph drew deeply on his pipe, and removed it from his mouth. 'And where do you come in?' he asked.

'I'm still working for the motor industry, hence the Germany trip, but at the same time, I'm doing some work for the Air Ministry. The current thinking is that the automobile industry could be mobilised to produce weapons of war, should we ever again be at war with Germany, or with anyone else, for that matter. It's early days, though.'

'By weapons of war, you mean what exactly?'

'The priority would be aircraft. The motor industry could be asked to manufacture aircraft components by using technology transferred from car production—making airframes as well as engines—plus associated equipment and armaments.'

Joseph gave a low whistle.

'A number of factories would be involved,' Philip went on. 'Each would manufacture a different part of the plane. No one factory would build the whole plane, so if one of the factories was bombed, only a part of the plane would be lost. And that part would have been under construction elsewhere, too.'

Joseph studied the bowl of his pipe, and then drew on it again. 'In terms of organisation, how would that work?'

'That's yet to be decided. But it's looking increasingly likely that in the coming years, the Air Ministry will take over valuable industrial space in order to create capacity. Factories that used to turn out cars or car parts would be adapted and equipped for a change of product, and they'd be staffed by those skilled in the motor industry as well as those familiar with aircraft production.'

Joseph let out a low whistle.

'But as I say, people are only just starting to think along those lines, and they're still hoping it'll never come to another war.'

Joseph nodded slowly. 'I'm beginning to see where this might be going.'

Philip smiled. 'I thought you might. We're looking at construction companies with a sound reputation. Linford & Sons is known for the quality of its houses and its good practice. And your work in the last war was also noted. It was suggested that I contact you.'

'Are we talking about building new factories?'

'In some regions, yes. We'll need factories with wide, clear gangways and good lighting—the roofs may have to be glazed—that are free of shafting and belt drives. The Government will see that they're equipped.'

'And funding?'

'Under the present proposals, there's government funding in the form of grants and loans for building these new production facilities. '

'I see.'

'It won't just be building new factories. In other regions, it might be possible to extend existing factory complexes in order to facilitate switching to aircraft capability. It's one of the things I'll be looking at as I visit different parts of the country.'

'And you think motor car companies will be able to turn their hand, just like that, to making engine parts?'

'Not without training, no. But they'd be given that training so that if war were to break out, the new factories were ready to go immediately into full production.'

Joseph frowned. 'Surely, you're not expecting to be able to keep such facilities secret?'

Philip shrugged. 'That would be hard. But in the event of hostilities, they'd be camouflaged.'

'And you think the motor industry would go along with such a radical change in production?'

'There'd be a substantial management fee.'

Joseph sat back in his chair and regarded Philip. 'I've got to take my hat off to you, son. How old are you?'

'Thirty.'

'That's some responsibility for someone as young as you.'

'It was a matter of being in the right place at the right time, and with the right experience. But at present, I'm merely sounding out people who could help the country prepare for a possible war. We're some way off signing contracts.'

He paused. 'If this plan is put into practice, you're very likely to be offered some contracts. I thought it something that you might want to start thinking about.'

Joseph puffed thoughtfully on his pipe for a moment or two. 'You're banking with Charles, I know,' he said. 'Is that in any way connected with your approach to me? It's the same family, after all, even though Charles isn't involved in the building side of things.'

'Only indirectly. I came upon Charles's bank a number of times while researching for a bank in which to place my money. Having been in the US at the time of the Crash, I'd seen a frightening number of banks fold for lack of funds, so I was looking for a solid bank.'

'You made a wise decision. Linford & Sons have banked with them for years.'

'After discovering Charles's bank, I came upon your company. That was an unexpected bonus, given my Air Ministry work. As was meeting Louisa last weekend.'

'I'll have to introduce you to my son, Robert,' Joseph said. 'He's now Chairman of Linford & Sons, but as you'll have realised, I'm still involved to some extent. Possibly to a greater extent than Robert would like, but he's far too polite to say so.' He laughed.

Philip leaned forward and picked up his glass. 'We should drink to the future,' he said.

Joseph smiled. 'Seconded, dear boy.' And he, too, picked

up his glass. 'I suspect that you're a man who knows what he wants when he sees it, and goes after it with the determination that brings success,' he added. 'I like that.'

He smiled. 'I trust that your trip with Louisa tomorrow will prove both enjoyable and productive.'

He raised his glass in a toast, and Philip noted in amusement that Joseph was still smiling as he put it to his lips.

27

The Zoological Gardens, Regent's Park,
the following day

'LIVER PASTE SANDWICHES!' Louisa exclaimed. Laughing, she took one from the plate of sandwiches that Philip was offering her. 'I've not had these since I was a child. I love them.'

He grinned. 'I thought you might,' he said. 'I do, too. I think a picnic should contain everything one likes, even if the end result is a meal that isn't as well balanced as we keep on being told a meal should be. Don't you agree?'

She peered into the wicker hamper on the wooden bench between them. 'As I can see that your likes include Twiglets and Custard Creams, I most definitely do agree.' She sat back and took a bite of her sandwich.

'There's some Cheshire cheese in there, too, that I think you'll like. I'm lucky that there's a place that sells cheese in Belsize Park. It's getting harder to find farmhouse cheese.'

'Why do you think that is?' she asked.

'With the Milk Marketing Board guaranteeing farmers a good price for their milk, there's no incentive for farmers to make cheese. If you're as keen on cheese as I am, the situation's frustrating.'

She nodded, her mouth full.

'I would've liked to have cemented my place in your good books by packing some chocolate, too,' he continued, 'but it would've melted in the sun.'

He leaned against the back of the bench, stretched out his legs, hooked his hands behind his head and looked up at the sky. 'It was the right decision, I think.'

As she finished the last of her sandwich, she glanced sideways at him.

The sun had caught the planes of his face and was highlighting them in gold. Her palms suddenly moist, she wiped her hands on her skirt.

'All of the decisions you've made for today have been the right ones.' She felt herself colour slightly, and she fixed her gaze on Three Island Pond, which lay on the other side of the path.

He glanced at her. 'You could have added "so far". There's more to see. We haven't yet been to the Reptile House.'

She gave a theatrical shudder. 'That sounds scary.'

'They're behind glass.'

'Glass has been known to break.'

'Then I'd put my arms around you and carry you away to safety,' he said.

She glanced at him. Their eyes met, and she turned quickly away.

'You've gone to a lot of trouble,' she said a few moments later, brushing some crumbs from her lap. 'Why?'

'Because I wanted you to have a good time.'

She felt herself colour more deeply. 'Why does that matter to you?'

He turned to look at her. 'Because if you don't have a good time, you won't let me take you out again. And I'd very much like to do so,' he said quietly.

She studied her feet. 'I don't know why,' she said, her eyes firmly fixed on her white round-toe shoes. 'You must have lots of friends who know masses more than I do, who can talk about interesting things. What do *I* know? Nothing!

'I'm sure that isn't so.'

'It is. I work for my uncle's company, one of a small group of people led by another uncle. All we talk about is house interiors, or Uncle Thomas is snapping at me to leave him be.'

He grinned at her.

'It's not funny,' she said. 'And it's not much better at home. Father always talks about banking things, which don't mean much to me. Mother used to have something to say about everything, but she's much quieter now, and that's down to me.'

'You told me you had an accident. No one's to blame for an accident, no matter how regrettable the outcome.'

'*I* was to blame for that accident.'

He frowned slightly. 'Some might say that it's self-indulgence to assume blame where blame doesn't exist, but I don't think that's you.'

She turned to him sharply. 'Nellie said the same thing, but neither of you know what I'm really like. If you did, you wouldn't make any attempt to save me if the glass broke and a giant cobra came charging towards me. You'd stand back, arms folded, and allow it to eat me.'

He laughed. 'I'm sorry, Lou, but that's a funny picture. If

you and the cobra confronted each other, my money would be on the cobra backing down first. And as for the part I play in the action, or don't play, I find it hard to picture myself acting in such a cowardly manner. When I see myself in my mind, it's usually in an heroic guise.'

She stared at him for a moment, and then burst out laughing. 'All right then, I won't make you so inactive. When it's scared me to the point of death, you can gallantly intervene.'

'That's more like it,' he said.

They smiled at each other, and then both turned to look towards the ornamental ponds.

'Would it help if you told me about the accident?' he said after a few minutes. 'We're going to be seeing each other a great deal in the future, and instinct tells me that this is something we should get out of the way.'

She looked at him. 'Who said we're going to be seeing each other again?'

'I did.' He gave her a long slow smile.

Her heart missed a beat.

She straightened up on the bench. 'I've only ever told one person what really happened six years ago, and that's my cousin Dorothy. She's the one in Germany.'

'I think it might help you if you told me, too,' he said gently.

'Maybe. Telling Dorothy has helped. We've been writing for a few years now. Not often, just occasionally. But I feel close to her. I think that in a funny way, although she's got a husband and two children, she feels on her own in some respects. I can sense it. It can't be easy to live so far from your family, and know you can't come back.'

He nodded. 'I agree.'

'My parents obviously know the truth about the accident. And also Uncle Joseph and Aunt Maud—Uncle Joseph always knows everything. But no one else knows. Not even Nellie.'

Her eyes filled with tears. 'I don't want to tell you, Philip. I don't want you to hate me.'

'That won't happen, Louisa,' he said quietly. 'Whatever occurred six years ago has stopped you from living a normal life, and it's made you think very little of yourself. While it's good for me that because you've hidden away, you've not already been led down the aisle, it's bad if you allow it to continue dominating your life. So tell me, Lou.'

'I can't,' she cried in despair.

'Yes, you can.' He took her hand. 'I'm not going to judge you, Louisa. Whatever it is, you've clearly suffered enough and your slate is clean. So, please, trust me.'

She pulled her hand away. 'All right, then. But you'll see that I'm a horrible person, who always pushes people away by being nasty to them.' Tears rolled down her cheeks. 'I don't know why I used to be like that, but I was.' Her voice caught in her throat.

'Tell me, Lou,' he repeated.

Then, her head bowed, she told him everything, including her years of bad behaviour towards her parents and Christopher, and towards the rest of the family, and the truth about the accident.

'That's it, then,' she said when she'd finished. 'You know everything there is to know. You can take me back home now.' She rose to her feet.

He gathered the litter from their lunch, put it into the hamper, closed the hamper and stood up. Holding the hamper in one hand, he held out his other to her.

She looked down at his hand, and then stared questioningly up at him.

He smiled. 'I'm hoping you'll hold my hand in case I get nervous in the Reptile House.'

'I don't understand,' she said in bewilderment. 'You've just heard that I'm truly the most unpleasant person you've ever met.'

'That's what you used to be like. But that's not who you are today. I think you got lost for some years, Lou, but you've now come to terms with it, and turned your life around. It's the future that matters, not the past. So now, unless you're concerned that the protective presence of the elephants, tigers and lions around us is insufficient compensation for the lack of a chaperone, shall we hold hands?'

Feeling lighter than she could remember feeling for years, she took his hand, stared down at it, and smiled.

'I THOUGHT we ought to round off the day properly with an afternoon tea, and the Carlton Tavern wasn't that much out of our way,' he said, smiling across the table at Louisa, who was pouring tea from a porcelain teapot into their bone china cups. 'And especially as chocolate hadn't yet made an appearance today.'

'It's a lovely idea. In fact, the whole day's been lovely. I've really enjoyed it,' she said, putting down the teapot and extending a cup to Philip. 'You're very easy to talk to, you know,' she added, and she blushed.

'I could say the same about you,' he said.

'I can't talk to anyone in the way I can talk to you—not even Nellie. Dorothy comes closest, but writing's very different from speaking to someone face to face.'

'I can see that.'

She picked up her cup, and sat back. Nursing the cup in both hands, she looked around the large rectangular

Luncheon and Tea Room, which they'd entered through a glazed door that led from the street. Her gaze settled on the brass fixtures around the room that were glinting in the reflected sunlight, and on the short curved bar at the far end of the room.

'I wouldn't recommend those fittings for any of our houses,' she said. 'They're much too garish. Oops!' Her hand flew to her mouth, and she giggled. 'Not so long ago, I was moaning that all we ever talked about at work was interiors. And now, listen to me.'

He laughed. 'Don't worry. I'm interested in interiors, too. After all, I'll be getting a house, won't I?'

'Have you told Uncle Joseph what sort of house you want?'

He shook his head. 'I don't yet know. It'd be nice to have made a decision before I go to Germany, but that's still some way off so I've got time.'

'D'you know if you're going anywhere near Dorothy? It would be marvellous if you could go and see her.'

'What was the name of her town?'

'Rundheim. It's only small, though. She told me that they'd started out in a town called Morbach, and then moved south of that.'

'I'll look on the map and see if I can find it. If I can get there, I will. But I don't want to raise your hopes. Germany's a large country, and I've a lot to do in a limited amount of time. Also, much as I'd like to visit Dorothy for your sake, I'd be reluctant to go too far to the east of Cologne. Or to go too far anywhere in Germany, for that matter.'

'And you mustn't do so. You're not to take any risks. When Father isn't talking about banking matters, he's talking about politics. You have to know what's going on in the world if you're a banker.'

'Your father is certainly very up-to-date in his knowledge of world matters.'

'Since I started writing to Dorothy, I've been listening whenever he talks about Germany, and it's scary what's happening there. I really wish Dorothy would come home. And I'm sure Uncle Joseph wants that, too, but he'd never say so. I don't think she will, though.'

'Would her husband be willing to come here, do you think?'

Louisa shook her head. 'Absolutely not. Franz was interned in the war, and that's turned him against England. And so did the treaty at the end of the war. Unfortunately, she'd never come back without him. And also, her two children must be more German than English. But I know she'd love to meet someone with a connection to the family. She often sounds really homesick.'

'I'll do my best, but I suggest you don't tell her I'm going to Germany. It's more likely that I won't be able to visit than that I will, and it would be better not to build up her hopes, just in case.'

'You always seem to know what's the right thing to do, Philip.'

He grinned at her. 'But I don't always do it. The right thing would be to leave a polite amount of time before I ask you out again—it's what your parents would expect—but I'm not going to do that.'

She felt herself blushing with pleasure.

'Would you come with me to the Palace Cinema in Kentish Town on Friday evening? They're showing *Facing the Music*. It's a musical comedy starring Stanley Lupino. I don't know anything more about it than that, but I thought we could use some light-hearted entertainment at the end of the week.'

She put her hands to her cheeks, which felt as if they'd gone scarlet.

'That's a yes, then, is it, Lou? To show you how pleased I am, I'm going to leave you the last little chocolate fudge cake.'

LOUISA STOOD in the front reception room, holding her straw hat in front of her, facing her parents. They'd looked up expectantly as soon as she'd come into the room, and had never once taken their eyes from her face.

'I told Philip everything,' she said, her face glowing. 'All about how horrible I used to be and about the accident. About what really happened.'

'And?' Charles asked quietly.

'And he wants to take me out again,' she cried. 'He really does, Father. He suggested next Friday. He's not been put off by anything I said.'

She burst into tears, spun round and ran out of the room.

Charles leaned back in his chair. 'Thank God,' he said.

28

O xfordshire,
Mid-December, 1933

CHARLES STOOD at the window of the reception room and stared out at the garden through a pane of glass etched with the intricate patterns drawn by the sharp morning frost.

The rays of the cold sun were creeping across a crystalline ground that glinted gold whenever it felt the touch of the sun. Everything in the garden looked so different beneath the glittering hand of frost, he thought.

Every bare branch had been painted with silver, every bush in the thickets, every stone in the wall, every cluster of berries—under its gossamer veil of frost, the garden had become an ethereal scene in a fairy tale world.

'You don't mean to say you're admiring nature.' Charles jumped at the sound of Christopher's voice behind him. 'And I do believe from what Mrs Spencer said that you've been up for an hour, yet you don't have a balance sheet in your hand!' Chris exclaimed in mock amazement as he moved to stand next to his father.

Charles glanced at Christopher. 'I know what they say about leopards, but this is a leopard that *can* change its spots. Even *I* think the garden looks lovely on a morning like this, and I was appreciating its beauty. In fact, it's almost as beautiful as that balance sheet you mentioned!' he added with a smile.

'But tell me, Chris,' he went on, 'how's the job going? Any regrets about not joining Linford & Sons? Your uncle Joseph was sorry you turned down his offer, and your mother and I were, too. But we all recognise that you're old enough to make your own decisions.'

'And I made the right one. I've learnt a phenomenal amount at Chapman's, and I'm enjoying every minute of it. They're nice people. I'm not going to stay there forever, though. When I've learned all they can teach me, I want to get a market garden of my own.'

'When do you hope to be ready for that?'

'Realistically, in two or three years at the most. After all, I've already leanrt a lot from helping on the farm.'

Charles assumed an expression of alarm, and patted his jacket pocket. 'Why is my wallet suddenly groaning?'

Christopher grinned. 'I'm delighted to know that our minds are running along the same leafy path.'

Charles laughed. 'We'll have to see about that. In the meantime, what're your immediate plans? Will you be staying here with your mother and me till after the New Year? Philip and Louisa are. I don't know about the rest of the family, but they'll be here a couple of days before Christmas, and they'll tell us then.'

'Good gracious!' Christopher feigned deep concern.

'That's an unusually long time for you to be away from the bank. Let's hope it doesn't fold because of your absence.'

'Your anxiety is duly noted,' Charles said. 'But I didn't really have a choice. Philip wants Louisa's advice about houses, so she asked Thomas if she could have the time off, and when he said yes, she asked Joseph if they could stay here. They plan to drive around areas that Philip has earmarked as possible places for a house, and also to look at one or two show houses for ideas.'

Laughter sounded from the garden.

'That'll be them. As they were going to stay here, Sarah obviously had to come, too, and I wasn't going to let her come here without me. I want to see that she doesn't overdo it, and to keep her company when Philip and Lou are out.'

At the sound of more laughter, they pressed closer to the glass and peered out. Philip was chasing Louisa across the glistening turf, waving his car key in the air.

Charles moved back and shook his head. 'He's determined to get her driving again. But I'm afraid he's fighting a losing battle.'

'I wouldn't be too sure of that. She isn't stupid. She'll need to be able to get around when he's away on one of his motoring trips.'

Charles looked at him sharply. 'The two of you are obviously closer these days, which your mother and I are delighted about. Has Lou confided in you? Are you saying they're engaged?'

'Not yet. But I'm sure they will be before much longer. Knowing Philip, he'll do the right thing and ask you for her hand and all that. But you only have to see them together to know that it's just a matter of time.'

Charles looked back at Philip and Louisa. 'What d'you think of him?' he asked.

Christopher shrugged. 'I like him. And so must you or you wouldn't have pushed them together. And Mother seems to like him, too.'

'You're right—we both like him very much. We want to see Louisa happy and settled, and if that's going to be with Philip, I hope he takes me aside before too long. It'd be good to have something to celebrate this Christmas.'

'Agreed.'

'It'll be a good distraction for Joseph, too. I know he's increasingly concerned about events in Germany, and how they might affect Dorothy, though he wouldn't admit it. And Nellie would relish advising Lou about planning a wedding. And that would be no bad thing—Nellie certainly got it right when she and Walter married.'

'D'you know, that's the only time I've been asked to be a pageboy? I wouldn't say no to repeating it.'

'Well, don't get your hopes up, son! I can't see Lou wanting you to don your sailor suit and follow her down the aisle. You've grown a bit in the past thirteen years and it must be too small by now. And like any other healthy fourteen-year-old, James would be horrified if he had to let you hold his hand while you and he toddled down the aisle together!'

They grinned at each other.

'Your mother and I were pleased that you managed to get a couple of weeks off so that you'd be here for the whole of the time we were, Chris. I suppose it's easier at this time of year. There can't be much to do at the moment in a market garden.'

'There is if you grow sprouts,' Chris said cheerfully. 'We pick sprouts throughout the winter months. And there are chairs to repair. And wood to saw and split. But I'd told them at my interview that I wanted to keep my hand in at the farm, and they saw that this was a chance to do so.'

'Are you going across there today?'

'Yes, when I've had another coffee. There's bound to be some digging and hoeing to do, and more digging and hoeing, and some scattering. You'd be surprised—the winter months can be very busy on a farm.'

'I'll admit that I *am* surprised. But you seem to be thriving on the work.'

'I love what I'm doing, Dad. There's nothing better than working outside in the open air. I'd hate to be stuck in an office all week.'

Charles clapped Christopher on the shoulder. 'I'm glad it's turned out so well for you, son.'

They heard the front door open, and a moment later, Louisa burst into the room, her cheeks red from the cold air, her face shining. 'We saw you through the window,' she said. 'We thought we might drive around the area north of Oxford, and have lunch out.'

'Would you both care to join us?' Philip asked, coming into the room after her. 'And Sarah, too, of course.'

Charles laughed. 'Don't look quite so panicked, Lou. We're not going to take up your kind invitation. Your mother hasn't even come downstairs yet, and Chris has just said that he's off to the farm. I think we can safely let you go on your own. Is it just the villages you're looking at, or a particular house?'

'It's too soon to look at an actual house,' Philip said. 'Joseph suggested we decide on an area, and then we discuss the house with him.'

Louisa glanced at him, and then looked quickly back at her father. 'It's partly research for me,' she said. 'I shall be looking at the extreme ways in which builders today are encouraging people to buy their houses. We've already seen offers of turfed and planted gardens, and extra kitchen equipment. One builder's even giving a car to everyone who buys a thousand pound house! Can you believe it?'

'Hey!' exclaimed Philip. 'I've had an idea! If I bought one of those thousand pound houses, it would sort out a car for Louisa, Charles.'

'It's certainly something to think about,' Charles said with a broad smile.

'WHY ARE you so keen on me getting behind the wheel of a car again?' Louisa asked, as she and Philip sat in his car in the centre of Charlbury. She'd thrown her rolled-brim cloche on to the back seat, and their heads were bent over a map of the area.

He looked up from the map. 'I suppose it's because it's a useful thing to know. You can never tell when you might need to be able to drive.'

'I see.'

They looked back down at the map.

'When you were talking to Father earlier on,' she remarked a minute or two later, her eyes still on the map, 'you said that we'll decide on an area and then we'll discuss the house with Uncle Joseph. You keep on using "we" whenever you talk about things to do with the house. But it'll be *your* house. So why?'

He shrugged. 'I just say what I'm thinking. Or perhaps it's what I'm feeling.' He paused. 'You must know I like you, Louisa.'

She looked down at her hands and bit her lip.

He gave her a wry smile. 'You're meant to say at this point that you like me, too.'

She looked across at him, her face reddening. 'You know I do. I wouldn't be here if I didn't.'

'There's like and like. How do you like me?'

She gave an awkward laugh. 'I think we should change the subject.'

'Because I know what I feel for you, Louisa,' he went on, and he picked up the map and folded it. 'I feel something considerably stronger than liking. And I say "we", and not "my", because I want it to be *our* house, not mine.'

She stared at him. Her lips parted, her heart racing.

He cleared his throat. 'I'd intended to wait till we were somewhere romantic, and I'd worked out the right words to say. It's not exactly romantic here, crammed inside my car on a chilly day—quite the opposite, in fact—and I haven't any beautiful words prepared. But I'm going to have to say it, nevertheless.'

He turned to face her more squarely.

'I never think in terms of "I" any longer—it's always "we". I love you, Lou, and I can't bear to think there might be a time when we're not together. I can't imagine anything more perfect than being with you every single day for the rest of my life, and I very much want to marry you to make that happen.' He took a deep breath. 'So, will you marry me?'

'Oh, yes!' she cried. Her face broke out into a radiant smile. 'Yes, I will.'

Impulsively, he took her by the shoulders, pulled her to him, and brought his mouth hard down on hers.

Drawing back, they faced each other, their eyes filled with love, their hearts beating fast.

'I love you, Philip,' she said.

'Oh, Lou.' He reached out again and his lips brushed hers.

Sliding her hands behind his head, she drew him closer still, and kissed him back with a fervent longing.

Then they pulled apart, their breathing ragged. Each gave a nervous laugh.

'I'll speak to your father later,' he said when he could breathe more easily. 'I want to do this properly.'

'He'd like that.'

He shook his head. 'I can't believe how lucky I am,' he said, gazing at her in wonder. 'For years, my focus has been myself and my work, and I'd thought that enough. But since meeting you, I've known the sheer joy of being with someone you love, and how it transforms each day. You complete my life.'

She smiled at him through tears of joy. 'For someone who hasn't prepared any words, you're doing very nicely.'

'Everything we've looked at so far, I've imagined you and me living in it. But I didn't want to scare you off by telling you that. Whatever we look at from now on, though, we'll both know that we're looking for a house for the two of us, and maybe more than two one day, and you've no idea how happy that makes me feel.'

She put her hand to his face and trailed her fingers down his cheek. 'I think I do. That's because I know how happy that thought is making me.'

He caught her hand, and kissed it. 'I'm going to do my best to see that you feel as happy as this every single day of the years ahead, if not happier,' he said. 'I promise.'

He shifted his position. 'A good place to start would be to get out of this car! It clearly wasn't made for romantic encounters. There's a place to eat opposite. Let's have a celebratory lunch.'

He got out of the car, went round to the passenger side, gave his hand to Louisa and helped her out. He locked the car door, and they stood on the pavement, holding hands, each staring into the face of the other.

For a long moment, neither moved. Then, at the same moment, they leaned towards each other, and their lips met.

'I WANT to marry you as soon as possible,' he said as the waiter moved away, having served him with a cognac and Louisa with a coffee. 'I want to go to bed with you and wake up with you beside me. It's killing me to have to exercise the restraint I've been exercising since I met you, so the sooner we marry, the better.'

'I don't want to wait too long, either.' She put her hand to her mouth. 'That sounded awful.' She laughed in embarrassment.

'Not to me, it didn't,' he said warmly. He swirled his cognac in the snifter. 'So when shall we marry?'

'I don't know—it's all still sinking in. What about soon after you get back from Germany, assuming that your trip isn't too far away?'

'That'd be ideal,' he said with a broad smile. 'We must now think seriously about where we want to live—whether we want our main home to be here or in London. And then we can think about the sort of house we want. It'd be good to have something ready to move into, or close to ready, by the time we marry.' He hesitated. 'I think I'll be going to Germany in April. Would that give you long enough to organise a wedding?'

'I'll make sure it does. I can't wait to marry you.' Blushing again, she put her hand to her cheek.

He reached across the table and took her hand.

'Nor can I,' he said. 'You're so beautiful, Louisa. I can't believe that in a few months, I shall open my eyes in the morning and see you. That I'll come back from work at the end of the day, and you'll be there. That I'll sit in my armchair listening to music in the evening, and you'll be next to me. And then we'll go to bed. I'm the luckiest man alive.'

'I'm the lucky one.'

He gave a theatrical sigh. 'Am I never going to be allowed to have the last word?'

'Not when you're wrong.'

'I suppose I'll have to accept that. When I met you, I knew that living with you would be interesting. You'd never be a doormat, which I'd hate, but you'd be a partner.'

'When did you decide you wanted to marry me?'

'That's easy. It was the evening I met you. You sat through the first part of dinner, scowling, but the moment you joined in with the discussion about the contents of my flat, your face became alive and vivacious, and I knew that I wanted to look at that face every day for the rest of my life.'

'Did you know that Father had this in mind when he invited you?'

'I did wonder. He seemed to find a lot of different ways to bring up your name whenever we had a conversation. And your expression at dinner that first evening told me that you, too, knew what he was up to, and were less than pleased.'

'I can assure you he's entirely forgiven,' she said happily. 'But about the wedding,' she added. 'I'd rather not have anything large and extravagant, if that's all right with you. I'd feel uncomfortable, given everything that's happened in the past.'

'I understand,' he said quietly. 'That suits me very well. Perhaps we should fix a date at the end of May or beginning of June.'

'And you're definitely going to Germany in April?'

'Yes, at the beginning of the month. My company's booking a ticket on a new boat called the "Twickenham Ferry". It's a train ferry with space for twenty-five cars. Annoyingly, though, it'll be sailing from Southampton to Dunkirk, and not from Dover. The new facilities in Dover aren't ready yet. I've friends in Dover and I'd have liked to have visited them.'

'Will you be driving through France to Germany?'

'Through France and Belgium.' He smiled at her. 'And yes, if it's at all possible, I'll go to Rundheim after I've finished in Cologne.'

29

*C*horton House,
    Two weeks later

'I SEE that you've managed to avoid the trappings of Christmas that are everywhere else in the house,' Philip remarked, looking around Joseph's domain.

A few sprigs of berry-laden holly lined some of the bookshelves, but apart from that, the only suggestions of Christmas were the aromas of nutmeg and cinnamon that spiced the air, and the plates of figs, preserved ginger, dates and mince pies that had been set out on the table between Philip and Joseph, flanked by a snifter of cognac for each. Next to the glasses stood an open bottle of Rémy Martin.

'Every year, it's the same,' Joseph said, stretching out his legs and making himself more comfortable. 'They can do what they like in the rest of the house, but this is my sanctuary.'

'I like that idea.'

'Take my advice, dear boy, as soon as you've moved into your house, select a room that'll be your own. Allow Louisa to do as she wishes with everything in the house except for your private haven. It's the way to a happy marriage.'

'I'll certainly need a room of my own—I'll need an office. But it'll have a comfortable chair or two, and I look forward to the day when I can entertain you to a cognac in my own territory.'

He leaned forward, picked up his glass and raised it in salute.

Joseph picked up his glass. 'I know that we all toasted you and Louisa this evening, but I'd like to say again how delighted Maud and I are that you're joining the family. Louisa's a very lucky woman.'

'And I'm a very lucky man, sir. In Louisa, I've found my ideal wife. My last few years were dominated by my work— you could use that old cliché and say that I was married to my job—but I've now reached the point in my career that I'd been aiming for, at a younger age than I'd expected, and to meet someone so perfect for me at exactly the right moment, is more than I could've ever hoped for.'

Joseph studied the depths of his glass. 'Louisa will have told you a little about events in the past, I imagine.'

Philip nodded. 'She did, sir. She told me how rude she'd been to all of you for a number of years, and about the accident. Not the official version, but what actually happened. I can appreciate that your feelings towards her will have been affected by her past behaviour—that's only normal.'

'I must admit, she was a difficult girl to like. And to be honest, we didn't like her. And we didn't like the way she ignored Christopher, who's always seemed a very pleasant lad. But in all fairness to her, she's sorry for what she did and has more than made up for her past transgressions, and we're genuinely delighted about your engagement, both for Louisa's sake and because it'll bring you into the family.'

'Thank you, Joseph. That's good to hear.'

Joseph took a sip of his drink. 'Have you settled on an area for your house?' he asked.

'We have. We'd like a place near Charlbury. You suggested once before that if we found a suitable house to buy, you'd be able to bring the interior up to scratch, and I'd like to take you up on that. Charlbury's a very pleasant little town—lots of thatched-roof houses and good road access to Oxford, London and Birmingham.'

Joseph nodded. 'I know it well.'

'And the station there is a bonus. Also, it'll always have good memories for us as it's the place where Lou agreed to marry me. But don't tell Charles that,' he added with a laugh.

Joseph smiled. 'I won't. No, it's a good choice of location for someone who needs to travel. And I'm sure it'll be a lovely place to live.'

'But there's been a slight change of plan,' Philip said with a wry smile. 'Marrying Louisa has rather altered things. I'll have to be away on occasions, and she'd be happier, I know, if she was in London at such times, near all of you.'

'That's understandable.'

'So the Charlbury house won't be our main home. It'll be to us as Chorton House is to you. I'm already living in London as you know, and I'll be very happy to carry on living in London.'

Joseph stared at Philip in surprise. 'You and Louisa are going to live in your flat?'

Philip laughed. 'Not exactly. I'm going to buy a house.

Linford & Sons have been building in and around Glenilla Road, I believe.'

'That's right. We've always kept a presence in London. Our focus after the war may have been building houses along the main arterial roads into London, but we've continued to build in various parts of London, too. Including Belsize Park, as you say. So you'd be interested in one of the Glenilla Road houses, would you?'

'Definitely. Admittedly, Louisa hasn't yet seen them, but I have. I looked at a couple before deciding that renting a flat was better suited to my immediate needs than buying a six-bedroomed house. But I like the area, and I'm certain they're the sort of house that both Lou and I would be comfortable in.'

'She *should* like the houses—she probably did the interiors,' Joseph said drily. 'I suggest that you, Louisa and I meet in Belsize Park as soon as we're back in London. We're fairly close to finishing one of the houses, and I think it might well suit you. If you liked it, both you and Louisa could be involved in any future decisions relating to the house.'

'That sounds a great idea. Thank you.'

Joseph picked up the bottle of cognac and refilled the snifters. 'Your house was one of the reasons I suggested we have a talk away from the others,' he said, putting the bottle back on the table. 'The other's a little more delicate.'

He paused, and then cleared his throat. 'It's about my daughter, Dorothy. You heard what was said a few weeks ago at dinner, so you know that we no longer consider her a member of the family. She married a German, you see.'

'I do remember that.'

'As Nellie told you, she lives in Germany, and I'm certain that Nellie's in touch with her. Dorothy told me in her first letter that she lives to the south of a place called Morbach.'

He cleared his throat again. 'When you mentioned Cologne, Maud and I looked at a map. Cologne's further north than Morbach—quite a bit so, in fact—but it's almost directly north. And the route between Cologne and Morbach looks fairly straightforward.'

Philip leaned forward and smiled. 'I'll make every effort to get down to Dorothy to check that she's all right, sir. If you or Maud would like me to take her anything, you have until April to give it to me. But there's a chance, of course, that it might prove impossible for me to get there, so it would be better that Dorothy wasn't told that I might visit.'

Joseph took his handkerchief from his breast pocket and wiped his forehead. 'That's very good of you, Philip. I don't expect her to come back—in fact, I wouldn't want her back. She's got a German husband and children, and Thomas's feelings must be taken into account. He's had a lot to put up with, what with his war injuries and the trouble with Alice.'

'Of course.'

'Much as her mother and I would like the situation with Dorothy to be different, there's nothing we can do about it. Or should do about it. I once interfered in Robert's life, and the consequences were dreadful. I've learned from my error. But we'd like to know she's safe. And that she's happy,' he added, and his voice broke.

Philip sat quietly, his glass in his hand.

'The thing is, you don't stop loving them,' Joseph said, blowing his nose, 'just because they do something damn stupid. She's thirty-six now or thereabouts, so I shouldn't be worrying about her at her age, but I do. She's still my daughter.'

'I understand, Joseph. You can be sure I'll do my level best to get there.' He hesitated. 'Are you telling Thomas that

I shall try to visit Dorothy? He knows I'm going to Germany, and might wonder.'

'Good point.' Joseph thought for a moment. 'I think I'd better. I'm not asking you to keep this a secret from Louisa—there've already been too many secrets in this family, and we don't need any more. Louisa sees Thomas most days, so he should be told. But I'll assure him that your visit, if you get there, will be solely to check that Dorothy's all right. There's no question of welcoming her back home.'

'I understand, sir.'

Joseph smiled. 'Now that that's decided, let's talk about Charlbury. Perhaps we should all go and look at the place before we go back to town. What d'you say?'

PHILIP LEANED across the breakfast table, helped himself to some butter from the dish and spread it across his toast.

'I see you're on your own.' At the sound of Nellie's voice, he glanced towards the door. 'I wondered if Christopher was still here,' Nellie said, coming into the room. 'But he must have had breakfast and gone.' She sat down next to Philip. 'You two are always the first ones up.'

'There are three of us today, it seems. You must count yourself, too, Nellie.'

She smiled. 'Three of us, then. Actually,' she said, pulling her chair closer to the table, 'it's just as well that Christopher's gone. There's something I wanted to ask you.'

'The answer's yes,' he said, and he took a bite of his toast.

She straightened up, and stared at him in amused surprise. 'That's a bit risky isn't it? You don't know what I'm going to ask.'

He grinned at her. 'Yes, I'll make every effort to get to Dorothy's, but I obviously don't know if that'll prove possi-

ble. I won't know till I get there. And in case it proves impossible, it'd be better not to mention to Dorothy that I
might go.'

She giggled. 'Louisa must've already asked you. I
should've guessed that she would have done.'

Smiling at her, he reached for the marmalade.

R undheim,
    beginning of April, 1934

DOROTHY STARED through the window to the road outside the house.

Traces of blackened snow lingered on either side of the track. And along the base of the walls of the opposite houses, intermittent banks of solid ice were yellowing. But the track itself was clear.

She smiled at the pane of glass.

With the bulk snow gone and the roads now clear, normal life in Rundheim would soon resume, and this was a distant date to which she looked forward at the start of winter every year.

The patch of window in front of her mouth clouded. With the corner of her pinafore apron, she wiped away the film, and turned from the view. After the long winter months, being able to move around the town more easily was something to celebrate, and she'd make Franz and the children the special lunch that Herta always made when something good happened.

Simple though it was, she knew she'd never be able to make it as well as Herta, but she also knew she'd improved. They'd all been quite complimentary about her last couple of efforts.

She went across to the worktop, scrubbed several potatoes and put them on to boil. Then she measured some linseed oil into a jar, spiced it with salt and pepper and set it to one side.

Reaching into the pantry, she took out a bowl of *quark*, and set it down next to the linseed oil. When the potatoes had boiled, she'd let them cool, and then all she'd have to do was pour the seasoned oil on top of both the potatoes and the creamed cottage cheese, and an easy, but tasty, meal would be ready.

She wiped her hands on her apron and looked restlessly around the empty room.

It would've been very pleasant to have had a mid-morning coffee with Herta, which they'd rather got into the habit of doing, the deep snow of the past few months having restricted how far they could go from the house.

But Herta had told her that she was starting on her annual spring clean immediately after breakfast, so having a coffee together wasn't going to be possible for the next few days.

And she wouldn't be seeing *Frau* Arnstein, who'd occasionally stopped for a coffee when delivering eggs. A week or two earlier, when Franz had gone to clear the ice from the steps outside her house, he'd returned saying that the house had been boarded up. A neighbour had told him that the Arnsteins had gone to live with family overseas.

Before the heavy snow had made walking down from her house treacherous, Ruth Weinberger had sometimes called in to say hello and to have a coffee. Hopefully, now that the thaw had truly set in, either Ruth would start visiting again or she'd go up to their house.

But that was for the future.

As far as the present was concerned, no one would be stopping by for coffee. And as it would be at least two hours before the children and Franz got back from school, she'd probably do well to follow Herta's example.

She sighed inwardly. The twice yearly house-clean wasn't something she relished, but it had to be done sooner or later. And as it was now warm enough in the house to remove the extra pane of glass from each wooden window frame, and to have a single pane only in every frame, it would make sense to begin with the windows in the upstairs bedrooms.

She went across to the stove, drained the potatoes and left them to cool.

Then she heated up some more water, and poured it into a bucket. Putting the soap for scrubbing the windows and a few sheets of newspaper with which to dry them into a second bucket, she went up the stairs, carrying a bucket in each hand.

She'd start with Dieter's bedroom, she decided, and she went into his room, put down the buckets and looked around.

Nothing was out of place. It was as neat and tidy as always. In *Jungvolk*, he'd been taught the importance of discipline, both in the orderliness of your room and in the presentation of your person, and invariably he tidied his room before he left for school.

It was too tidy, she sometimes thought, and on occasions

she'd caught herself longing to find his room the disorganised mess her brother Robert's bedroom had been when he'd been nine years old like Dieter.

She stared at the large frame hanging above the table that stood against the right-hand wall of his room. On it were pinned the many badges and medals that Dieter had earned since joining *Jungvolk*. Her gaze dropped to the table, and to the neatly folded uniform on the corner of the table.

His black shorts had been arranged at the bottom, under his brown shirt. On top of the shirt was the black kerchief that he wore around his neck, threading it under his chin through a toggle-like leather knot.

The short red and white cord that ran from the shoulder of his brown shirt to the buttonhole in his left-hand shirt pocket had been placed very carefully on top of the pile.

He'd been given the cord when he'd been put in charge of a small unit of ten boys. That was quite an achievement for someone of his age, she'd been told on more than one occasion.

The uniform on the table, and the frame of achievements on the wall above it, spoke of Dieter's pride in his success, a pride shared by Franz.

Frowning slightly, she stared at the table for a moment longer. Then she roused herself, went across to the window and reached up to the corner of the window frame.

Leaning against her bedroom door, she looked wearily at the pile of panes stacked up on the landing, ready for Franz to put them back in the attic where they'd stay for the summer months.

She'd been right to do the windows that morning, she told herself. Because she'd already prepared the lunch, she'd been able to work throughout the morning, and she'd removed the second panes from all of the upstairs windows, and cleaned all of the glass.

She'd have to stop now as school would soon be over, but she was back in a spring-cleaning mood, and she'd do the downstairs windows the following morning.

She bent down to pick up the buckets.

'*Mama!*' she heard Elke scream from outside the house.

Footsteps pounded up to the house, and she heard the front door fling open.

'*Mama!*' Elke screamed again.

In a panic, she straightened up, ran to the edge of the landing, and saw Elke standing at the bottom of the staircase. She stopped abruptly.

Elke was staring up at her, panting heavily. Her face white, tears were streaming down her cheeks. The bottom of her school coat was torn.

Fear gripped her.

Her knees threatening to give way, she ran down the stairs as fast as she could, caught Elke in her arms and hugged her close.

'What's the matter?' she asked, her heart beating fast.

'It's Sofia. She's gone,' Elke sobbed, clinging tightly to Dorothy. 'I ran home to tell you. I ran so fast I slipped on the ice.'

Her arms tightened around Elke. 'What d'you mean, gone?'

'Men came and took her,' Elke cried, weeping uncontrollably.

'Men in uniform?'

Elke shook her head. 'No,' she said, her voice muffled against Dorothy's chest.

A gust of chill air blew into the room. Glancing above

Elke's head, she saw Franz come into the house, closely followed by Dieter.

'Close the door, Dieter,' Franz said, a hint of suppressed urgency in his voice. He took off his thick coat, hung it next to the door, and put his gloves into one of the pockets.

Dorothy slid her arm around Elke's shoulders, moved her towards the table and helped her sit down. She sat next to her, her arm still around her. 'Elke said that Sofia's been taken from the school, Franz. Is this true?'

His face pale, he nodded.

'And Karl?' she asked with a sense of dread.

'Yes, Karl, too. And we didn't see Hans after that.' His voice caught.

'Oh, Franz.' Her eyes flew beyond him to the window that looked out on Karl and Herta's house. She opened her mouth to frame the question she feared asking.

Franz frowned slightly and indicated the children. 'I'd like a coffee, Dorothy,' he said, his voice strained. 'The children can have a glass of milk and then go to their rooms until lunch is ready. Take off your coats, children.'

Dieter hung up his coat, and then turned to face his father. 'No, *Vati*,' he said, standing with his back to his coat, his arms at his side. 'I want to know what's happened. I'm old enough.'

'And I do, too,' Elke said, pushing Dorothy's hand away. 'Sofia's my friend.'

'And Hans is mine,' Dieter said firmly.

Franz looked helplessly at Dorothy.

'Sit down, Franz,' she said, getting up. 'You, too, Dieter. I'll make a pot of coffee and bring some milk.'

She prepared the coffee and put the pot on the table. Then she gave each of the children a glass of milk, and sat down opposite Franz. 'Here, Franz,' she said, pouring him a coffee, and then pouring one for herself.

'Where's Sofia, *Vati*?' Elke asked, her milk untouched.

Franz shook his head. 'I don't know, *mein Liebling*. I wish I did, but I don't. All I know is that *Onkel* Karl and Sofia have gone, and it seems that Hans might have been taken, too.'

'What happened, *Vati*?' Dieter asked.

'It was during the first lesson, and we were teaching in classrooms next to each other. All of a sudden, I heard his classroom door open, and his room went silent. The pupils in his class had been reciting a poem, but they instantly stopped. All of them did. Then the door closed again. The silence lasted a few minutes longer, and then loud talking broke out. The pupils would never have talked in such a way had Karl been there—he was a much-respected teacher. Then I heard the voice of the Head of the school, and the children fell silent again. There was no further sound during that lesson.'

'Didn't you immediately look for *Onkel* Karl?' Elke asked, her face accusing.

Franz glanced at Dorothy. 'No, I didn't,' he said quietly. 'I had many anxieties in my mind, many things I'd liked to have found out, but I didn't move. I sat with my class till the end of my lesson. And then I went to the staff room, as I always do. As Karl always does. But not today. And then I went to my next lesson. And the next.'

'You should have looked for him? He's your friend, like Sofia's mine,' Elke shouted at Franz, and burst into tears again.

Dorothy took Elke's hand. 'Is that what happened to Sofia, Elke?' she asked gently. 'Did people come and take her from your classroom?'

Elke nodded.

'Do you think they were the Gestapo, Franz?' Dorothy asked.

'Probably. The Gestapo don't always wear a uniform on such occasions.'

Dorothy's free hand went to her mouth.

'Do something, *Vati*,' Elke begged. She pulled her hand away from Dorothy and wiped her face dry with both her hands.

'I think it better to stay indoors for the rest of the day,' he said.

'I don't!' Elke slid off her chair and headed for the front door. 'I'm going to see if they're home yet. *Tante* Herta won't mind.'

'Hans is my friend. I'm going, too,' Dieter cried, and he turned to the door and reached for the handle.

Franz pushed hard against the door, and caught hold of Elke. 'I'm sorry, *Lieblinge*, but you must stay here.'

'I won't! I want to see Sofia,' Elke yelled at him.

'Well, you can't. You and your brother are going to sit here with your mother.' He hesitated. '*I* shall go across and see what's happening, not you.'

Dorothy rose to her feet, her eyes anxious. 'You'll be careful, Franz, won't you?'

'I promise.' He attempted a smile. 'While I'm talking with Herta, the two of you can be drinking your milk. Now go and sit down,' he told Elke and Dieter.

He walked the children to the table, and waited until they'd picked up their milk. Then he went across to the door, took his coat from the hook, and went out.

A few minutes later, he was back, his coat still over his arm.

Three faces stared questioningly at him as he hung his coat on its hook.

He sat heavily down at the table. 'I took one look at what was happening, and came home,' he said quietly. 'I suspect all our neighbours did the same as there was no one to be seen, except for the men who were emptying Karl's house. There were two trucks, and they were loading boxes of books and papers into them. And furniture, too.'

'And Herta?' Dorothy's voice was a whisper.

He shook his head slowly. 'Nowhere to be seen. She must have already been taken away. It means that the whole family will probably now be together, and that's good,' he added, forcing a note of brightness into his voice.

'Why did they take them away?' Elke asked, her eyes filling again with tears.

Franz and Dorothy exchanged glances.

'Was it because *Onkel* Karl was teaching the children in his class something he shouldn't?' Dieter asked.

'What makes you say that, Dieter?' Franz asked.

'Some of the others in my class said that.'

'He was an inspiring teacher, Dieter,' Franz said. 'He was teaching what he'd taught at the school for many years. It's true, though, that he'd recently been advised to teach a different poet, but it was hard for him to accept that.'

Dieter frowned. 'But if he was told not to teach it, he shouldn't have done, should he? That was wrong of *Onkel* Karl, wasn't it?'

Franz hesitated. 'Perhaps unwise would be a better word,' he said at last. 'There are lots of angry things being said about Jewish people at the moment, and they're being blamed for everything that's wrong. As a result, Jewish people can no longer live as they used to, and the books they've written aren't being read. Indeed, many such books have been burned, as I think you know.'

'They told us in school that it was good that they were burned,' Dieter said.

'*Onkel* Karl was very brave. He didn't agree with the ban on Jewish authors, and he continued to teach the work of the poets he admired, even if they were Jewish. I imagine they've now stopped him from teaching because of this.'

'Will you be able to find out where he is?' Dorothy asked.

He nodded. 'I'll try. I'll—'

A knock at the door silenced him.

He and Dorothy exchanged frightened glances.

There was another rap on the door.

Elke started to cry, and the blood drained from Dieter's face.

31

Franz took a deep breath, got up, walked across to the door and opened it.

'*Frau* Weinberger?' he exclaimed, and he opened the door wider. 'And Leah. Do come in.'

Elke jumped up from the table, flew across the room to Leah, and they hugged each other.

Dorothy stood up. 'You must both have something to drink,' she said.

Her face tired and drawn, Ruth Weinberger gestured her refusal, and stayed standing. Dorothy sat down again.

'I mustn't be long,' Ruth said, 'as we're leaving Rundheim this evening, and we've much to do first. We plan to leave when the townsfolk are eating their evening meal. But Leah refused to go before she'd said goodbye to Elke, and I wanted to tell you how much we've enjoyed having your friendship.' She paused. 'We're trusting you, you see, by telling you that we're leaving today,' she added, a tremor in her voice.

'You know you can trust us.' Dorothy's brow creased in anxiety. 'But where are you going? And how?'

'We're doing as the Arnsteins did, going to America. My husband has family there. We shall go to England, to a town called Southampton, and we'll get a boat from there to New York. We have addresses for people in New York.'

'But how will you get to England?' Dorothy asked.

'By car. We had some jewels from both our mothers. My husband sold them and bought a car yesterday. There's some money left over, so we've the money for tickets to New York and a little to help us settle there.'

'I'm so glad you were able to sell the jewels,' Dorothy said.

Ruth nodded. 'It was a relief. We were worried that we should have done so sooner. While our decision to leave has come suddenly, we've known for a while that we'd have to leave Rundheim at some point. My husband is an excellent dentist, but no one visits him. How long could we live like this?'

'Can't you stay a bit longer,' Elke said. 'Sofia's gone, but Leah and I can still do things together.'

Ruth smiled at Elke. 'I wish we could, Elke. We'd intended to go at the end of the week, before people realised we had transport—people like *Frau* Schmidt. But Sofia and her family being taken in such a way has made us feel that we shouldn't wait even a week.'

'Oh Ruth,' Dorothy said sadly.

'We won't feel safe now till we've left Germany and are in Belgium, on the way to the coast. Perhaps you can write to Leah, though, Elke. When we're settled in America, Leah will send you a letter, and you can write back. That way, you can stay friends.'

Her face wet with tears, Leah nodded. 'I'll do that, Elke. You'll always be my best friend, wherever we live.' And they hugged each other again.

'Come, Leah. We must go,' Ruth said.

Dorothy crossed the room to Ruth. 'You can be sure we won't say a word. I really wish you well. I'm so sorry, Ruth; so very sorry.'

'You have nothing to be sorry for. Some in Rundheim, yes, but not this family.'

They hugged each other.

Franz stepped forward and shook her hand. Then he went with her and Leah to the front door and opened it. Ruth paused in the doorway. She and Leah turned to look back at the family.

'Goodbye, my friends,' she said, her voice trembling with emotion.

Then, with Leah at her side, she walked out into the street, turned right and headed for the north of the village.

A leaden silence weighted the room.

Then Dorothy moved. 'Sit down and finish your milk,' she said briskly, and she went across to the cutlery drawer.

Dieter returned to the table. 'Why did they have to leave? They weren't doing anything wrong. Not like *Onkel* Karl.'

'Nor were Sofia and Hans doing anything wrong, or *Tante* Herta. So why were they taken away, too?' Elke asked.

Franz sat down opposite them. 'This is difficult to explain in a way that you'd understand,' he said. 'But I'm afraid that *Onkel* Karl's disobedience will have meant that his family was classified as undesirable. Undesirables don't fit into the system we have in Germany today, so the system removes them. It puts them where they can't cause any trouble.'

Elke kicked her chair. 'And is Leah's family undesirable, too? Is that why they're leaving?'

'I suppose you could say that they are.' He leaned

forward and put his forearms on the table. 'Listen to me carefully, children. Much as we would like the country we live in to be perfect, no country *is* perfect. Hitler's strength is that he's improving life for ordinary Germans, which is very important. His weakness is his unreasonable dislike of Jewish people.'

'Why doesn't he like them?' Elke asked. 'Leah's nice.'

'He needs someone to blame for everything wrong in the past, and he's blaming Jewish people. We voted the government into power so they could act for the general good, but unfortunately we let in some destructive elements, too. The brutality of Hitler's supporters is one such element. A strong anti-Jewish sentiment is another.'

'It's not fair.' Elke's face was sullen.

'I agree, Elke. But—and I deeply regret having to say this —but in future, when we disagree with something the government does, which most people do at some point or other in their lives, it would be better not to speak aloud our thoughts. We can do so inside the house when just the family is here, but never outside. Do you understand?'

She nodded.

'And I think we mustn't talk outside the house about Herta and Karl again, or about Sofia and Hans. Or the Wein-bergers. It's essential that no one knows that *Frau* Wein-berger came to see us before leaving. If people knew she did, they might accuse us for not reporting them and stopping them from going.'

Dieter stared at his father. 'But if it's wrong for them to go away, shouldn't we tell someone?'

'It isn't wrong of them to want to visit their family in America, and there's no reason why they shouldn't do so,' Franz said steadily. 'But some people wouldn't see it like that. Because of those people, we mustn't say anything.'

'*Vati*'s right,' Dorothy said quickly. 'What if I wanted to visit my family in England one day, Dieter? There'd be nothing wrong in that, would there?'

He shrugged. 'I suppose not.'

'But as with the Weinbergers, there are people here who might feel differently,' she went on. 'So we mustn't tell anyone that they came to say goodbye. Not ever.'

'There's one other thing to bear in mind, children. It's hard to know what one person will make of the actions of another. If we informed the Party that the Weinbergers were leaving, we'd have to say they visited us and told us.'

Dorothy nodded. 'That's right, children.'

'And despite us reporting them, the fact that a Jewish family felt comfortable enough in our company to tell us what they were doing, might make the Party look closely at us, and we wouldn't want that, would we?'

Elke and Dieter's fear lay heavy in the air.

'We can still love our friends, and keep them in our hearts,' Dorothy said. 'But not on tongues.' She paused. 'Do you both understand?'

Their faces ashen, they nodded.

'Well then,' Franz said with false heartiness. '*Mutti* will give us our dinner, and after that, you'll do your homework while I prepare my lessons for tomorrow.'

DOROTHY LOOKED AT HER WATCH. It seemed much longer than it actually was since Franz had left for the pub.

They'd agreed after dinner, while the children were upstairs doing their homework, that they'd have an early supper, and Franz would go to the pub after that to see if he could learn anything at all about the whereabouts of Karl and Herta.

But they decided not to tell the children what he was doing.

Accordingly, as soon as they'd finished their evening meal of sausage, cheese and black bread, he'd announced that he was going out for a short walk to clear his head.

He wouldn't be out long, he'd assured Elke and Dieter in an effort to quell their cries of alarm at the thought of him leaving the house at that time of night, when so many frightening things had happened that day.

Dorothy had assured them, too, that it was perfectly safe for their father to go for a short walk, and she'd asked them to get ready for bed.

Franz had been certain that there'd be no better place than the pub for information. Someone would know the story behind the events of the day, and would be eager to show off that knowledge.

And even if there wasn't such a person, Karl was well liked, and was bound to be the main topic of conversation that evening. By listening to the general discussion around him, he had a chance of finding out more, and of doing so safely.

He'd also be interested to hear if anyone mentioned the Weinbergers, who would have already left in their car.

Eventually, Franz returned home, looking both depressed and exhausted. He sat down heavily at the table. Dorothy moved her chair so that she was sitting next to him.

'Were we right that this was about Karl's teaching?' she asked.

Franz nodded. 'I'm afraid so. It seems he'd been discussing Heine's poems with his Class Four yesterday, and he'd set them a homework last night to write about the poems. Apparently, one of the boys from a village south of Rundheim, whose father owns a bakery, was busy writing the essay when his father looked over his shoulder to see what the boy was doing.'

Dorothy drew in her breath in horror.

'The man took one look at the homework set for his son, picked up the boy's book and walked off with it. The father was the leader of his village's Nazi Party.'

She put her hand to her mouth.

'Given his position, it's not surprising that he informed on Karl,' he went on. 'And that's why the Gestapo came to the school this morning and took Karl and the children away. They drove up and collected Herta immediately afterwards. No one knows where they've gone, or when they'll be back. Or even *if* they'll be back.'

Dorothy sat very still, staring at the table.

'Say something, Dorothy.'

She turned to him, her eyes wide open, her fear palpable. 'I'm frightened,' she said, her voice shaking.

His mouth stretched in a smile that failed to reach his eyes, she noticed. 'There's no need to be, *mein Liebling*. I teach only what is allowed. No one will be coming for us.'

'But is this any way to live?' she asked, her voice hollow.

He gestured helplessness. 'This is the only way we can live. Rundheim is our home. And things are looking up in Germany. People are happier now and they're laughing again. They're buying more watches and jewellery, and shop owners are buying cars. The economy is good, and getting better all the time. They're even installing telegraph poles ready for telephones, so soon you'll be able to speak to Nellie and Louisa. There's still much that is good in Germany today, Dorothy.'

'Not if you're Jewish,' she said flatly. 'Or believe in free speech. And don't like violence.'

'No, not if you're Jewish. I don't like what's happening

any more than you do. But unfortunately, it's the bad that we have to take with the good.'

He put his fingers beneath her chin, and turned her face gently towards his.

'We must look only to the future, *mein Liebling*, and stop worrying about Karl and Herta. They were saying at the pub that the family will have been taken to a camp for re-education. Sofia and Hans will continue their schooling there. After that, they may well come back to Rundheim. Karl will know not to teach Heinrich Heine, but he'll have had the reason explained to him, and he'll be reconciled to it.'

He kissed her lightly on the lips, and put his arms around her. 'I love you so much, my Dorothy. I can't bear to see you looking so worried.'

His arms tightened around her.

Her head on his shoulder, she stared beyond him to the front door, her eyes wide open.

32

R undheim,
  beginning of May, 1934

PHILIP DREW the car to a halt a little way down the hill that led south from the crossroads in the centre of Rundheim.

When Nellie had told him that Dorothy's house was on one of the corners of the crossroads, it had been a relief to know that his choice was limited to one of four.

As he felt around in his pocket for the piece of paper on which Louisa had written brief details about Dorothy's family, he glanced out of the car window at the half-timbered houses meandering up both sides of the hill. Hitler flags were hanging from at least one of the windows in every house.

Feeling himself the subject of scrutiny, he turned towards the house on the opposite side of the road.

A woman who'd obviously been cleaning her downstairs windows, had stopped what she was doing, and was standing still, rag in hand, staring at him in undisguised curiosity. He inclined his head towards her. She hastily resumed the polishing of her window.

A movement at the back of his car caught his eye.

An old man, who'd clearly been walking down the hill past the car, had paused and was peering curiously through the window. Philip smiled at him. The man looked quickly away, and continued rapidly down the hill, pulling behind him three young goats that he'd tethered to a string.

Strangers were obviously a rarity in Rundheim, he thought in amusement.

What must it have been like for Dorothy, he wondered, to have moved from a city as large as London into a village as small as this? And to have a life as narrow as her life must have become?

And what must Rundheim's residents have made of her when she'd first appeared in their little community, a community made up of people, most of whom would probably not have gone further in their lives than the neighbouring village?

The smallness of the place was something of a surprise. He'd expected somewhere a little larger, somewhere closer in size to Morbach where he'd spent the night.

He'd reached Morbach just before lunch the previous day, the drive south from Cologne having taken a little more than three hours.

Since his time in Cologne had been filled with research into the factory's plans for future cars, and with meetings with area officials on a wide number of issues, he'd been very ready for a break, and had decided to spend the night in a hotel in Morbach. In addition, he'd felt it would be politer to call upon Dorothy in the morning.

After he'd checked into a small hotel near the centre of

Morbach, he decided to look around the town in which Dorothy had started her married life, and he'd had a pleasant stroll through the streets, pausing every so often to look up at the colourful half-timbered houses or into the windows of one of the numerous small shops.

When he'd got back to the hotel, he'd remarked to the owner about the large number of Hitler flags.

They'd been up since the celebrations for Hitler's birthday towards the end of April, he'd been told, and the owner had given him one of their remaining celebratory Hitler Rolls.

They tasted no different from Kaiser Rolls, the owner had remarked with a shrug of dismissal as he'd covered up the plate. He'd then clapped his hand over his mouth in obvious annoyance at himself for having commented thus to a stranger.

When he'd finished his lunch of *Bratwurst*, a sausage he particularly liked, and *Sauerkraut*, he'd decided that as it was a beautiful afternoon, he'd walk to Burg Baldenau, a ruined castle to the east of Morbach, which the hotel owner had assured him he shouldn't miss. Apparently, it was known locally as the Water Castle owing to the fact that it had once been surrounded by a moat.

He'd enjoyed wandering around the ruins, and had returned to the hotel invigorated after several hours in the open air. Greatly refreshed by his break, when he'd woken that morning, he'd found himself looking forward to meeting Louisa's cousin.

He glanced down at the piece of paper Louisa had given him, made a mental note of the names and ages of Dorothy's children, and her married surname, and then tucked it back in his pocket.

Since he hadn't driven far past the crossroads, he

decided that he might as well leave the car and walk the short distance back, and he got out. He'd start at the house south of the crossroads, and if it turned out to be the wrong house, he was sure they'd direct him to the correct one.

But as he neared the house closest to him, he saw a girl of about thirteen or fourteen polishing a bicycle that had been propped up against the wall of the house on the far side of the crossroads.

That might be Elke, he thought, with a sudden surge of excitement, and he walked past the first house, crossed over the road and went straight up to the girl.

He cleared his throat. 'Hello! Are you Elke?'

She spun round, took one look at him, and screamed '*Mutti!*' in visible fear.

Dropping the rag, she ran into the house, leaving the front door wide open.

He hesitated, wondering whether to go up to the doorway or stay where he was until the girl's mother came out. Presumably, that would be Dorothy.

Wondering what they were saying, he tried to pick out some words from the rapid exchange he could hear inside the house.

One word stood out clearly. That word was Gestapo.

A moment or two later, a woman wearing a pinafore over a pale grey dress, and a dark grey kerchief round her head, came to the doorway and stood there, staring at him. Elke was hovering behind the woman, her face frightened.

The woman, too, looked terrified.

'I don't think the Gestapo hire people who're English,' he ventured with a half-smile.

'You're English,' she said, and her face relaxed. 'English,' she repeated, her voice taking on a note of wonder. She took a step forward. 'You're really English?'

He nodded. 'That's right. I'm Philip McAllister. And I think you must be Dorothy Linford, now Dorothy Hartmann. You and Nellie bear a strong resemblance to each other.'

She went closer still. 'You know my sister?'

'Yes, I do,' he said.

She put out her hand as if to touch his face. Then she pulled it back, took a step backwards and put both hands in front of her mouth. She tried to speak, but her voice was lost in a sob.

'I'm engaged to your cousin, Louisa. You and Louisa write to each other, I believe.'

'*Mutti*?' Elke asked questioningly.

As if suddenly remembering Elke's presence, Dorothy glanced round at her, with tears in her eyes. She took Elke's hand and pulled her gently forward. 'Louisa is your cousin, too, Elke. Say hello to *Herr* McAllister. You can speak English to him.'

'Hello,' Elke said, shyly.

Philip held out his hand to Elke. Elke put her hand solemnly in his, and they shook hands.

Dorothy wiped her eyes with her fingers.

He smiled at Dorothy. 'It's lovely to meet you at last. Louisa has spoken about you.'

She took a handkerchief from her apron pocket, and blew her nose. 'You must forgive me,' she said, trying to steady her voice. 'This is so unexpected. But such a pleasure. You've no idea how happy it's made me to see you.' Her eyes watered again.

'I think I have,' he said gently. 'I also realise that this must be a shock. I wasn't sure I'd be able to get here, so I asked Lou and Nellie not to tell you that I might come.'

She held out her hand to him, palm down, and tried to

laugh. 'See. I'm not trembling as much now. We thought you might be the Gestapo. And then finding out you came from home. Yes, it's such a shock. Such a pleasant one, though.'

She put her hand to her throat. 'Louisa's mentioned you in a couple of letters, but she's not said much about you. I'd like to hear more. And for you to tell me all about them. I miss them so.' Her eyes brimmed.

'I'd be happy to do so, in as far as I can.'

'And you must meet my family. My husband's still at school. He's a teacher. And Dieter's at school, too. Elke wasn't feeling so well so she stayed at home today. She's fine now, though,' she added quickly.

Philip nodded.

'But why are we standing here?' Dorothy asked, with a laugh. 'I'm forgetting my manners. Come in and have coffee. And you'll stay for lunch, won't you? And perhaps stay tonight, or for longer. You will stay tonight, won't you?'

Her voice shook.

'I want to hear everything about England. Nellie and Louisa tell me a great deal, but there's so much more to know. Little things. Things you wouldn't put into a letter because you'd think them unimportant. I want to hear those things, too.'

'If it's not too much trouble, I'd love to stay until tomorrow. I think I might be doing so under false pretences, though—I haven't known the Linfords for very long, so there's probably not much I can tell you that you don't already know. I'll have to leave tomorrow morning, as I must get back to England.'

She glanced over his shoulder to the car a little way down the road.

'Is that your car? If it is, why don't you drive it closer to the house? You can then bring easily into the house what you need for tonight. I'm so glad you can stay.'

Her voice cracked, and tears rolled down her cheeks.

'Ignore me—I'm being silly. But just seeing someone from England, who knows my family, after so many years, it's lightened me. Does that make any sense, Mr McAllister?' she asked.

Elke put her arms around her mother.

'Yes, it does, *Frau* Hartmann. Or rather, Dorothy, if I may call you that. Believe me, I *do* understand.'

She wiped her face with her pinafore. 'I'll go and make us some coffee while you're moving the car. And you, Elke.' She smiled through her tears at her daughter. 'You must finish cleaning your bicycle and then bring it in. And *Vati* left you some schoolwork to do. You can take your milk upstairs and do your lessons while I talk to *Herr* McAllister. You can talk to him at dinner.'

Philip turned to go to the car. 'I'll see you in a minute, then. In the meantime, Dorothy, you can practise saying Philip,' he said with a smile. 'And you, too, Elke, if you wish.'

'I WISH there was more I could tell you about everyone, but I've known them for less than a year, and some I've hardly met, if at all,' Philip said as Dorothy refilled his mug with coffee, and then pushed a plate with slices of *Stollen* closer to him. 'If there's anything you'd like to know, and I don't know it, I'll try to find it out when I get back home. Louisa can write and tell you.'

'That's very kind, Philip,' she said. 'I might jot down one or two things.'

He looked around the room, and then his gaze returned

to Dorothy. 'Did you find it difficult to settle here?' he asked. 'Rundheim is so much smaller than London.'

'It wasn't so much the size of the place that was difficult to adjust to—after all, I was still young when I left England and I hadn't really been out in the world. I'd effectively been confined to my home in the years before the war.'

'You were a nurse, weren't you?'

'That's right. When the war started, I learned how to nurse people, became a VAD and moved away from my family. But I was always in a nurses' hostel or at the hospital. As I'm sure you know, it's how I met Franz.'

'Louisa told me. She'd heard from her mother what happened. It sounded very romantic.'

She laughed. 'We met over an infected ulcer. So not so romantic. But when I looked up from his leg, and saw his lovely blue eyes, well that was a romantic moment.'

'It must have been. I'm sure there are many such moments in the pages of the novels that Nellie reads,' he said in amusement.

'I'm not surprised, from what I remember of Nellie,' she said with a laugh. 'No, what was very strange at first, apart from the language—I could hardly speak to anyone so I did a lot of smiling and nodding—wasn't the size of Rundheim. It was having to do all the things in the house that someone used to do for me.'

'I suppose it must have been,' he said, glancing around the room.

'Without even realising it, families like mine take it for granted that servants will do the work. And also, things here were more ... more primitive. Primitive is a good word. Things today are more advanced, but we're still far behind the large towns in Germany even, let alone England.'

'The years immediately after the war must have been

very difficult,' he said, 'with your sharply rising inflation. In England, things were difficult, too, but my understanding is that it was far worse over here.'

'That's right. Hitler came to power on the back of peoples' sense of grievance. Germany expected to pay to some extent for the war, but not to be treated so unfairly.'

'A lot of people in England would agree that Germany was badly treated.'

'But we're a small community here in Rundheim, and everyone helped everyone else, so we managed. And things have now much improved. Franz and I dislike a lot about Hitler, but we recognise that life in Germany is much easier now. If you're not Jewish, that is.'

'Are you talking about Leah?' Elke called from halfway down the stairs. She bounded down the last few stairs and came and sat at the table. 'I've finished the work *Vati* set,' she said, and she waved her schoolbook in the air.

'No, we weren't, Elke. But if you've finished your work, perhaps you'd do something for me, would you? If I give you a short list and some money, would you go to the shops for me?'

'I hope I'm not making too much work for you,' Philip said anxiously.

Dorothy shook her head. 'You're not,' she said. 'It's such a pleasure to have you here. But Germans eat their main meal at midday—but you must already know that—and I should like to add one or two more things to the table.'

She got up, went across to the kitchen cupboard, took out a piece of paper and wrote down several items. Then she took some money from the bag on the shelf beneath the glazed upper cupboard, and went back to the table. 'Here you are, Elke,' she said.

Elke took the note and money with obvious reluctance,

got down from the table and went across to the door. She picked up a wicker basket from a small table next to the door, and went out.

Dorothy waited until the door had closed behind Elke, and then turned back to Philip. 'That'll keep her busy for a while. I didn't want her to hear me tell you about Leah and her family. And about our friends Herta and Karl. She's only just beginning to sleep through the night again, and I wouldn't want to set her back. What happened terrified her. And Dieter, too.'

And she recounted the taking of Karl and his family, and the departure soon after that of the Weinbergers.

'It's unbelievable,' Philip said slowly when she'd finished, 'that people should be treated like that. There aren't words to describe it. It must have been absolutely terrifying for you and Franz, as well as for the children.'

'It was,' Dorothy said quietly. 'We miss our friends very much, and we worry about them.'

'That's inevitable. And you can't find out where they are?'

She shook her head. 'We wouldn't dare try. I can't believe I'm actually saying this, but we're scared to say freely what we think. If people can be taken from their homes without good reason, we must be so careful what we say to our neighbours.'

He frowned. 'That sounds quite awful.'

'The butcher's daughter is married to a Brownshirt. Brownshirts are thugs. We don't like the butcher's wife, Olga Schmidt—we never have done—but we go out of our way to be friendly to her.' She shook her head. 'It isn't easy to live like this. It's actually worse than when our inflation was sky-high.'

He looked down at his coffee, and then he looked back

at Dorothy. 'If you want to return to England, I could fit all of you into my car. You won't have a passport, but I've connections and I can deal with any formalities.'

'That's very kind of you, Philip, but no. Our home is here in Rundheim. Franz was interned in London during the war. He found his experience humiliating. It disillusioned him about England, and dented his affection for the country. He'd never go back. I love him, and my home will always be where he is. And the children are German through and through, even though they can speak English, too. Dieter is especially German with his fair hair and blue eyes.'

'Of course.'

'I'm very grateful to Franz that he's never attempted to turn the children against England,' she added, 'but I'm sure they've sensed how he feels about England these days, and they've never shown any interest in going there, nor in knowing anything about their English family.'

'Does that bother you?'

'It's upsetting, I must admit. Whenever I receive a letter from Nellie or Louisa, they just shrug. So with my family here not interested in anything to do with England, I'll never go back. And really, there's no need for us to be afraid. Violence grows out of suffering and anger, but the economy's improving, and people's lives are getting better, so we shouldn't be seeing any more of the actions that have recently seemed so fearful.'

'That's good to hear.'

'So, in all honesty, I've no desire ever to go back to England,' she said, and she gave him a reassuring smile.

33

'You've two fine children,' Philip said, as he and Franz sat with a *Schnapps* while Dorothy was upstairs, making up Dieter's bed for Philip, and putting pillows at the top and bottom of Elke's bed for Dieter to sleep in there that night.

'Thank you,' Franz said. 'We're proud of them. Elke is near the top of her class, and Dieter has risen to a high rank in the *Jungvolk*. For someone of his young age, that's quite an achievement. You saw his badges and emblems.'

'I did, and very impressive they are, too. Your Hitler Youth movement sounds very similar to a movement we have in England, which started about twelve or thirteen years ago. It's called the Boy Scouts. It's for boys over eleven, I believe, but there's now a Cub Scouts for younger boys. And the girls have a similar thing, too—Girl Guides, with Brownies for the younger ones. I think it's excellent for youngsters to camp out, and learn a variety of practical activities.'

Franz nodded. 'That's what Dorothy and I think.' He

paused. 'In England, do you hear much about what's happening in Germany today?'

'A bit. Mainly about the economy. And we've also heard about some of the violent incidents in recent years. Obviously, not here in Rundheim, though. This seems a very peaceful village.'

'It is. It's one of the things we like about it.'

'But the book burning appalled us, as it must have done you, a teacher. And also the restrictions placed on Jewish people. I was shocked to hear how the new laws were being put into effect. Dorothy told me about your friends, the Arnsteins and the Weinbergers.'

'And they're not the only ones who've left. A number of our Jewish community have left Germany, but I think the general feeling among those who remain is that with the economy thriving as it is, Germany will settle down, there'll be an end to violence and we'll go quietly back to the peaceful way in which we used to do things.'

'That's good to hear.'

Franz smiled at him. 'Our progress in your field, the field of automobiles, illustrates well the growing strength of our economy. It's three years only since your Henry Ford and our Mayor of Cologne, Adenauer, laid the foundation stone for the Cologne Ford Plant, and two years only since the first Cologne-produced Ford came off the production line.'

Philip smiled. 'You're very informed.'

'And I know, too, as you must, that an increasing proportion of the Ford vehicles sold in Germany have been made in Germany, and not imported from Britain. That's progress.'

Philip nodded. 'It is indeed. I was hugely impressed by the plant in Cologne, and by the company's plan for the future.

Also by your government's strong backing for the industry. It's not just the tax benefits for car owners that Hitler's announced, but also his major road expansion programme.'

'In some matters, Hitler can't be faulted,' Franz said quietly.

'His vision for the future is admirable. I hear he's supporting the construction of a cheap, simple car for the masses. With such improvements to transport, the German economy will expand even further.'

Franz smiled. 'And you'd also like to know, I'm sure, that the Nazi Party much admires the British Empire. There've recently been a series of articles in our newspapers that have praised the British imperial history. Hitler looks upon Britain as a friend, and wants close ties in the future. It means that we need not fear a return of enmity between us.'

'I'll drink to that,' Philip said, raising his glass. Franz did the same, and they both took a drink of their *Schnapps*.

'So, have you enjoyed your visit to Germany?' Franz asked.

'Very much. Cologne went well, and the icing on the cake has been meeting Dorothy, you and the children. I'll be able to tell Joseph what a lovely family Dorothy has, and how pleasant Rundheim is.'

'Joseph!' Franz exclaimed. He sat upright. 'He knows you're visiting Dorothy, and he doesn't mind? But he spoke so harshly to her.'

'That was years ago. He's her father and he loves her. He asked me to come here if I possibly could. He wants to know she's all right.'

Franz frowned. 'Does he think I can't look after my wife?'

'Not at all,' Philip said hastily. 'But he's read about the violence in Germany, and he's worried. Newspapers like to make things sound worse than they are and, knowing that I wouldn't be too far from here, he asked if I'd try to visit you. And it wasn't just Joseph who asked. So did Nellie and Louisa. Dorothy is loved by the family.'

'And she's loved by me, too. I'd never let anything harm her. I do everything I can to keep her safe.'

'I'm sure you do, Franz. I can see how much you love her, and how much she loves you.' He hesitated. 'Perhaps I should put your mind at rest about something that might be worrying you—all Joseph wants is news about Dorothy. He's not hoping I'll bring her back. In fact, he doesn't want her to return.'

He saw Franz's shoulders imperceptibly relax.

'They're protective of Dorothy's uncle Thomas, you see,' he went on. 'He's Joseph's brother. From what I can gather, Thomas hasn't had an easy time since the war. His leg and most of his hand were blown off in the fighting, and it's affected him deeply, as one would expect.'

'That's understandable.'

'They're all very conscious of the fact that if whenever the family got together, Thomas was obliged to see the niece who'd chosen to marry a German, and live with Germans, it could be most distressing for him.'

'I shouldn't say this as it makes me sound an awful person,' Franz said ruefully, 'but I'm glad about that. I'd never go back to England, and I wouldn't want Dorothy to be able to blame me, or me to blame myself, for the fact that she couldn't go back if she wanted to.'

'Well, it won't come to that,' Philip said with a smile. He glanced at his watch and finished his drink. 'I think I'll go to bed now, if you don't mind. It's been a long day, and I've a couple of days' driving ahead of me. Plus another long drive when I get back to England.'

'How will you go?' Franz asked as they got to their feet.

'Through Luxembourg to Belgium. I'm sailing from Dunkirk, which is close to the Belgian border.'

Hearing footsteps on the stairs behind him, Philip turned and saw Dorothy coming down the last few steps. She went and stood next to Franz, and he put his arm around her shoulders.

'Your bed is ready,' she said. 'We've very much enjoyed your visit, Philip. If you come to Cologne again, you'll let us know, won't you, and you must come and stay with us, perhaps for a little longer.'

'I'd like that very much,' he said.

'We won't say goodbye now. With no school tomorrow, we'll all be here to see you off,' Franz said.

'It's bound to be a good journey—it's very direct. Well, goodnight, then, both of you. Thank you for making me feel so very welcome.'

'Thank *you* for coming,' Dorothy said, her voice trembling. 'You've taken me back to England in my mind.' Her voice broke, and she pressed her fingers hard against her lips.

Philip saw Franz tighten his arm around her, steadying her.

With a slight wave, he turned away and went across to the stairs.

STANDING at the window of Dieter's room, he ran his fingers idly up and down the length of the wooden window frame that smelled slightly of damp.

As he did so, he stared up at the darkening sky, mesmerised by a single silver star that grew larger and brighter as the darkness around it deepened.

Moving closer to the window, he looked up the street to the right, towards the jumble of roofs that belonged to the houses to the north of the village.

That was the street down which he'd driven on his way into Rundheim. It had been very empty of people, he recalled, with little signs of life in the houses. Now he understood why.

Somewhere among the roofs silhouetted against the indigo sky, there was a synagogue, Dorothy had told him. In her early years in Rundheim, Christians and Jews had helped each other, and the two communities had been friends.

But that felt a very long time ago, she'd said, her voice heavy with sadness.

She couldn't really pinpoint when Christians had stopped going to the area north of the crossroads, had stopped visiting the doctor or dentist who practised there, had stopped calling in on the people who lived there and who'd been their friends, but at some point they had.

And now, a number of their Jewish friends had quietly moved away. And those who'd remained did their best to keep out of the sight of the non-Jewish residents of Rundheim.

It had all happened without anyone really noticing, she'd said, as if thinking aloud, rather than talking to him.

As he stood there, looking out, the last of the houses to the north was swallowed up by the black mouth of night.

So this was Dorothy's home.

A village shrouded in dread and fear. A village around which, despite the optimism that Franz expressed about the future, he could feel that shroud tightening.

And there was nothing he could do to loosen it.

34

T*he following morning*

PHILIP LEANED AGAINST THE DOORPOST, and stared out at the stillness of the early morning.

There was movement in the blacksmith's forge, where a red fire blazed deep within, but the road both ways was empty of people and animals, with the exception of a solitary pig that nuzzled among the heap of damp leaves that had gathered at the foot of the wall of what he'd been told was Karl and Herta's house.

Instead of a sense of abundant life, there was bleakness and desolation.

He felt a sudden powerful longing for the journey home to be over, for him to be back in England, back with Louisa. To be miles away from the naked fear he'd glimpsed in Dorothy's eyes.

After his conversations of the day before, he hadn't been

surprised that breakfast had been a somewhat sombre affair, despite his one or two attempts at lightening it.

Dorothy had looked drained, as if she hadn't slept much in the night. Franz had seemed on edge and anxious, and had kept glancing surreptitiously at Dorothy. Dieter had been unnaturally quiet for a boy of his age, and although, from time to time, he'd glanced from one parent to the other, he'd said little.

Only Elke had seemed untouched by the oppressive sense of melancholy that lay heavy in the air. Wearing a russet dress and with her hair tied back, she'd sat reading her book, rhythmically kicking the table leg as she did so.

'You shouldn't read at breakfast, Elke,' Dieter had said at one point in irritation. 'Should she, *Vati*?'

Franz looked across at Elke. 'Your brother's right, Elke. Put your book away, please.'

'It's not fair,' she said, sulkily. 'Just because he doesn't like reading.'

Dieter opened his mouth to answer her back, but Philip cut in. 'That's a very pretty dress, Elke,' he said. 'The colour suits you.'

She beamed at him. '*Mutti* made it for me.'

'Your mother's obviously a good needlewoman.' He glanced at Dorothy. 'Did you bring the skill with you to Germany, Dorothy, or is it something you learnt here?'

She smiled. 'Definitely not from England, if you discount being able to sew up a wound. In England, all of our clothes were made for us. And if we tore our skirt, for example, a maid would repair it. But I don't miss that at all. No, being able to make clothes and mend them is something I learned here. My friend Herta taught me. I find it a very satisfying activity. And it's good not to have to rely on other people to do essential things for you.'

Philip nodded. 'I agree entirely. Although I'm afraid that my life in the past, and I suspect my life in the future, in no way reflects that ideal. I dread to think of Louisa's response if I gave her a roll of material, a needle and scissors, and suggested she made her own dress,' he added with a laugh.

Dorothy smiled. 'I can well imagine it! If she's anything like her mother, I wouldn't want to be around to hear it.' She hesitated. 'I'm afraid that breakfast today hasn't been the most cheerful of meals,' she said with a tinge of awkwardness. 'I think we've all enjoyed your visit so much that we're sad to see you go, and that's lowered our spirits.'

'And I'm sorry to have to leave you so soon. I've very much enjoyed my stay.'

He'd smiled around the table, and had then resumed his breakfast of rye bread, salami and cheese.

After breakfast, he'd swiftly packed the few items he'd taken from the car for his overnight stay, put his bags in the car, and was ready to leave. All that remained was to say goodbye.

Standing in the open doorway, he could hear Dorothy in the house behind him, clearing the dishes from the table, and then the clattering stopped.

He glanced over his shoulder to see if this would be a good moment at which to take his leave.

Dorothy was standing next to her chair, staring across the room at the cupboard that stood against the opposite wall.

Franz was in the middle of taking a pile of schoolbooks from his bag and putting them on to the table. Elke was reading her novel, and Dieter was rubbing a badge against his shirt in an effort, Philip assumed, to make it shine more brightly.

'I think I ought to set off now,' he said, and he took a step into the room.

Dorothy turned her head and looked at him, wide-eyed.

'I lied!' she blurted out.

He stopped abruptly, and stared at her. Her face was stricken.

He glanced quickly at the others.

Franz was standing very still, a schoolbook in his hand, his eyes on Dorothy. Dieter had stopped polishing. His badge in his hand, he was frowning at his mother. Elke had looked up from her book and was staring at Dorothy, surprise giving way to trepidation.

His gaze returned to Dorothy. 'I'm sorry?' he said, his words forming a question.

'I lied, Philip, when I said I didn't want to go back to England. I do. I want to go back very much.' Her voice was trembling, but clear.

Franz dropped his book. The sound of it hitting the floor reverberated around the room.

'This is our home,' Franz said, his face ashen.

She turned to him. 'Dearest Franz, it felt like home in our first years here, but it hasn't for a long time now. Germany's changed. First it was the big towns. We saw that from the newspapers. Then the poison spread to villages like Rundheim. It feels as if we're living under a threatening cloud.'

She took a step towards him. 'I'm frightened for us, and for our children. I don't want them to grow up in an atmosphere of hatred and fear. Not when there's no need to.'

He gestured helplessness. 'But things are getting better in Germany. You know they are.'

'Economically, yes. But not in other ways. And it's the other ways that really matter. In those ways, things are getting worse, and I believe they'll get still worse. And we'll never have peace of mind.'

Franz turned from Dorothy to Philip, who was standing just inside the room, uncertain what to do.

'This is your fault,' Franz said, his voice ice-cold, his blue eyes glittering with anger. 'Dorothy was settled and happy. Then you got here. And now she isn't.'

Dorothy moved forward and put her hand on his arm. 'No, I wasn't, Franz. I was frightened. I've been frightened since the day you joined the Party even though you didn't want to. And everything I've heard and seen since then has made me even more afraid.'

He stared at her in surprise. 'But there's nothing for people like us to be fearful about.'

She dropped her arm, took a step back and stared at him in disbelief. 'Are you truly saying that it's all right for some people to live in fear? So long as it isn't us? A year ago, you wouldn't have said such a thing.'

'You're misunderstanding me.'

'I don't think so. And you're wrong in thinking we've nothing to fear. Karl being taken shows that everyone is at risk. Every day I'm afraid that one of us—you, me, the children—will say or do something we shouldn't, without even knowing we shouldn't. That's all it would take. And then we'd be taken away.'

'*Mutti*!' Elke cried out. She burst into tears, and ran to Dorothy.

Dorothy put her arm around her.

'Karl knew he was doing something that wasn't allowed,' Franz said quietly.

'He was teaching a poet he loved, whom he'd taught for years, who happened to be Jewish. And the whole family was punished for it. That doesn't alarm you? You don't think it's terribly wrong?' she said, in rising incredulity.

'Of course I do. But I accept two things. Firstly, we should obey the government, and secondly, every government will make at least one mistake as they come to terms with governing.'

'A mistake? Burning the books of authors just because they were Jewish was just a mistake, was it? And those of Bertolt Brecht and Karl Marx because they believed in communism? And of Ernest Hemingway, a so-called corrupt foreign influence? And of Thomas Mann because he warned of the dangers of dictatorship? Anyone who thinks for himself is at risk under this régime, Franz.'

He opened his mouth to speak.

'But we should be encouraged to think for ourselves,' she cried, 'and be allowed to disagree with something if we want. To do so now, though, would endanger us.'

'You've been upset by our visitor from England, Dorothy, so you're exaggerating the situation. You've also forgotten that your father doesn't want you back. And if he doesn't want *you* back, he certainly won't want your family.'

'Then we'll manage without him.' She went up to him. 'Dear Franz, tell me you're not now acutely aware of every word you say in the school, and whenever you meet friends in the street or the pub, and every time you go into a shop. Tell me that you feel able to take the Hitler flag from our window. Tell me, Franz.'

White-faced, they stared at each other.

'The Franz I used to know would open his eyes, face the truth, and do everything in his power to protect his family,' she said quietly.

He ran his hand through his hair. 'What would you have me do?' he cried in despair. 'Return to England, the country that locked me up for years merely because I was German? And which might lock me up again, and our children, too? Is what Hitler's doing so much worse than that?'

'But you wouldn't be locked up as there won't be another war, will there? Germany's turning against some of its own citizens, but not against England.'

Franz straightened up. 'I will not leave my country again. Germany is my home. And it's the home of my children.'

The ticking of the clock was the only sound to be heard in the room.

'I can't take back the words I've said, Franz,' she said at last, 'and I don't want to. It's what I truly feel. This town has changed since the days we started living here, and I'm frightened by that change. I want us all to go to England.'

'Well, I don't,' he said bluntly. 'And I won't go.'

'We've been given a chance that we might never have again,' she pleaded. 'And I'm going. If you won't come with me, the children and I will have to go without you. But we'd rather not do that.'

'No!' Dieter shouted, and he stood up. 'I'm staying here. I'm German, not English. I'm a unit leader. I'm staying with *Vati*.' He ran to his father.

Side by side, the two of them faced Dorothy.

'And you, Elke?' Dorothy said. 'What do *you* want to do?'

'I miss Sofia and Leah,' she said. 'And what happened to them has made me afraid. I'm always scared that we could be taken away like Sofia. I don't want to leave *Vati*, but I don't want to stay here any more.' She looked at her father. 'I'm sorry, *Vati*,' she said and she started to cry.

Her face deathly pale, Dorothy stared at Franz and Dieter.

Franz held out his arms to her and she walked into them.

Tears streamed down his cheeks as he tightened his arms around her, and hugged her to him. Then he pulled off her kerchief and buried his face in her hair.

'I shall always love you, Dorothy,' he said, his voice muffled. 'And I shall live with the hope of seeing you again. This is not goodbye for ever. It can't be. It would be like cutting off a limb. One day, you and Elke will come back to us. This I know. And Dieter and I will be waiting for you, our hearts full of love, a love that will never die.' He broke off with a sob.

She nodded, unable to speak. Then she gently eased herself out of his hold and moved sideways to Dieter. Leaning down, she kissed him.

'My darling, darling Dieter,' she said, stroking his face. '*Vati* will write and tell me how you are, and you must write to me, too. You have a place in my heart, just like *Vati*, and you always will.'

'Why d'you have to leave us, *Mutti*?' he cried. He flung his arms around her. 'I love you.' She hugged him as hard as she could, and then she let him go.

Almost blind with tears, she turned towards Philip. 'Elke and I will get a few things, and be down again in minutes.'

She put her arm around Elke's shoulders, and each supporting the other, they hurried up to their bedrooms, both of them weeping.

'Why did you come? You shouldn't have done!' Dieter shouted at Philip. 'I hate you!'

Pushing past Philip, he ran out of the house, turned to the left and ran past the smithy and butcher's shop, and out of sight as fast as he could.

'He's right,' Franz said. 'You unsettled Dorothy. You didn't mean to, but you did. You reminded her of England when she was feeling low at the loss of Herta and Karl, and she wasn't able to think clearly. She loves me, and she loves her children. But now, because of you, our family is broken.'

'I'm so sorry, Franz.'

'Because of you, our children won't grow old together, and I won't grow old with my Dorothy.' His voice broke. His pressed his knuckle to his mouth.

'I didn't for one minute expect this, or want it,' Philip said quietly. 'And I'm deeply saddened that it's come to this.'

'You think going back to England will make her happy?' Franz said, drawing slow steadying breaths. 'Well, you're wrong—it won't. Dorothy will never be happy away from me, just as I will never be happy away from her. You'll be responsible for both of our misery, and that of our children. Such a person as you is not welcome in my house. I want you to wait outside.'

Philip turned, left the house, and went and stood next to his car.

As he waited for Dorothy and Elke, Joseph's words flooded his mind. He definitely didn't want Dorothy home again. Not at all. Protecting Thomas was his priority, and it always would be.

Leaning back against the car, Philip groaned.

35

An hour later

HAD she done the right thing in leaving Rundheim, Dorothy thought in rising panic as they neared the border with Luxembourg.

She and Elke would very likely be rejected by her family. If they were, she'd hate it, but she knew she'd be able to cope with it. Elke wouldn't, though. She'd suffer terribly.

Should she have risked that happening to Elke?

And if they *were* rejected, how would she manage to support them both?

She should have thought more about what she was doing before she'd turned their lives upside down, she berated herself. Before she'd taken Elke from her father and brother. Before she'd left the husband and son she loved with all her being.

She inwardly shook herself. She must stop thinking like that!

She hadn't had the luxury of time in which to consider her options. It had all happened so fast, Philip arriving, and having to leave so soon, and with a car into which they would all fit.

And she'd been so afraid for so long.

Feeling as she did, she hadn't really had any choice when faced with a way of gaining peace of mind.

The knowledge that they could all escape the fear that had become their daily companion had overwhelmed her, and she'd been incapable of seeing beyond that.

But from the moment she'd told Franz she was leaving, and he'd refused to go with her, she'd felt numb.

Full of love for Franz and Dieter, and dread that she might never see them again, she'd sat in the back of the car, paralysed by anguish, her arms around Elke, holding her close, trying to shield her from the same cold emptiness that had lodged within her.

Franz had been at the centre of her life from the moment they'd met.

She'd never failed to feel cherished and protected by him. They'd shared so much together, the wonderful moments when the children had been born, and the intense grief each time she'd lost a child in an early stage of pregnancy. And he'd been an excellent father to Elke and Dieter.

But now, just as she was going to have to find a way of living without him at her side, Elke was going to have to adjust to life without a father.

And both would live with the fear that at any moment, Franz and Dieter might fall foul of Hitler's government or the Brownshirts.

Had she stayed, she'd might have been able to prevent

Franz from taking unnecessary risks, and she could have helped to make sure that Dieter knew always what was right and what was not.

The closer they'd come to the border with Luxembourg, the weaker her certainty that she was doing the right thing for both her and Elke.

She could be making a terrible mistake.

Franz had been sure that she was. He believed she'd got everything out of proportion. Could he have been right, and she have been wrong?

And what about Elke? Was she being unfair to Elke, taking her to an environment that would be totally strange to her, that might not even accept her?

Hugging Elke tightly, she felt her panic grow.

It was at its height as they reached the border.

A few minutes after they'd passed through the border, Philip steered the car into the side of the road and brought it to a stop.

She gripped the door handle, her knuckles white.

Elke sat up and gasped aloud.

Philip turned to them, and smiled reassuringly. 'No cause for alarm. I just thought you might want to stretch your legs for a moment or two.' And he got out, opened the back passenger door and helped them out.

Then he went to the edge of the road and faced Germany.

She exchanged curious looks with Elke, and they went and stood next to him.

He pointed ahead. 'Over there's Germany. The border's just out of sight, but it's very close and it would be easy enough to go back.' He turned to them. 'I suspect you're wondering now if you've made a huge mistake, Dorothy. Am I right?'

She nodded.

'I thought you might be. That's only normal. Sometimes we think we want something, and then when we have it, we realise we don't want it after all. It had been a dream that had seemed more attractive than it was because of the unlikelihood of it ever coming true.'

Holding Elke's hand, motionless, she stared in the direction of Germany.

'Well, this is a dream that *has* come true,' he continued. 'You've now left Germany and you're on your way to England. I want you to think hard, both of you, if this is what you still really want. If you feel you've made a mistake, we can return to Rundheim. I'll willingly take you back.'

A picture of Franz filled Dorothy's mind. His clear blue eyes were looking at her with love, as they always did, morning, noon and night. And as they'd looked at their children, too, as side by side with her, he'd watched them grow.

She hesitated. Then she turned to Elke.

'This is your decision, too, Elke. You're nearly fourteen, so you're old enough to understand the implications of what we're doing, and to know your own mind. If we go to England, you'll have to speak English outside the house all the time.'

'I know that.'

'And you'll have to get used to a very different style of life from the life you've known so far. You'll go to an English school, and as well as the friends I hope you'll make, there'll be those who don't like you merely because of your German blood. It's not just Uncle Thomas who was injured in the war. Many men were injured or lost their lives, and they were all someone's husband, father, son, brother.'

Elke looked up at her, her face chalk-white.

'And then there's your father and brother,' Dorothy went

on. 'We would obviously write to them regularly, but letters are a poor substitute for the genuine thing, and there's a real chance we might never see them again. I want you to think hard, Elke, and tell me honestly if you'd prefer to go back to Rundheim. We're going to do whatever you want.'

Elke turned to look again towards Germany.

'I feel safe now,' Elke said, her voice firm and clear. 'And I haven't felt safe since long before *Onkel* Karl and *Tante* Herta were taken away. Leah used to tell Sofia and me that her parents were always frightened of what might happen, and that made both of us frightened, too. So I've been scared for a long time now.'

'Oh, Elke,' Dorothy whispered.

'There are worse things than not being liked,' Elke went on. 'I'm sure that Sofia and Hans would rather be in a school where no one liked them than be locked away wherever they are. I shall keep asking *Vati* and Dieter to come to England, too, and I'll keep hoping they agree, but I want to go to England.'

'Darling Elke,' Dorothy said, tears welling up. 'When did you become so strong and so sensible? I don't think I've ever been prouder of you.'

She looked up at Philip, her vision blurred. 'Thank you, Philip,' she said. 'You've helped us both accept that although we love Dieter and Franz with all our heart, our fear is too great to stay in Germany, and we want to leave.'

He nodded. 'That's all I needed to know. Let's continue on our way, then.'

Primrose Hill

.   .   .

PHILIP DREW up alongside the kerb, and pulled on the brake. Across the road on the right were the green slopes of Primrose Hill, and to the left of the car was a line of imposing houses.

Filled with a trepidation that had been building as they'd approached Primrose Hill, Dorothy stared through the car window at the five-storey house on her left.

The brick walls were warm in the early afternoon sun. Against them, the white wooden frames of the sash windows dazzled.

'It hasn't changed at all,' she said slowly. 'It seems as if time has stood still for the past fifteen years.'

'I suppose it must do. This isn't an area where people move in and out. Once they're here, they tend to stay. And they're the sort of people who like everything to remain as it is.'

He looked at his watch. 'Stopping for something to eat on the way was a good idea. We wouldn't have wanted to arrive just as they were about to sit down for lunch. But I imagine they'll have finished by now.'

She stared at him in surprise. 'Does Father have lunch at home, then? He used to be at Kentish Town all day, or out on a site somewhere. He'd have lunch wherever he was.'

He smiled. 'The house may not have changed, but your father has. He's retired now, isn't he? Mind you, he's still involved in much that goes on in the business, so it isn't your typical retirement. But all the same, I gather your mother has laid down certain rules, and having lunch together is one of them.'

'I've kept up with the family's news through Nellie and Louisa, but somehow you still see everyone's routine as it used to be. And the people, too. In my head, my parents look as they did when I left. It'll be strange seeing them as they are now.'

She turned to Elke. 'Well, we're here now,' she said. 'This is the house where I grew up.'

Elke leaned closer to the window. 'It looks huge,' she said. 'And so do all the other houses in the road. It's not like Rundheim.'

'We can sit in the car and talk all day, thereby putting off going inside,' Philip said gently. 'Or we can do what you're naturally nervous about doing, and let your parents know you're here.'

She gave him a wan smile. 'Was it that obvious?'

'Yes, but it was understandable. May I suggest that the two of you stay in the car, while I go in and let Joseph and Maud know that you've both come back with me? Assuming they're at home, that is.'

'Thank you,' she said, shakily, and she gripped the door handle, her knuckles white.

The last time she'd seen her father, he'd told her bitterly that she was no longer a daughter of his, and he'd physically turned his back on her. He'd refused even to meet Franz. And beyond the letter telling her that her grandfather had died, he'd never written to her in all the years since she'd left.

Asking Philip to visit her, and wanting to know that she was well, didn't mean he wanted her back.

And she wasn't just back—she was back with a German daughter.

She watched Philip cross the pavement and go up the few steps to the front door. She couldn't see who opened the door, but she saw him go inside, and the door close behind him.

Her eyes on the door, her heart thumped wildly.

Several minutes later, the door opened, and Philip came back down the steps.

'They're in,' he said, opening the car door for her. 'I won't be leaving till I'm sure you don't need me again. I'll be in the room at the back. Mrs Morley's going to bring me a coffee. You'll find your parents in the front reception room. So, shall we go in?'

Her face pale, she drew in a deep breath, and put her foot on the pavement.

36

With Elke following nervously, Dorothy was ushered into the front reception room by Mrs Morley, who closed the door behind them.

Hearing the door click shut, Dorothy hesitated. She glanced over her shoulder at Elke, gave her an encouraging smile, and then turned to her father.

Joseph faced her, his legs astride, his back to the fireplace.

Her mother had risen, too, and was standing in front of one of the armchairs that flanked the marble fireplace.

'Hello, Father,' she said, her voice trembling. 'And Mother.'

Joseph took a step forward, and stopped.

Instinctively, Dorothy moved back and grasped Elke's hand.

With a rustle of rayon from her pale blue dress, Maud moved gracefully across the room to her daughter and granddaughter.

She put a hand on each of Dorothy's shoulders, and for a long moment, stared into her face.

'Darling,' she said, her voice shaking with emotion. And she hugged Dorothy close to her. 'My darling girl,' she repeated. Drawing back from her, she touched Dorothy's face, as if in disbelief.

Then Maud moved to Elke, took her hand and pulled her gently forward. 'So, you're our granddaughter, are you? Well, we're delighted to meet you.' She embraced Elke warmly, and then straightened up and looked back at Joseph. 'Aren't we, Joseph?'

'Yes, we are,' he said, his voice breaking. His gaze on Dorothy's face, he went up to her. 'At last, you're where you belong,' he said gruffly. 'We can now stop worrying about your safety. You're home, Dorothy.'

He drew her close to him and hugged her hard. Releasing her, he took a handkerchief from his jacket pocket, and Dorothy saw that his eyes were glistening.

She felt herself relax.

'I didn't know if you'd want us back,' she said, filling with emotion.

A tear ran down his cheeks. 'Forget everything I said. You're my daughter, and nothing can change that.' He hugged her again, and then wiped his eyes.

'And this is *my* daughter, Elke,' she said, smiling at Elke through blurred vision. 'She's almost fourteen.'

He blew his nose, and looked solemnly at Elke. 'Hello, Elke. Does she speak English?' he asked, glancing at Dorothy.

'Perhaps you'd like to answer your grandfather's question, Elke.'

Elke gave him a shy smile. 'Yes, I do. I always spoke English with *Mutti* in the house, and I spoke German with *Vati*, and also at school and outside the house.'

Joseph nodded. 'That's good. It means we can talk to

each other. You look very like your mother did at that age, you know,' he added. 'Very like her.'

His voice broke, and he wiped his eyes again with his handkerchief.

'I'm very glad you're back, Dorothy, and I don't mind telling you, relieved. Philip told us only that this was a sudden decision to leave Germany, and that your husband and son chose not to come with you.'

'That's right.'

'You and Elke must stay here while we get to know each other again. At some point, when you've had time to think and to take stock of what's happened, we'll talk about where you might like to live. But there's no hurry for that. Your home is here with us for as long as you want. And I suggest we find Elke a suitable school near here.'

'I don't want you to feel obliged to do anything that makes you uncomfortable, Father,' Dorothy said quietly. 'I remember your words when I married Franz.'

'And if he'd been here, things would be different. I'm not going to pretend they wouldn't. I wouldn't be able to invite him into the house. You haven't seen Thomas since he came home from the war so you won't know how badly affected he was by his injuries, and still is, and how damaged he was by seeing his closest friend blown to bits in front of him. I don't know if you remember David.'

'Only vaguely.'

'Well, the last years have been difficult for Thomas, and we must recognise that, and protect him from anything that could further distress him.'

'Of course.'

Maud put her hand on Joseph's arm. 'I imagine that Dorothy and Elke are in need of a rest, Joseph,' she said firmly. 'Philip tells us you've had lunch, Dorothy. We'll see that your luggage is taken from the car, and we'll ask Mrs Morley to prepare your rooms. Then I suggest that you and Elke go upstairs and freshen up. You can then have a short rest, and come down again in time for afternoon tea.'

'We brought very little with us,' Dorothy said. 'It all happened so quickly.'

'Don't worry about that,' Maud said, with a dismissive wave. 'Tell Mrs Morley what you lack, and she'll see you have everything you need. If you feel sufficiently rested by tomorrow, we'll add to your wardrobe.'

There was a knock on the door, and Mrs Morley came into the room. 'Mr McAllister has taken Miss Dorothy's luggage from the car and is ready to leave.'

Maud stepped forward. 'Would you be kind enough to prepare rooms for Miss Dorothy and Elke, Mrs Morley, please?'

'I took the liberty of doing so while you were talking to them, ma'am. Their rooms are ready.'

'Thank you, Mrs Morley. That was well anticipated by both you and Mr McAllister,' Maud added with a smile.

'Ask Mr McAllister to come in, would you, please?' Joseph said.

Philip appeared in the doorway. 'I thought I'd get off now, sir. I wouldn't want to intrude.'

'And you wouldn't be. Dorothy and Elke are going upstairs—they can thank you another time—and Maud's going up for rest, too. She always does at this time. I'm about to have a cognac in the library, and I'd be very pleased if you joined me. If you're not anxious to get away, that is. I'd understand if you are—you've had a long journey, and also you must want to see Louisa again.'

'Indeed, I do, but I know she'll be working at the moment, and I'd rather not go to Kentish Town. Not till

Thomas knows that Dorothy's back. And you'll want to be the one to tell him that, I'm sure.'

He smiled at Dorothy and Elke, and then turned back to Joseph.

'I shall go to the flat first, and see Louisa this evening. A cognac with you before I get back on the road sounds very pleasant. Thank you.'

'I MUST ADMIT, I'M SURPRISED,' Joseph said, tapping his pipe on the ashtray, 'that Dorothy left her husband, and came back to England without him. I'm delighted she did, of course,' he added quickly. 'If he'd come back with her, I couldn't have had them stay here. And I doubt that the family would've wanted to see them. Having Dorothy by herself is quite a different matter.'

'It's not that she no longer loves him, if that's what you're wondering—I'm certain she does. But fear's a difficult thing to live with. Her anxiety about events in Germany had been building up for a long time, and at some point, that anxiety became real fear for her family's safety.'

He recounted in brief what had happened to Karl and Herta, and how their Jewish friends had been quietly leaving the village.

'There doesn't seem to have been any actual aggression towards the Jewish people in Rundheim,' he concluded, 'but the townsfolk had obviously been influenced by what they'd read in the newspapers, and Jews were being ostracised, from what I could gather.'

'It sounds a highly undesirable environment in which to bring up a family.'

'It was. My visit to Dorothy gave her the chance to come back, and she took it. Franz thought she was worrying needlessly, and refused to go with her. His decision will have been influenced, I'm sure, by his period of internment here. And Dieter didn't want to come, either.'

'Maud and I have certainly been very concerned about things we've read in the papers, and so has Charles. He's been watching the situation in Germany very closely.' He took the pipe from his mouth, and stared at Philip. 'As you must have been, too, Philip.'

'Indeed,' Philip said. He leaned forward and picked up his snifter of cognac.

'You've told me you work for the Air Ministry, too, Philip. You must tell me if I'm out of line, but I suspect that your visit to Germany wasn't just to look under the bonnets of numerous cars. This will have been related to those dual-purpose factories you were talking about.'

Philip gave him a wry smile. 'How very perceptive of you.'

'So I imagine you'll have some idea if Dorothy was right to be apprehensive.'

'She was certainly right that anyone who questions the German Government risks being taken away—and their family, too. They're being sent to camps for re-education. There's plenty of proof of that.'

Joseph frowned. 'So why doesn't Franz share her alarm?'

'He does, but not to the same extent. He thinks the government will calm down when it's been in power a little longer.'

'Is he right?'

Philip hesitated.

Joseph stared Philip squarely in the face. 'You have my word that I'd never repeat anything you told me.'

Philip leaned forward. 'No, I don't think he is. If I had to put money on it, I'd say that Germany was preparing for war.'

Joseph straightened up.

'Before the war,' Philip went on, 'they had the third largest colonial empire after Britain and France. At the end of the war, they'd lost control of their colonies, which were confiscated under the peace treaty. There's a lot to make one suspect that Hitler wants to regain Germany's lost colonial possessions, and that means war.'

'And that's your way of thinking, too?'

Philip nodded. 'Yes, it is. As far back as three years ago, the journalist Ossietzky was talking about the reality of clandestine German rearmament, and just over a year ago, at his first cabinet meeting after coming into power, Hitler said that re-armament was going to be the top German priority.'

Joseph frowned. 'But is that happening, despite the peace treaty?'

'I'm afraid it is. There've long been rumours that pilots are being secretly trained in glider clubs, for example, and also in the Soviet Union, and Hitler's now openly said that Germany has begun to construct an air force. We know for a fact that he plans to bring back conscription, and this can only be to build up an army.'

'That *is* a cause for concern.'

'It's also rumoured that although amassing arms is forbidden under the treaty, orders are being placed through dummy companies. We've all condemned Hitler's actions, but we haven't penalised him for them. And it seems to have given him free rein to do what he wants.'

Joseph studied the bowl of his pipe for a moment. 'So you really believe that Germany wants another war, do you?'

'I do. Of course, a lot is still speculation, but it has the ring of truth, and I'll be reporting that what we're hearing should be treated as well founded, and that we should speed up our precautionary preparations for war. I'm only a small voice among many, though, so who knows what the Government will decide.'

'I can see we've even more reason to be grateful to you for bringing Dorothy back to us than I'd realised. If there'd been a war against England while she was still in Germany, I dread to think what might have happened. From the bottom of my heart, I thank you, dear boy.'

'It was my pleasure, sir.'

'The family must be told she's back, and as soon as possible,' Joseph said. 'You'll obviously tell Charles and Sarah this evening. Louisa will be pleased, but I imagine that Sarah will be quite hostile.'

'I think that might be so.'

'And you're right that I should be the person to tell Thomas, and I'll go there later this afternoon. I'll call in at Walter and Nellie's on the way home, and tell them, too.' He stared thoughtfully at Philip. 'That's the easy part. The hard part is what we're going to do with Dorothy and her daughter?'

Philip smiled. 'I think you may find that Dorothy will have some suggestions to make. She'll have changed over the years, many of which were a hard struggle. Her home was very different from this.'

Philip gestured around him.

'She didn't have servants to wait on her for a start. She's not the girl who left England. I'd leave it to her to tell you what she'd like to do. Once she gets over the shock that this must have been, of course, and has had time to think about the future.'

Joseph nodded. 'Wise words. And yes, I'll do what you

studiously avoided saying outright—I'll tread cautiously. One thing I *can* do, though, without Dorothy knowing, is find out her position in law. I like to be prepared for every eventuality. That's just the way I'm built. Since I'll be calling in at Nellie's this evening, it won't hurt to have a quick word with Walter about Dorothy's situation. He's never yet let me down.'

'As I say, from the little I've seen of Dorothy, she'll know her own mind, sir, and she won't hesitate to tell you what she wants when the time is right.'

Joseph beamed. 'In other words, a chip off the old block, dear boy. But talking about knowing one's own mind, Louisa's made a number of decisions about the interior of your house, and I'm happy to say it's now finished. She has the keys, and I know she's keen to take you to see it as soon as possible. She wants you to see inside the house before her parents do.'

Philip smiled broadly.

He finished his drink, and stood up. 'I ought to get off now,' he said. 'We both have people we want to see before night falls.'

37

K entish Town

'IT'S MR LINFORD, SIR,' Mrs Carmichael announced, and she held the door open for Joseph to go into Thomas's office.

Thomas was sitting in the wheelchair in his favourite position, his back to the door, facing his view of the street, which was framed by the tall sash window.

Joseph glanced above Thomas's head to the scene that his brother saw daily.

The plane trees that grew along the edge of the pavement on the opposite side of the road were coming into new leaf, but their star-like leaves were not yet large enough to hide from sight the ugly row of rundown shops that lined the back of the pavement.

'You'd think they'd pull down those old shops and build something more attractive for you to look at,' Joseph remarked.

Thomas grinned at him over his shoulder. 'You came all this way to tell me that? Next you'll be telling me that you know just the building company to buy and develop the land.'

Joseph laughed. He went forward, pulled up a wooden chair from the side of the room, and sat down next to Thomas.

'Would you like me to bring you tea, sir?' Mrs Carmichael asked from the doorway.

Thomas glanced sideways at Joseph. 'Tea or something stronger?'

'The something stronger sounds good. Whisky would hit the spot.'

Thomas raised his eyebrows. 'Make that two whiskies, Mrs Carmichael, please,' he called to her. 'Pull up that coffee table, Joseph and put it between us. So this is a whisky visit, is it? What's it about? Or should we make small talk while we wait for our drinks? You're looking particularly dapper today in your dark blue suit, if I may say.'

Joseph laughed again. 'If that's your best attempt at small talk, I think we'll give it a miss. Has Louisa finished for the day?'

'Thank God, yes! Without Philip here as a distraction, she's been smothering me even more with her desire to help. Every minute of the day, I feel her eyes boring into me as she tries to anticipate my every need. I live in fear that one of these days, when my stump is really playing up, she'll try to stop me from having to put any weight on it by offering me a chamber pot! I don't dare let myself wince with pain for fear of that ultimate humiliation.'

Joseph chuckled.

'Here you are, sir,' Mrs Carmichael said coming into the

room. She put their drinks on the coffee table, stood an open bottle of whisky next to the glasses, and left the room.

Joseph picked up his glass. 'Cheers!' he said, and he took a drink.

Thomas's glass remained on the table, untouched. 'What is it, Joseph?' he asked. 'I know you well enough to be able to tell when there's something you've got to say to me, and you think I won't like it.'

Joseph put his glass back on the table. 'You're right. There *is* something, and I don't think it's anything you'd have chosen to hear.' He cleared his throat. 'Dorothy's back. Philip visited her when he was in Germany, and she came back with him.'

'Dorothy and?'

'And her daughter, Elke. She's almost fourteen.'

Thomas stared intently at Joseph. 'And?'

'There's no one else, Thomas. Dorothy's husband chose to stay in Germany, and so did her son. He's nine, I believe.'

Thomas turned back to the view across the road. 'You're right,' he said at last. 'They ought to knock down those shops. They're an eyesore.'

'Is that all you've got to say?'

Thomas shrugged. 'What else is there to say? She's your daughter so she's part of the family. And so is her daughter. While I'd rather not see them, I realise that our paths will probably cross at Chorton and at Robert's monthly lunches. I shall be civil, so you've no need to worry on that score. But as for sitting next to her at the dinner table, I'd prefer to sit next to Louisa.'

'It's good of you to be so understanding, Thomas. Maud's delighted she's back, as you can imagine.'

Thomas nodded. 'And it's not as if her husband is with her. If he'd come, too, that would be entirely different.' He picked up his glass. 'So what brought her back after all this time?'

CAMDEN TOWN

'I'M sorry to interrupt your evening,' Joseph told Nellie and Walter, 'but there's something I wanted to tell you. And also I'd like some advice. They're connected.'

He leaned back in the armchair, stretched out his legs, and picked up his glass of whisky.

'Maud would be most annoyed with me if she knew that having had a cognac after lunch, and then a whisky with Thomas, I'm now having a whisky with you. She'd have me on milk for the rest of the week.'

All three laughed.

'I hope you'll add wine to your day's alcoholic intake,' Walter said. 'You'll stay and have dinner with us, won't you?'

'That's very kind of you, dear boy. If it's no trouble.'

Nellie stood up. 'Of course, you must stay. I'll have a word with Cook, and then I'll telephone Mother and tell her you're eating with us this evening.'

'So you've been to Kentish Town, have you?' Walter remarked as Nellie went out. 'How was Thomas?'

'Amusing when it got to the subject of Louisa's ministrations. Much as he moans about her, I think he's actually quite fond of her. He realises that his irritability makes him the only person upon whom she can demonstrate the sincerity of her remorse, and he finds it quite entertaining. At least, he *was* the only person. There may be another contender now.'

'Contender for what?' Nellie asked, coming back into the

room and sitting down on the sofa next to Walter. 'I hope you weren't saying anything interesting in my absence.'

She paused. 'I'm sorry to tell you, Father, that Mother didn't sound in the least bit upset that she was going to have to dine by herself this evening.'

'That's because she won't be eating alone. That's what I wanted to tell you. Philip's back.'

Nellie clapped her hands in glee. 'Oh, I'm so pleased! Did he see Dorothy? Please say that he did. Is that why he's visiting Mother this evening, to tell her all about Dorothy? Is Louisa there, too?'

Joseph smiled at her. 'Yes, he did see Dorothy.'

'And how is she? What did she say? Had she changed much? Is she still as pretty as she was? Well, he wouldn't know that. But what are her children like? Do they look like Dorothy or Franz?'

'Perhaps we should allow your father to tell us in his own way, Nellie,' Walter said in amusement. 'I'm losing track of the questions, as I imagine Joseph must be.'

She beamed at Joseph in excitement. 'Well, Father?'

'It isn't Philip who's with your mother this evening. He did better than bring back information about Dorothy—he brought her home with him.'

Walter and Nellie stared at him in momentary silence.

'I want to shout out how delighted I am at the thought of seeing her again, and I really am. And I'm going to go and see her first thing tomorrow. But what about Uncle Thomas?' Nellie asked, her face anxious.

'Only Dorothy and her daughter came back with Philip. For some time now, Dorothy's been living with fear about what's happening in Germany, all the violence. Philip offered her a way out, and she took it. Her husband preferred to stay. And so did her son.'

Nellie put her hand to her mouth. 'Oh, poor Dottie. And poor Elke. They must be so unhappy? Oh, how awful to have had to leave Franz and Dieter like that. But how dreadful to have been so frightened that you ended up leaving the people you loved. All of them must be distraught.'

She stared at Joseph in dismay.

He nodded. 'I'm sure that's true. At the moment, everything's happened so quickly for Dorothy that it hasn't yet sunk in. When it does, I imagine she'll go through a very hard time, trying to come to terms with leaving them.'

And Joseph told them everything he'd learned from Philip. He finished by adding that Elke seemed a pleasant girl, who was the image of her mother at that age.

And then he told them Thomas's response to the news.

'Had she come back with her husband, it would have been infinitely more difficult,' he concluded by saying. 'But she didn't, so we don't have to worry on that score.'

'I take it that Dorothy is the other possible contender for Louisa's attention,' Walter remarked.

'That's right. Philip is going to see Louisa this evening, and he'll tell Sarah and Charles that Dorothy's back. Sarah's been constant in her criticism of Dorothy for marrying a German, and I can't see her changing her attitude merely because Dorothy's back.'

'But *you've* changed,' Nellie said. 'Despite what you said when Dottie married Franz, you've welcomed her back. Sarah might have changed, too.'

'I wonder. But whatever Sarah thinks, Dorothy must be included in any family get-togethers, which means there could be some awkwardness. And if there is, I've a feeling it won't come from Thomas, but from Sarah. Louisa may well find another role for herself, and that is protecting Dorothy.'

He paused, and glanced sideways at Nellie.

'She's certainly well placed to do that,' he added, 'having been writing to Dorothy for years.'

Nellie gasped aloud. 'How d'you know?' she exclaimed.

'Haven't you learned yet that your father knows everything, Nellie?' Walter said with a smile.

Nellie giggled, and glanced quickly at her father.

Joseph looked back at Walter. 'Not quite everything, son. I don't know how to protect Dorothy financially from any claims her husband might make on her. And also on the family, for that matter. She's still young enough to have a future with someone else if she wants, which would mean divorcing Franz. I'd be grateful for your advice.'

'Wouldn't she have to accuse Franz of adultery if she wanted a divorce?' Nellie asked.

'That's right, Nellie,' Walter said. 'And she'd have to come up with some sort of evidence. We'd have to fabricate that evidence in a way that didn't look obvious. There must be no hint of collusion.'

'Dorothy would never agree to that,' Nellie said firmly. 'She loves Franz, and she'd never lie about him.'

Walter nodded. 'I'm sure you're right. Another option is to apply for a declaration of nullity, but I can't see her wanting to do that, either. Franz would lose his right to inherit from her, should she die first, and both would be free to marry again, but their children would be considered illegitimate.'

'She wouldn't want that, and nor would we,' Joseph said. 'What about an annulment, then?'

'That, too, would be far from ideal. Yes, it would protect Dorothy's rights, and keep the children legitimate, but neither she nor Franz would be able to marry again unless the other dies. She's very young to be put in such a position.'

Joseph sat back. 'Both sound somewhat drastic, and I certainly won't bring up the subject until Dorothy does. But it's good to be prepared. Whatever Dorothy may feel at the moment, she's a good head on her, and she'll come to see the importance of a settlement that protects her financially. And that protects the company from any demands that Franz might make in the future.'

'There's always the possibility of a legal agreement between them,' Walter added. 'But that would require the co-operation of her husband, and I would imagine this is all too recent, and too painful, for such co-operation to be forthcoming, and it could be difficult to effect over such a distance.'

'So what would you advise, Walter?' Joseph asked.

'That you do nothing for two or three years. After all, there would seem to be no urgency to act. Waiting will give us a two-fold advantage. Dorothy will have had time to know what she wants to do—it's conceivable that she might even want to return to her husband.'

'And the other advantage?'

'It will allow time for the changes that I suspect are going to come about in the law regarding divorce. If the changes under discussion were to be implemented, it would help Dorothy's situation.'

Joseph looked at him in surprise. 'What changes?'

'I don't know if you've come across a book called *Holy Deadlock*. It's a satirical novel by an author called A.P. Herbert. I rarely have time to read novels, but I made time for this one.'

'What's it about?' Joseph asked.

Walter grinned. 'The many perceived inadequacies and absurdities of the divorce law today. Basically, it takes the unusual line of treating divorce as a way of relieving misfortune, rather than as a crime, and it demonstrates how the current system encourages perjury and adultery. It's more than likely that the book will pave the way for statutory reforms, helped by the fact that women are now able to vote.'

'Which means?' Nellie asked.

'That in a year or two, we may see a new Matrimonial Causes Act, one that allows more grounds for divorce than just adultery. Cruelty, desertion and incurable insanity are being increasingly mentioned. If this comes about, and if Dorothy decides she wants a divorce, despite the stigma, one of the new grounds could come to her aid.'

Joseph sat back and smiled in satisfaction. 'I told Philip this afternoon that you'd never let me down, Walter. And indeed, yet again you haven't. I'm most grateful to you, son.'

38

K nightsbridge

'GOOD EVENING, MR PHILIP,' Mrs Garner said. 'Come in, will you. I'll tell Mr and Mrs Linford that you're here.'

'Thank you, Mrs Garner,' he said, stepping out of the column of amber lamplight and into the entrance hall. 'You're well, I hope.'

'Indeed, I am, sir,' she said, closing the door behind him.

'Philip!' He heard Louisa's scream of delight.

A moment later, she came running from the dining room. 'I heard your voice,' she cried. 'You're back!'

He took a step forward, held out his arms and she ran into them.

'I've missed you so much, Lou,' he said, folding his arms around her and hugging her tightly to him.

She pulled back and gazed up at him through tears of pleasure.

'And I've missed you, too,' she said, her voice breaking. 'I thought about you every single minute of the day. I hope you never ever have to go anywhere again without me.'

'Philip.' Sarah appeared in the doorway of the dining room. 'How lovely to have you back with us,' she said warmly, coming towards him. 'But you're very naughty not to have telephoned. You could have joined us for dinner. Can I ask Cook to prepare you a plate?'

'It's very kind of you, Sarah, but I grabbed something when I went back to the flat.'

Charles came and stood behind Sarah, and put a hand on each of her shoulders. 'I was about to have an after-dinner brandy while the girls have their coffee. You'll join me, won't you?'

'Thank you, sir. I'd like that.'

With Louisa clinging to his arm, her face wreathed in smiles, he followed Charles and Sarah back into the dining room. Sarah went to her seat at the end of the table, and he and Louisa sat down next to each other.

Charles crossed to the mahogany sideboard, poured a brandy for each of them, came back with the drinks, and sat down at the head of the table.

'We're very unbalanced in our seating,' Sarah said glancing around the table, and she got up. 'I shall come opposite you, Louisa. I want to hear all about Philip's trip, and it'll be easier to do so if we're closer to each other.'

Louisa turned to Philip. 'And I want to hear everything, too—all about the cars you saw and the places you visited—but before you begin, you must put me out of my misery and tell me if you saw Dorothy.'

He smiled at her. 'Yes, I did see her.'

'Oh, I'm so pleased!' she cried out happily, and she

leaned across and hugged him. 'I can't wait to hear all about her family and her life. And what her house is like.'

'How was she?' Sarah asked, a little stiffly.

'Very worried about the things that are happening in Germany at the moment, and have been for a while,' he replied.

'I'm not in the least bit surprised,' Charles remarked. 'Anyone who's been reading the newspapers on a regular basis over the past few years would be very concerned about the intentions of that man Hitler. There's a worrying amount of violence towards those who oppose him.'

'That was at the root of her fear. Her alarm grew out of an accumulation of events, rather than just one event.'

Louisa frowned. "What d'you mean?'

He told them about the events that had happened in Rundheim. 'From everything I heard and saw, she was right to be afraid,' he concluded.

Sarah cleared her throat. 'It's no secret that I was appalled that Dorothy married a German, and still am, but I'm sorry to hear that she's less than happy in her chosen life. I wouldn't have wished that on her.'

Charles nodded in agreement. 'No one would.'

'She was very happy with Franz,' Philip said. 'It was what was happening around her that was the worry.'

They heard the front door close, followed by footsteps.

'That'll be Christopher,' Charles told Philip. 'He was working late tonight.'

The door opened, and Christopher came in.

He saw Philip, stopped short, grinned at him, and went across and shook his hand.

'It's good to see you, Phil. If I'd known you were here, I'd have come home sooner.'

'I haven't been here for long. I only got back today. But I

couldn't wait to see Louisa.' He smiled at her, and she beamed back at him. He turned again to Christopher. 'How are the sprouts?'

Christopher laughed. 'Picked. It's now about earthing-up potatoes and planting quick-growing carrots. The bounty of the British spring must make you glad to be back,' he added, sitting down in the chair that Sarah had vacated.

Philip glanced at Louisa. 'While the attractions of a speedily emerging carrot are undeniable, there are other even stronger reasons why I'm glad to be back.'

Louisa looked into his eyes, and slowly smiled.

Dragging his gaze from Louisa's face, he turned to Charles and Sarah. 'I'm afraid that I've something to tell you that I don't think you're going to like.'

Louisa stared at his profile in surprise.

Charles frowned. 'What is it, son?'

'I didn't return on my own. Dorothy and her daughter, Elke, came back with me.'

There was a moment's silence.

'Elke?' Louisa said in amazement.

He nodded. 'That's right.'

He explained that Franz and Dieter had chosen to stay in Germany.

'And what about Thomas? Don't his feelings matter?' Sarah said sharply. 'Whether or not the German's with her, she chose to marry someone from the country responsible for Thomas's disability, and I find that unforgivable. I can't imagine how Thomas will feel when he knows she's back.'

'He'll know by now,' Philip told them. 'Joseph was going to tell him this afternoon. Joseph and Maud are delighted that Dorothy's back, and they obviously hope that the family will welcome both her and her daughter. After all, Franz isn't with them.'

'As far as I'm concerned, I've no interest in seeing Dorothy,' Sarah said, her back ramrod straight, a red spot on each cheek, 'or in meeting her child.'

Charles leaned across and took Sarah's hand. 'Don't agitate yourself, my dear.'

'Well, *I'm* interested in seeing her, Mother, and also in meeting Elke,' Louisa said firmly. 'And you should be, too. They're members of our family. Robert's her brother and he runs the company we all benefit from. Nellie's her sister, and you're very close to Nellie. How would Nellie feel if you refused to be in a room with her sister?'

'Lou's got a point, Sarah,' Charles said.

'And what if the others followed your example?' Louisa continued. 'It would be awful for Dorothy to be made to feel that her family didn't want her. You heard what Philip said about the dangers there. Would you prefer her to have stayed where she was in danger?'

Sarah sat, stony-faced.

'Thomas is the only one with a genuine reason not to see her. I'm going to visit her tomorrow.' She sat back in her chair, her eyes glittering.

Philip put his arm around her shoulders.

'I think we should listen to Lou, darling,' Charles told Sarah. 'Perhaps this is something to sleep on.'

He glanced at Philip and Louisa. 'We'll leave the subject of Dorothy for the moment, and talk about the situation more generally. When you were in the Cologne factory, Philip, and meeting colleagues over there, did you see or hear anything that made you think there could be another war?'

'Heaven forbid!' Sarah exclaimed, pulling her hand away from Charles. 'Of course, there won't be. We haven't got over the last one yet. Don't even suggest it. Why, Christopher would be conscripted into the army if there were to be a war. It doesn't bear thinking about.'

'I wouldn't fight,' Christopher said bluntly.

'Don't worry, you wouldn't have to,' Charles said. 'Farmers and growers were exempt from fighting during the last war, and I'm sure it'd be the same if there were to be another war. Someone has to grow the food to feed both army and country.'

Christopher looked at his father in surprise. 'I'm not worried. I would refuse to fight, and that's that.'

'You seem very certain that you don't want to fight, Christopher. If it came to a war, you might feel differently,' Philip said with a smile.

'I wouldn't. I'd never kill anyone. Killing is evil. You can't overcome one evil with another.'

'I don't know what to say to that, Chris,' Charles said slowly. 'And I certainly hope I never have to find out.'

Philip hesitated. 'To answer your question, Charles, there's certainly a lot of mistrust among the Germans, but it seems to be directed towards each other, and not at us. Hitler's spoken warmly about Britain, and there's no reason to think he'd turn on us. But he's unpredictable, and I wouldn't like to bet on anything.'

Charles smiled. 'Spoken with the caution of a banker or a lawyer. You could be in the wrong profession, Philip.'

They all laughed.

Philip turned to Louisa. 'What have you been doing in my absence, Lou?'

Her eyes shone. 'Nellie's been giving me some advice about weddings. Ours won't be as large as hers, but it'll be as lovely. And we've been talking about the whole family going to Chorton at the end of May. It'll be the last time we all get together before our wedding.'

'But before that, it's the lunch at Robert's next Sunday, Philip,' Charles told him. 'And then a walk on the Heath, if the weather permits. You're invited, too, of course. After all, you'll officially be family soon enough.'

'Thank you; I'd like that,' Philip said. He glanced at Louisa, and then at Charles and Sarah.

'If you don't need Lou on Saturday, can I borrow her? I know the Charlbury house isn't yet ready, but Joseph tells me Glenilla Road is. I thought Lou and I could take a look at it together. In fact, I don't believe you and Sarah have seen the inside yet. Perhaps you'd care to join us, and Christopher, too. We could have lunch in Hampstead afterwards.'

'We'd love that. Wouldn't we, Sarah?'

'Thank you, Philip. Yes, we would.' She hesitated. 'About Robert's lunch on Sunday. Do you know if Dorothy will be there?'

He shook his head. 'I've no idea. But if I had to hazard a guess, I'd say yes. She and Elke are staying with Joseph and Maud for the time being, and he'll want to see her back among the family. And if she hasn't already seen Robert, she'll certainly want to see him. But you'd have to ask Robert if you wanted to be sure.'

'If she's going, I'm not.'

'You *must* go, Mother,' Louisa insisted. 'Whatever Uncle Thomas decides is up to him, and would be understandable. But *you* haven't lost a leg.'

'We all have to do what we think right,' Sarah said icily.

'Just think what Dorothy must be going through, having had to leave her husband and child. If you can't be sympathetic, at least don't do anything to make things even harder for her.'

Sarah rose to her feet. 'I think I'll turn in now,' she said.

'No, don't get up, Philip. There's no reason for you to leave just yet.'

She walked across the room, went out into the hall and firmly closed the door.

'That's your mother all over. Once she's taken a position ...' Charles gestured helplessness. 'But I don't think you need to worry, Lou. She has a good heart, and when she's given this more thought ... Well, I'm confident she'll be there on Sunday, and won't cause any embarrassment.'

'I do hope so,' Louisa said anxiously. 'It'd be so wrong of her not to go.'

Charles smiled reassuringly. 'And furthermore, I'm equally sure that Joseph will have the foresight to suggest that Robert puts her at the opposite end of the table from Dorothy.'

39

P rimrose Hill,
       Sunday morning, mid-May

DRESSED and ready to leave for the family lunch at Robert's, Dorothy stood at the window of her former nursery and stared out at the view on the opposite side of the road.

The sunlight that filtered through the clouds had polished each blade of grass, and the meandering walkways that cut through the fields were flanked with carpets of brilliant green.

It was May, she thought, the time of year for new beginnings. So why did she still feel such a sense of loss? Why had there been no hint of rebirth? After all, she'd done the only thing she could.

She turned and looked around the room in which she'd spent so much time in her early years.

The *Sleeping Beauty* wallpaper had gone, and the walls had been painted a pale apple green. And the heavy brocade curtains of her youth had been replaced with velvet drapes in a deep shade of green.

But the dolls' house, toy pram, rocking-horse, children's table and chairs, and Robert's alphabet blocks, were all still there. They'd been arranged neatly in one corner of the room, permanent reminders of the childhoods spent within those walls.

Hers had been a happy enough childhood, she thought. She remembered feeling wistful at times, and disappointed, and perhaps a little left out, but she hadn't felt unhappy.

She'd understood that she couldn't compete with Robert, the longed-for son, or with Nellie, her lively, exuberant sister, who'd commanded the attention of all around her, and she'd been content to sit back and observe. But she'd no recollection of feeling sad.

How did she feel now, she wondered, having been in London for just over a week, a week in which she'd been re-acquainting herself with a style of living she'd long ago ceased to have.

Basically, did she feel happy?

She'd certainly felt out of place throughout the week. It was as if she no longer belonged, she realised with a start.

It now felt uncomfortable, having someone to take her clothes from her at the end of the day, and either launder them or put them away; to set out a breakfast buffet each morning, replenishing it as needed; to put plates in front of her at the dinner table, offer her food from tureens and pour her drinks, and then remove the empty plates and wash them; to ring a bell if she wanted anything.

After so many years of looking after Franz and her children, she'd got out of the habit of being waited upon, and it had felt surprisingly unsettling to be back in that world again.

And nor was she used to having nothing that needed to be done between meals, such as shopping for food, preparing and cooking the meal, serving it and clearing up afterwards, or cleaning the house, or washing and repairing the family's clothes. Or even making their clothes.

All the things she'd willingly done throughout the past fifteen years for the family she loved.

Of course, the hours between meals in England could be filled by any number of activities.

Her mother, Nellie and her aunt Sarah approved the day's menus, and then entertained friends who'd stopped by for morning coffee or afternoon tea. Or they went out to the houses of friends for morning coffee or afternoon tea, or met them in stores like Harrods.

In addition, her aunt and her mother were on numerous committees that claimed their time and gave them a purpose.

But such activities didn't attract her.

She'd had a genuine role to play when she'd been a nurse, caring for her patients, a role that had been immensely satisfying.

And after that, she'd had a real purpose in Rundheim, too. Her job had been to look after Franz, her children and their house, doing for them whatever needed to be done. Not to supervise someone else doing the work. It had been hard work, yes, but it had been rewarding, and she'd loved caring for her family.

But now, back in England, she felt as if she was rudderless and drifting.

And it wasn't just not having anything meaningful to do in the day that was difficult. Getting used to the structure of the English day again was demanding.

In Germany, school finished for the day at the end of the

morning, and Franz and the children had come straight home for what was their main meal of the day.

In the evening, they had a light meal only—rye bread or pumpernickel, a selection of cheeses and a variety of cuts of sausage. Occasionally they'd have *frikadellen,* the meatballs Franz loved, with perhaps a potato salad, but usually it was just the bread, cheese and sausage in the evening.

Now she had to get used to eating a light meal at midday and a large meal in the evening.

And she no longer liked doing so.

And Elke didn't, either, she knew.

Poor Elke, thrown into a world so very different from the world in which she'd been raised. And without her father or brother at her side.

If, despite it having been the style of life with which she'd grown up, it all now felt so very strange, it must be feeling even more so for Elke.

And they both of them had been somewhat stunned by the degree of choice in the shops, she thought, her gaze settling on the large oak wardrobe at the side of the room. There were so many different products displayed on the shop shelves, and hanging from rails.

Two days after her return, she and Elke had been taken by Maud to Hampstead and Knightsbridge, the areas in which Maud liked to shop when she wanted to buy ready-made clothes, which she'd told them she was doing increasingly frequently rather than go to a dressmaker.

When her mother had taken them into the first shop and urged them to select a few outfits that would be suitable for their new life, they'd stared in amazement at the seemingly endless array of dresses from which people could choose, and of cardigans, jumpers, coats, hats, gloves, all in every imaginable colour and style.

They hadn't known where to begin, and in the end they'd had to rely upon Maud to decide for them. It had been a relief when they were finally back in Primrose Hill.

She thought back to the clothes she'd worn in Rundheim—to her plain cotton dresses, her cover-all pinafore and the kerchief she wore daily on her head.

She'd had several changes of workday clothes, all of which she'd made herself, and a couple of dresses she'd wear on a special occasion, such as for a wedding in the village or the Polterabend on the eve of a marriage ceremony, but that was all. She hadn't needed more. No one in Rundheim had.

But she was once again in England, and there was no point in looking back with nostalgia, if that's what she was doing, at the very different life she'd left behind.

Her question to herself had been, was she happy now?

She pulled herself up mentally. How could she possibly be happy? Happy was far too strong a word. She'd never be completely happy again—not without Franz and Dieter.

She missed them desperately.

Franz was in her mind first thing every morning when she woke. She'd lie in bed, seeing his face, unwilling to cause it to fade by getting up and going downstairs. And he was in her mind last thing at night as she lay between the sheets, forcing herself to stay awake, just to feel near to him for that little bit longer.

If Franz and Dieter had been with her and Elke, the past week in England would have been so different. She could have laughed with them and made light of the difficulty she was finding in getting used to her pre-nursing life.

If she'd had at her side the people she loved so much that just to think of them was sufficient to reduce her to tears, she could have been happy.

But without Franz and Dieter, there was a gaping hole in her life, and in that of Elke's, too.

She felt a lump come to her throat, and she swallowed hard.

She must focus solely on the good things that the move to England had given her, not on the misery it had left in its wake.

The biggest thing was that she was no longer afraid in the way that she'd been in Rundheim, and she could see that Elke, too, had lost the terror that had been eating into them. Now that the fear with which they'd lived for so long had gone, peace of mind was bound to come.

And she'd very much enjoyed seeing Louisa and Nellie again.

Both had arrived, overflowing with joy and excitement, within minutes of each other on the morning after her return.

Joseph and Maud had taken Elke for a walk across Primrose Hill, leaving Nellie and Louisa alone with her, allowing them time to get to know each other again.

Although they weren't really getting to know each other again, were they, she'd later told herself. She was getting to know them for the first time.

She'd loved, admired and envied Nellie from the time that Nellie had been born, but it wasn't true to say that she'd known her.

She'd certainly learned something of the grown-up Nellie through their exchange of letters, but Nellie had written mainly about what had been happening in the family, and not about the way she was feeling.

Her love for Walter had shone out of her letters, and her happiness with him, but there'd been no sharing of her innermost thoughts on matters of importance. Nor indeed, any indication about what was important to her.

And she'd really liked the Louisa she knew from her letters.

There'd definitely been a time when she'd had something in common with Louisa.

Louisa had felt herself rejected by the family, owing to the way in which she'd behaved and to the accident she'd caused, and she, Dorothy, had been cast off by the family because she'd married the man she deeply loved.

But the Louisa who'd thrown herself at her in delight that first morning at home had been very different from the Louisa who'd first written to her about six years earlier.

The Louisa today was in love with Philip, and knew herself to be deeply loved by him. And she clearly knew, probably without ever consciously thinking about it, that her family had seen the genuineness of her remorse, and had taken her to their hearts, possibly for the first time in their life and hers.

As she'd sat with Nellie and Louisa, after they'd greeted her with initial exchanges of surprise and wonder, and she them, and after they'd exclaimed with pleasure at the thought of meeting Elke, she was acutely aware that they'd come to the end of the obvious things to say.

The day would come, she was sure, when they would all engage in a deeper conversation. They were bound to have concerns about what was happening in the world around them, and she'd be interested to hear what they were. And when that happened, she'd know them better.

But it had clearly been too soon for matters of more import than the details of her journey back to England, for discussions with them about the sort of things that she and Franz had regularly discussed together.

She'd also briefly seen Robert. Her brother had stopped by for a few minutes on the day after Nellie and Louisa's visit, and he'd stayed to have a cup of tea and a slice of fruit cake with her.

But he'd been visibly tired, and his conversation had been limited to the bungalows being built by Linford & Sons.

In the early days, before Linford & Sons had become interested in constructing them, bungalows had been cosily rustic buildings, quaint and rural-looking, he'd told her, their use confined to the upper classes and wealthy professionals.

She made a polite noise to indicate interest.

'But the bungalows that the company's building at the moment', he'd told her enthusiastically, 'are small, compact houses on one floor, which give the buyer the best of both worlds. They combine the advantages of modernity with the rural dream shared by so many people. And since they're cheaper to furnish and easy to run, they're fast becoming popular as a main home among people at all social levels.'

By the time he'd finished singing the praises of his bungalows, it had been time for him to leave, and also for her and Elke to go clothes shopping with Maud.

With luck, the lunch at his house that day would give her a chance of finding out more about him than about bungalows, she thought ruefully.

And it'd be interesting to meet his wife, and also James, Robert's son, who'd one day take over the running of the company.

She knew from Louisa and Nellie's letters that the last few years hadn't been easy for any of them, and at some point in the future, but not on a family occasion such as the lunch would be, it might be something he'd want to talk about.

And those who hadn't already met Elke, would have the chance to do so.

So far, during all the introductions and re-introductions that had been taking place, Elke had either been out, or had kept in the background, sensing that it was her mother the visitors wanted to see, and wanted to welcome back.

But now that they'd seen her, it was time for them to take notice of Elke, and appreciate what a delightful young girl she was.

Elke and Robert's James were not so different in age, so it should be pleasant for them to meet each other.

There was a hesitant knock on the door. As she took a step towards it, the door opened and Elke's head appeared in the gap.

'Grandfather said to tell you we'll be leaving shortly,' Elke said, and she came further into the room.

'You look very nice, Elke,' she said with a smile.

She stared at Elke, trying to see her as the family would see her.

She was so obviously her daughter, but there was also a touch of Franz. Her expression, and some of her gestures, were pure Franz. She was a gentle girl, kind, loving and in her own quiet way, a firm believer in doing what was right. She hoped from the bottom of her heart that her family would see Elke for the lovely person she was.

Feeling suddenly very emotional, she felt herself flush. 'Your grandmother was right about that shade of yellow suiting you very well,' she said quickly, 'your hair and eyes being dark.'

Elke glanced down at her dress. 'It's a nice dress. *Vati* would like it.'

Dorothy nodded. 'Yes, he would have done.'

'I shouldn't have said *Vati*,' Elke said, smoothing down the skirt of her dress. 'Grandfather's asked me not to. He said I should say Daddy or Father. And you should be Mother or Mummy. He said *Mama* was all right, though, but not *Mutti*. He doesn't like me sounding German, does he?'

'If that's what he's said, he can't do. It's because of the war, you see.'

'*Vati* didn't fight against England. Leah's parents didn't fight, and nor did *Onkel* Karl and *Tante* Herta. Not every German wanted to fight the English.'

'That's absolutely true, Elke. But when there's been a war, everyone from the aggressor country tends to get blamed. Your grandfather obviously doesn't want the family to see you as a German—he wants them to see you as Elke, my daughter, and his granddaughter.'

'But I'm also *Vati*'s daughter. *Vati*'s German. I love *Vati* so why would I not want to be seen as German as well as English?'

Dorothy hesitated. 'You're right, of course. But your grandfather has made us very welcome, despite the fact that I did something which displeased and, I'm sure, greatly distressed, him. He and Grandmother want you to be loved by the family, as you deserve, so it's not really such a big thing they're asking, is it?'

'I suppose not. But I don't like it.' Elke paused. 'Will your uncle Thomas be there today?'

'He'll have been invited, but I don't know if he'll go.'

'I hope he doesn't. He'll hate us, won't he?'

40

H *ampstead*

THERE WAS a low buzz of conversation from all corners of Robert's main reception room.

From her seat on the sofa between Nellie and their mother, Dorothy glanced around the room.

The Hampstead house, formerly the home of her grand-father, Arthur Joseph Linford, who'd founded Linford & Sons, and her grandmother, Bertha, wasn't so different from the way she remembered it from her early years, when she and her parents, and later her brother and sister, too, used to visit their grandparents.

Her grandfather would have been pleased that the char-acter of the house had remained essentially unchanged, she thought. The walls were now painted a delicate green, instead of the former dark green wallpaper, but the black cast-iron fireplace remained, and the gilt-framed oil paint-

ings still hung from the picture-rail that skirted the upper
part of the walls.

The mahogany-framed three-piece suite, with its plush
pink velvet upholstery, had gone, and in its place there was a
less-ornate mahogany-framed sofa that had been uphol-
stered in a deep green velvet, and two armchairs uphol-
stered with a floral print, the dominant colour being green.
The mahogany occasional table at each end of the sofa and
next to each of the armchairs had been her grandfather's.

It had always been a large, elegant room that had
managed to be comfortable, too. Perhaps there was slightly
less elegance now, and slightly more comfort, but it still
easily accommodated the fifteen there'd be for lunch
that day.

There would have been sixteen, Robert had told them
apologetically before he'd gone out into the garden with
Charles and Sarah to discuss the landscaping, but his wife
was upstairs, lying down in an effort to shake a crippling
headache. If she succeeded, she'd come down later as she
was very keen to meet Dorothy.

The Sunday lunches in Hampstead had long been a
fixture in the family's calendar. It had been their grandfather's idea to start hosting a monthly lunch on Sundays as
Joseph, Charles and Thomas had grown older and were
close to moving away and setting up their own homes.

He had been keen on the family remaining close to each
other and the lunches had continued until his death, by
which time she was living in Germany.

There'd been a slight hiccup in family harmony, Dorothy
had learned in her first letter from Nellie, when Robert had
inherited the Hampstead house, which they'd all assumed
would have been left to Arthur Joseph Linford's sons.

But by then, Joseph and Charles already had homes of their own, and Thomas would, too, when he returned from the war, so they'd accepted the decision, and their sense of family had overcome any reservations about Robert being favoured over the other grandchildren.

'How are you liking being back in London?' she heard a voice ask, and she looked up and saw a young man standing in front of her. 'I'm Christopher, by the way. Louisa's brother.'

'I'll leave you with Christopher,' Nellie said, getting up. 'I think I ought to find out what Emily's telling James and Elke. Their eyes are sticking out like stalks. I dread to think what it is. And I want to remind Walter that when Thomas gets here, we're going to ask him to drop off some catalogues when it's convenient. Will you excuse me?'

'It must be very strange,' Christopher continued, moving closer, 'being in a big city like this after living in what I hear was a large village. At least, that's how Philip described it to us.'

'It is,' she said. 'It's not so much being in a village that's so different, although it is, of course, but it's the way one lives over here. Or rather, the way my family lives. Not everyone in England has such a comfortable life as the Linfords.' She gave a slight laugh. 'I can't get used to there being nothing in the day that I actually have to do.'

He smiled. 'I must say, I'd hate doing nothing. But then I'm not a woman.'

'Amazingly, Christopher,' Louisa said, coming up behind him, followed by Philip, 'lots of women these days have moved beyond the confines of needlepoint and the supervision of servants. And I don't just mean women who're so poor that they've no choice. And women are actually trusted to vote!' She threw up her hands in mock horror. 'The temerity of it!'

He laughed. 'I take your point, Lou. I think I'll remove myself from the line of fire, and have a word with Walter. I've great plans for the future, and I need some advice. Who better than Walter?'

'How are you getting on?' Philip asked as Christopher moved away, and Louisa sat down where Nellie had been sitting.

'I was telling Christopher that life here's very strange after my life in Rundheim.'

'Nice strange or nasty?' he asked.

'To be honest, I don't know,' she said slowly. 'I'm desperately missing Franz and Dieter. They were so much part of my life over there that I can't separate them from the way I lived. And as I love them ...' She felt her eyes fill with tears. 'I think we'd better change the subject,' she said, with a watery smile. 'I haven't yet got over them not being with me.'

'It's early days,' he said, sympathetically. 'We'll change the subject to our house in Glenilla Road, then. Louisa and I took Charles, Sarah and Christopher to see the house yesterday, and we'd like to show it to you, too. Wouldn't we, Lou?'

'Definitely. You must come and see it.'

'Perhaps you and Elke would let us take you there next week—on Saturday, maybe?' he suggested.

'We'd like that very much. Thank you. Ah, here's Father!'

'Charles and Sarah have just come in from the garden with Robert, and Robert has asked us to go to the table,' Joseph said, coming up to them. 'We're not going to wait for Thomas. There's no certainty that he'll come, despite grudgingly accepting the invitation. But that's Thomas for you.'

. . .

DOROTHY SAT at the far end of the table, to the right of Robert, who sat at its head. Elke sat opposite her, on the other side of Robert. At Robert's suggestion, James sat next to Elke. Being so close in age, Robert had said, it would be nice for them to get to know each other.

Joseph sat at the other end of the table from Robert, and Thomas, who'd arrived just as they were making their way into the dining room, had gone straight to the chair next to Joseph's, and had sat down on the same side of the table as Elke.

Despite the fact that Thomas was wearing his prothesis, and also using a cane, he was moving awkwardly, she noticed. A glove on his right hand hid the damage.

She would have liked to have gone along to him, to have broken the ice before the meal began. But to do so, she'd have had to disturb those sitting between them, and walk the length of the table, and the last thing she wanted to do was go up to him with Elke and the rest of the family watching, when she didn't know how he'd react.

So she tried to catch his eye, ready to smile when she did.

Thomas resolutely avoided looking towards her. Turning to Joseph, he immediately engaged him in conversation.

Sarah, who was sitting halfway up the table, opposite Charles, looked first at Thomas, and then back at Charles. She raised her eyebrows, but said nothing.

'How old are you, James?' Dorothy asked.

'Almost fifteen.' He turned to Elke. 'How old are you?' he asked.

'Almost fourteen,' she said.

'Emily's twelve,' he said. 'Aren't you, Em?'

Emily, sitting next to Nellie, nodded.

'I got a Leica for my birthday last year, as well as a bicycle,' James said. 'When we've eaten, we can go up and look at some of my photographs. I took a lot at Chorton. If you'd like to, that is.'

Elke nodded. 'Yes, I would. Thank you.'

'How lovely that the children are of a similar age,' Maud remarked to Nellie, leaning slightly in front of Emily to do so. 'It leaves the adults free to talk to each other. Of course, not so many years ago, children of that age wouldn't sit down at the table with the adults—they'd eat in the nursery, and then come down for a short period of time later in the afternoon.'

'With a child as demanding as Emily, there are certain attractions in that way of doing things,' Nellie said lightly. 'I'm joking, Em,' she added quickly.

As the meal drew to an end, Dorothy glanced along the gleaming mahogany table at the silver salvers piled high with fresh fruit, at the purple and gold boxes of Cadbury's Milk Tray that had been placed between the salvers, at the white bone china cups that had been filled with coffee, and at the wine glasses, some full, some empty, that sparkled the length of the table.

How strange this all now felt.

Joseph sat back in his chair and undid the lower button on his waistcoat. 'That was an excellent meal, Robert,' he called to Robert. 'Once again, everything was done to perfection. And you're to be congratulated on the menu. That piquant sauce with the poached salmon was truly delightful.'

Robert looked pleased. 'I'm glad you liked it. A lighter meal, given the spring-like weather, seemed a good idea.' He smiled at Elke. 'Did you enjoy the meal, Elke? I imagine it was very different from the food you're used to.'

'I liked it, thank you.'

'Did you do any cooking at home? When you were in Germany, I mean.'

Elke nodded. '*Mutti* did the cooking, but I sometimes helped. *Vati* and Dieter didn't cook. Because they're men, you see. Well *Vati* is. Dieter's not yet nine.'

Robert nodded solemnly.

'*Mutti*'s a very good cook,' Elke went on. 'Not as good as *Tante* Herta, though. *Tante* Herta and *Onkel* Karl lived opposite us. Their daughter, Sofia, was my closest friend. Along with Leah, who lived in the north of the village.'

Sarah leaned slightly forward. 'I understood you'd been asked to use only English words, Elke,' she said. 'You speak excellent English, after all. There's no need to say *Mutti* and *Vati* when you know to say Mummy and Daddy. You're in England now and you need to leave all that behind you.'

Elke turned to look at Sarah. She paled slightly, and moistened her lips with her tongue.

'I'm used to saying *Mutti und Vati*. Sometimes I also say *Mama* and *Herr Vater*. I know I'm English as well as German, but perhaps I'm a bit more German than English because I was born there and I've lived there all my life. And my father is German and I love him. So I don't want to pretend that I'm not at all German.'

A low indeterminate hum arose from around the table.

'Why did you leave Germany, Elke?'

At the sound of Thomas's voice, silence fell.

To a person, they looked at Thomas, and then at Elke.

Elke glanced along the table to Thomas.

'Because we were afraid,' she said, a tremor in her voice. 'We got more and more afraid. Leah and her family left

Rundheim because people stopped being friendly to them, and other Jewish families left, too. One day they were there, the next they weren't. And *Onkel* Karl and *Tante* Herta were taken away by the police and sent with Sofia and Hans to a re-education camp. The Gestapo came to the classroom and took them.'

'Why did they take them?' Thomas asked.

'Because *Onkel* Karl taught poems he shouldn't have done. *Vati* said they were by a Jewish poet. We had to be careful what we said and what we did. And because Frau Schmidt's daughter was married to a Brownshirt, we had to be even more careful. *Herr und Frau* Schmidt lived three houses from us.'

She glanced quickly at Dorothy, and then back at Thomas.

'And my brother, Dieter, told me something he didn't tell *Mutti* or *Vati*,' she added. 'He told me that at *Jungvolk*, they were asked to listen to what their parents said at home, and also to what their neighbours said, and if anyone said anything against Hitler, they had to report them.'

'You didn't tell me that!' Dorothy exclaimed.

'You would've been even more frightened if I had,' Elke told her, and then she turned again towards Thomas. 'But if I can't use German words here because if I did, people would know I was German and would hate me, it's not so different from having to watch every word we said in Rundheim.'

'Didn't your father want to come with you? And your brother?' Thomas asked.

'I'll answer that,' Dorothy said. 'Franz thought I was exaggerating the risk. He said it was a new government and that it would settle down, and the violence would lessen. And Dieter loved *Jungvolk*.'

'What's that?' Emily asked, cutting in.

Dorothy smiled at her. 'It's like Boy Scouts. He'd recently been given a promotion, even though he's very young, and he was extremely proud of that. Also, he wanted to collect more badges, which is one of the things they do.'

A trace of defiance crept into her voice.

'Elke's right,' she added. 'She's both German and English, and I'm not going to ask her to disown a part of herself. I hope you can all accept that. If you can't, I'm afraid there isn't a thing I intend to do about it.'

'Well!' Sarah's exclamation conveyed deep disgust.

41

P rimrose Hill,
        later that evening

DOROTHY AND ELKE, who was dressed ready for bed, stood side by side at the nursery window.

The curtains undrawn, they watched in silence as twilight deepened into night and the trees, bushes and fields across the road dissolved into a single mass of grey.

'What did you think of today, Elke?' Dorothy asked at last.

Elke shrugged. 'It was all right. But I didn't like the lady who told me off about using German words.'

'That was Aunt Sarah,' Dorothy told her. 'Uncle Philip's marrying her daughter. That's Louisa.'

'Then I'm sorry for Uncle Philip. She doesn't seem very nice.'

'What about Thomas? What did you think of him? He was the one who asked why we left Germany.'

Elke thought for a moment. 'I know he wasn't friendly to us, but I liked him. It was a better question than asking how old I am, if I like school or what my favourite lesson is. He wouldn't have asked if he hadn't been interested in knowing. He didn't just look at us, and think, Ah, they're German so they're horrid.'

Dorothy looked at her. 'What a very perceptive answer,' she said slowly. 'How grown-up you're becoming, Elke.'

'What did you think of today, *Mutti*?'

'Well, it was difficult because I was anxious about Uncle Thomas and what he'd say to us, if anything. And I was annoyed that Aunt Sarah said what she did. I thought you answered her very well.'

'I said what was true.'

Dorothy nodded. 'We've been here for the best part of two weeks now. Do you think you can be happy here? Not in this house, of course. We'd get a place of our own. Father has told me that he'll help us with that.'

Elke shrugged her shoulders. 'I like not feeling afraid,' she said at last. 'But I miss *Vati* and Dieter. I miss them more than I felt afraid when we were in Rundheim. I can make myself a bit happy here, but I could never be completely happy as they aren't with us.'

Dorothy's eyes watered. 'I could have said those same words,' she said. 'I miss your father and brother so much. Oh, Elke, if I'm truly honest, I want to go home.'

Elke threw her arms around her mother, and burst into tears. 'So do I, *Mutti*. When can we leave?'

THEIR BREAKFAST the following morning finished, over a last cup of tea Dorothy told Joseph that they were going back to Germany. His head bowed, he listened to her in silence.

'Is this to do with what I suggested to Elke about her vocabulary yesterday, and a result of what Sarah said at Robert's?' he asked when she'd finished. 'If it is, it isn't important. She must use German words if that's most comfortable for her.'

She shook her head. 'It's an awareness that's been building up. Yesterday may have crystallised things a little, and speeded up my decision, but I know I'd have come to this conclusion at some point. I miss Franz and Dieter so much that it hurts. I don't want to live apart from them.'

'Naturally, I'm disappointed, but I won't pretend I'm surprised,' he said at last. 'I've seen the way in which you've been struggling to adjust. I think you no longer feel part of our world. You've tried to belong, but you don't feel as if you do. And you aren't even sure that you want to. That's not a criticism—it's a fact.'

Dorothy gave him a wry smile. 'That's an acute observation, Father,' she said. 'I could have got used to a version of your world if we'd moved into a house of our own. And although Elke and I would have lived more simply than you, we'd have had greater physical comfort here than we could have in Germany.'

'But?'

'But mental comfort matters more. It's very simple—I miss Franz, and I miss Dieter. And Elke does, too. And we'll never have mental comfort if we aren't with them.'

Joseph stared at her, his face pale. 'You'd be going back to the same situation. It won't have improved, and it may well have got worse. You'd be living in fear, at risk of being taken away at any moment, and you'd always have to guard your tongue. You know what Dieter was told.'

'Don't think I haven't thought of that. But Elke said she missed her father more than she'd felt afraid in Rundheim.

And I feel the same. If I stayed here, every time that I read about an act of violence or aggression in Germany, I'd fear for the safety of Franz and Dieter.'

He nodded slowly. 'I can understand that.'

She gave him a wry smile. 'I suppose it's my fate to live with fear, one way or another. And in that case, I'm opting to be afraid alongside Franz.'

He leaned forward and grasped her hand. 'But what if there's another war? Every day, the papers say something about warlike preparations in Germany. Where would that leave you, an English woman in a German town? I beg of you, Dorothy. Give yourself a little longer to see if you can settle here.'

She enclosed his hand in hers. 'There won't be a war between England and Germany, Father. Hitler seems to like England.'

'You can't trust that man! Also, and I know it's selfish of me, but I can't bear the thought of seeing you go, and your mother will feel the same, too. We've only just started to get to know you again, to get to know you as an adult, and to know Elke, who's a granddaughter to be proud of.'

He withdrew his hand, took out a handkerchief, and blew his nose.

'Thank you, Father,' Dorothy said quietly.

'For what?'

'For what you said just now, and for what you didn't say. That means more than you'll ever know. Don't think it'll be easy to leave you again, because it won't.' She touched her chest. 'But you're here in my heart, dear Father, and you'll ever be with me. And mother, too.'

He nodded, and wiped his eyes. 'When are you thinking of going?'

'I know from what Philip said that the Twickenham

Ferry sails on Thursdays. We'll use buses to get from Dunkirk to Germany. I thought we could have just over one more week here, going round to see different members of the family, and then leave for Southampton on Wednesday the following week. We'd arrange our passage when we got to Southampton, stay overnight and sail the following morning.'

'It sounds very soon.'

'We'll have been here for almost a month. It may not sound long, but we'll have caught up with everyone, and given them our address. Maybe Louisa and Nellie won't be the only ones who write to us in future. I hope you'll write, too.'

She paused, and gave him a half-smile. 'D'you remember that letter I wrote to you after Grandfather died? You left that letter out so that Nellie would see my address, didn't you?'

'I wanted someone to keep in touch with you. I knew Nellie would.'

'Thank you, Father,' she said. 'That was a very great kindness.'

'I do understand why you're going, believe me.' He leaned across the table and took her hand. 'There's something I want you to promise, Dorothy,' he said, his tone very serious.

'If at any time it looks as if Germany might be about to declare war on England—if there seems to be the slightest chance of that happening, no matter how remote—you must come home, even if you have to do so alone.'

She made as if to speak.

'Just as your husband was interned here during the war,' he went on regardless, 'I'm sure the Germans would intern anyone English if they were at war with England. I've read about the violence meted out to Hitler's opponents, and I'm certain your experience would be very much worse than your husband's. Promise me you'd come back before war broke out, and you wouldn't leave it to the last minute, by which time it could be too late.'

She nodded. 'I promise, Father.'

'And you mustn't worry about Sarah,' he added. 'I'd see that she toed the line. She'll never upset you or Elke again.'

He paused.

'I'm going to give you a farewell present,' he said. 'For that I'll enlist Philip's help. He mentioned in connection with Louisa a small car that was easy to maintain, and I intend to get you that car.'

She opened her mouth to protest.

He raised his hand to silence her.

'I'm doing it for myself. I don't want to think of you having to rely on buses to get back to Germany, and having to struggle with your luggage, and I need to know that you could always get into a car and come back to England if you felt that things were deteriorating at an alarming rate in Germany.'

'That's extremely kind of you, Father, but there's a tiny problem. And that's—'

'—the fact that you can't drive.' He finished the sentence for her.

'We'll see that you learn. You may have to stay here for a week longer than planned as you need to be completely confident behind the wheel, but your journey will be shorter and easier as you'll have your own transport.'

'Yes, it will. Thank you so very much.'

He brushed away her thanks. 'Staying a little longer will

also give you time to talk to Philip. He can show you what you need to know about looking after the car, and he can familiarise you with the route.'

'I don't know what to say. That's very kind of you, Father, and very generous.'

'Nonsense! Apart from the fact that I would have helped you with a house, you've never been a drain on my wallet in the way your sister has,' he added, attempting to laugh. 'This will go a small way towards redressing the balance. I'll contact Philip this morning.'

Dorothy rose to her feet. 'I'm so grateful to you. I must go and tell Elke—she'll want to thank you, too. Mother's still upstairs, so I think Elke and I will go for a walk over Primrose Hill. We can tell Mother our plans when we get back.'

'I'll leave it to you to do so.'

She hesitated. 'You will write, won't you? Even though you're not completely retired, you've more time now.' She paused. 'I'm really going to miss you, Father.' Her voice caught.

He stood up.

'Your mother and I will miss you, too,' he said gruffly. 'And I very much hope that we see you again, and not just because there's a war. And that's not impossible.'

'Of course, it isn't.'

'As time goes on, it'll become easier to travel overseas. After all, as they now fly letters between countries, they're bound to get better at flying people, too. And when they do, we'd no longer have to do a long drive in order to visit each other.'

Impulsively, she leaned forward, slid her arms around him and hugged him hard.

Both of their faces were wet with tears when eventually they pulled apart.

'Forget everything I said when you married,' he said hoarsely. 'You're part of this family, and always will be. And your children, too. And your husband.'

42

P rimrose Hill,
        Wednesday, three weeks later

THE FRONT HALL was filled with movement.

Dorothy and Elke's luggage had been carried downstairs and lined up in front of the door, and Mrs Morley was going backwards and forwards with boxes of food to sustain them throughout the first part of their journey.

Maud had brought down a bag containing a couple of dresses and several cardigans that she thought Dorothy might find useful, having learnt how cold it was in the winter, and she was trying to persuade Dorothy to take the clothes back with her.

Joseph was hovering at the entrance to the reception room, waiting for Dorothy to be ready to leave. He'd asked everyone in the family to stay away from the house that morning as he thought that saying goodbye was going to be greatly distressing.

They'd said their goodbyes during the extra week that Dorothy had stayed, he'd told them, and he felt it should be left at that.

A few days earlier, he'd suggested to Dorothy that he and Maud go down to Southampton with her, and stay there the night, too, so that they could wave her and Elke off in the morning. They could then return by train.

But Dorothy had told him that she'd be finding it hard enough to leave the family she'd just got to know again, and it would be easier for her and Elke to go to Southampton alone.

She'd added, with a glimmer of a smile, that they'd have to be at the boat fairly early on the Thursday morning, and for her mother to have to be up at so early an hour could be a terrific shock to her system.

In the end, Joseph had to be content with giving her the tickets for Twickenham Ferry, which he'd bought her without her knowing, and the details of the hotel into which he'd booked her and Elke for dinner and an overnight stay, the bill for which he'd already arranged to settle.

'That's everything,' Dorothy said, coming down the stairs with Elke. Both had clearly been crying.

'I've checked our rooms and we haven't forgotten anything. You wouldn't have fitted into the car, Father,' she said, trying to smile. 'You and Mother have been so generous that there won't be an inch of seat without something on it.'

'Well,' he said. 'That's it, then. We'd better put your luggage into the car.' He paused. 'You're really sure you want to go back, Dorothy?'

She nodded, unable to speak for the lump in her throat that threatened to choke her.

His eyes moist, he went to the front door, and pulled it open.

FRANZ LEANED FORWARD in the car and stared anxiously beyond the front seat to the windscreen.

There hadn't been a moment when the road ahead of them had been clear of cars, and time was getting short.

The driver, obviously aware of Franz's anxiety at their frequent hold-ups, had called back apologetically several times that the traffic that morning seemed even worse than usual.

Franz glanced at his watch. It was already just after half past eleven, and apparently they were still some distance from Primrose Hill.

With Dorothy planning to set off at noon, it looked as if he might actually miss her. To have come so far, and then be too late, would be devastating.

He'd follow her to Southampton, of course, but there was no certainty that he'd find her till the next day. Although her family might be willing to help him, knowing that she'd decided to return to him, they might not know where she'd be staying.

He glanced at Dieter, who was slumped next to him, staring out of the window at a world that was so much larger and so much busier than the world they'd left behind.

Dieter looked bewildered and exhausted, and that wasn't surprising, their journey having been arduous. For Dieter's sake, if not for his, they needed to be with Dorothy as soon as possible, and for their travelling to be at an end.

Oh, if only he'd decided to leave Rundheim when Dorothy had!

He'd known he loved her deeply, of course, but he

couldn't have known how much she was a part of him, how essential she'd been to his happiness—to the happiness of them all.

And he couldn't possibly have known how desperately he'd miss her, how completely distraught he'd feel, how he'd wake up each morning, a black cloud hovering above him that refused to disperse throughout the day.

Why, oh why, had he allowed his experience in the internment camp to poison his mind and prevent him from seeing what really mattered? Why hadn't he realised sooner that there was no way on earth he could live without Dorothy?

FROM THE MOMENT she'd gone, he'd felt the pain of loss. He'd foolishly thought his anguish would subside with the passing of the days, but it hadn't—it had grown stronger.

Her aura was in the air he breathed, in the scent of the soap-laundered sheets, in the spices that emanated from the pantry every time that he opened the door, in the aromas that hovered above the stove, in the coffee beans she'd ground for breakfast on the morning of Philip's visit, that he hadn't been able to bring himself to use.

The kitchen cupboard, its shelves lined with the crockery given her by her grandparents when she was younger, that she hadn't been able to pack in the one bag she'd taken back to England, had cried out Dorothy.

As had the drawers that were filled with the letters she'd received from Nellie and Louisa.

And as had her chair. Motes of dust danced daily in the shaft of light that fell through the window on to the chair where she'd sit and read the letters from home. Which she did regularly.

Everything in the house they'd shared so happily was a daily reminder of the woman he loved with all his heart, and couldn't stop loving.

He and Dieter should have gone back to England with her.

As for what would have happened if he'd been in England and there'd been another war with Germany, well he and Dieter would have been interned, but they'd have got through it. It would have been a small price to pay for being with Dorothy again.

He'd been so very blind, and so very stupid.

The disadvantages of being an internee paled into insignificance against the fact that she'd lived with an increasing degree of fear for a number of years.

No one should be asked to do that if it could be avoided.

He should have taken her anxiety far more seriously, instead of dismissing it by casually saying that the Government would settle down and change.

There'd been no indication that there might be any such change in the future, as Dorothy had seen.

On the contrary.

The violence in the country had been increasing, and intensifying, and its targets more numerous. Dorothy had been right to take the opportunity to leave with Philip. And he'd been wrong not to agree. But he fervently hoped that it wasn't too late to show her how much he regretted letting her go with Elke, without him and Dieter at their side.

And he'd been so unfair to Dieter.

He should have immediately sought to make Dieter change his mind before Dorothy left and it was too late to do so.

He should have pointed out the advantages of what Dorothy was proposing, and the feeling of safety it would bring them, rather than standing by while Dieter centred everything on *Jungvolk*, and then ran out of the house in despair and misery.

After Dorothy and Elke had left, Dieter had become worryingly quiet and withdrawn, and although he'd gone to all the *Jungvolk* meetings, it seemed as if he was doing so with less enthusiasm.

He, too, must be greatly missing Dorothy, he'd reasoned. A boy of his age needed his mother.

And then, one evening when he'd finished washing the dishes after their supper, he'd realised that Dieter had gone outside. Dropping everything, he'd gone quickly after him. To his surprise, Dieter was standing at the crossroads, staring down the hill that led to the south.

'What's wrong, Dieter?' he asked, going up to him.

Dieter shrugged. 'Nothing.'

'I see,' he said. And standing next to Dieter, he, too, had stared down the hill.

'Is it *Jungvolk*?' he'd asked at last. 'Are you not enjoying it? Is it that it's somewhat changed since they introduced those training programmes? Or are you just missing your mother, as I am?'

He'd shrugged again. 'Both, I suppose.'

'Talk to me, Dieter,' he said quietly. 'If something's wrong at *Jungvolk*, I might be able to help.'

Dieter rounded on him. 'You shouldn't say that, *Vati*—it's dangerous. Someone might hear you. We have to report anyone who says anything against Hitler, or against anything to do with Hitler. We're meant to spy on people, even our parents and friends. I don't want to do that,' he said, and he looked away.

Dieter's lower lip was trembling, he noticed.

His stomach lurched with a sense of shock, and he

stared at Dieter. 'I'm glad you feel like that, Dieter,' he said at last. 'That's a very wrong thing to be asked to do.'

Dieter caught his arm in visible fear. 'Don't say that, *Vati*.'

He attempted a smile. 'All right. I won't say anything else that could be taken as a criticism.' He put his arm round Dieter's shoulders.

'And I don't like some of the things we've started doing now,' Dieter went on, moving closer and putting his arm around his father's waist. 'We've started doing things with weapons, you know. Like soldiers do. What we used to do, things like cycling, swimming and badge collecting, used to be fun. But now they seem to be trying to teach us to fight, and I don't like that. It's frightening.'

He nodded. 'I wouldn't, either.'

'I think it's also not fun because *Mutti* isn't here. I miss her.'

'So do I, Dieter. Very much.'

Dieter pointed down the hill in front of him. 'She went that way with *Onkel* Philip, didn't she?'

'That's right.' He paused. 'And *we* could go that way, too. Shall we?'

The expression on Dieter's face, the sheer joy and relief with which he gazed up at him, was his answer.

FRANZ GLANCED AGAIN at his watch. It now said quarter to twelve.

Was that really all it was?

It seemed so long ago that he and Dieter had left the boarding house where they'd stayed the night after stepping off the ferry, and with the instructions to her house that

Nellie had sent to Dorothy in his pocket, had headed for Southampton Terminus Railway Station.

But, in fact, it was a lot less time than it felt.

Nellie's instructions had been very clear, and their journey to Camden Town Station, and thence to Nellie's house, had been accomplished without difficulty.

Confident that if Dorothy wasn't there, Nellie would know where he'd find her, he'd knocked at Nellie's door.

The woman who'd opened the door to them—the housekeeper, she must be, he thought, remembering what Dorothy had said about the people who worked for her family—had looked surprised when he'd asked for Nellie in his accented English.

He couldn't quite remember what he'd said, but the woman had understood, and he and Dieter had been shown into the hall.

He'd heard the housekeeper announce to the family that a Mr Herr Hartmann was in the hall, and a moment later, a dark-haired woman a few years younger than Dorothy had appeared in the doorway, breathless with excitement, but also clearly full of trepidation.

She'd introduced herself as Nellie.

After a brief moment of obvious anxiety on Nellie's part, she'd taken him and Dieter into a large room and had introduced them to the two men there, who'd risen to their feet as they'd come in.

One of them was Walter, and the other was the man he'd least wanted to see, Thomas.

'We're having the house redecorated, *Herr* Hartmann, and Dorothy's uncle Thomas has bought us some catalogues,' Nellie said, with a badly disguised attempt at hiding the nervousness she felt.

Franz and Thomas had stared at each other.

Neither spoke. Neither moved.

He'd found his gaze slipping to Thomas's legs, and he'd felt himself colouring.

Nellie had taken control. She'd asked them all to sit down, and had sent for refreshments.

Why had he come, she'd asked while they were waiting.

Avoiding looking at Thomas, he'd explained his unbearable sense of loss, and that although England had treated him badly, it was not nearly as bad as not being with Dorothy.

He and Dieter, who desperately missed his mother, had come to stay. He only hoped that Dorothy would forgive his stupid refusal to accompany her when she came back with Philip.

But she's going back to Germany, Nellie had exclaimed. She was going that very morning, she'd said. She'd got a car and was going to drive to Southampton.

He'd heard Dieter cry out.

He'd jumped up, and said that he and Dieter must leave at once to find her.

Walter had instantly risen to his feet and volunteered to drive them to Primrose Hill.

But Thomas had stood up, told Walter to stay where he was, and suggested that Walter try to get his telephone repaired at once. If he succeeded, he could ring Joseph and tell him to stop Dorothy from leaving.

And he'd announced that George, his driver, would take them to Joseph's, and that he'd go, too.

He'd tell George they were leaving, he told them, and he'd walked out.

He had been vaguely aware of the surprise in the glances that Walter and Nellie had exchanged, but he'd been only too glad to have the chance of reaching Dorothy before she left.

Having apologised that they were leaving before the refreshments arrived, adding that he was sure they would understand, he and Dieter had headed quickly for the door. They'd picked up the bags they'd left in the hall, and followed Thomas out of the house.

And now they were minutes from the house where Dorothy's parents lived, in a car with Thomas, who hadn't said a word, who must truly hate him, but who was helping him be reunited with Dorothy.

He couldn't really understand it.

'Not far now,' George said.

Looking through the windows on both sides of the car, he saw an expanse of fields across the road on the right, and a line of tall brick houses on the left. A few moments later, he felt George pulling into the kerb and starting to bring the car to a stop.

He found himself tightly clutching the door handle, ready to fling it open the moment they arrived.

'Are we there?' Dieter asked. Leaning forward, he hugged his bag more tightly to his chest.

'We are, son,' George called to the back, bringing the car to a halt behind another car. 'I think that might be Dorothy's car. I'm not sure, though. If it is, it means you're in time. But let your father get out first.'

His heart thumping fast, Franz depressed the door handle, opened the door and stepped quickly on to the pavement. He paused, and looked up.

A line of black wrought-iron railings fronting a large house faced him. Behind the railings, cream-painted bricks on the walls of the lower half of the house framed a large bay window on either side of the slate blue front door. On the upper part of the house, the brickwork was soft-toned cream and grey.

This was what Dorothy had given up in order to come and live with him! How she must have loved him!

Please let that be her car, and let her still be there, he cried out inwardly. Please, please, don't let her have left already.

Before he could move, the front door opened. A tall, broad-shouldered man of about sixty filled the doorway.

Dorothy's father, he thought.

Her father started to come out of the house, but stopped abruptly at the sight of a man with very blond hair and striking blue eyes, who was standing on the pavement, looking up at him with hope.

He stared down at Franz in utter amazement.

His gaze slid to Dieter, who'd stepped out of the car and was hovering by the car door. And amazement gave way to a look of pure relief.

With a broad smile, he turned towards the house. 'Dorothy,' he called.

He felt a slight movement of air next to him. Glancing sideways, he saw that Thomas was standing next to him.

'There are no hard feelings on this side, Franz,' Thomas said. 'When it's a war, you do what you have to. And people get hurt. That's the way it goes. But all that's in the past. I imagine we'll be seeing a lot of you in the future, and I look forward to getting to know the man my niece loves so much that she's prepared to live in danger rather than live without him.'

To his huge surprise, Thomas held out his good hand to him.

Franz took it with both of his hands. 'Thank you,

Thomas,' he said, his voice trembling. 'Thank you from the bottom of my heart.'

Then he turned and looked up the steps.

Her face bemused, Dorothy was standing on the top step, her father just behind her. He had his hand on Elke's shoulder. All three were staring down at Thomas and Franz.

Releasing Thomas's hand, he took a pace forward.

So did Dorothy, her expression still disbelieving.

As then, realising in a moment of blinding joy that Franz was no vision, but reality, her face erupted with sheer delight.

With a cry of utter exaltation, she started to run down the steps at the same moment as Franz began to run up the path towards her.

They met at the foot of the steps, and stopped, breathing heavily.

For a long moment, each stared at the other, the eyes of both filled with wonder.

'Dorothy.' He said her name, his breath caressing her. '*Mein Liebling* Dorothy.'

'Oh, Franz.'

He opened his arms, and she fell into them, and two became one again.

AUTHORIAL NOTE

British shadow factories were the outcome of a plan devised in 1935, which was developed by the British Government in the years before WW2, with the aim of meeting the need to increase the number of aircraft by using technology from the motor industry.

A directorate of Aeronautical Production was formed in March 1936 with responsibility for the manufacture of airframes as well as engines, associated equipment and armaments. Herbert Austin headed the project, which was developed by the Air Ministry under the name of the Shadow Scheme.

Under the project, the Air Ministry took over industrial space in order to increase production capacity. Aircraft production was the priority, and a number of factories that had been making cars or car parts were adapted and equipped for the manufacture of aircraft.

In addition, many more factories were built as part of a dispersal scheme designed to reduce the risk of a complete collapse of production if what would have been a major facility were bombed.

Philip McAllister is an entirely fictional character, and the job that I gave him in the novel is a product of my imagination. I think it more than likely, however, that there were people employed at that time to do exactly the work that Philip was doing, since, I feel sure, such groundwork will have been an essential part of the preparations for the Shadow Scheme.

One final point I should like to make. Morbach is a real town, but Rundheim is fictitious.

In devising Rundheim, I've drawn upon my knowledge of the large villages in the area in which Rundheim is located. I'm afraid, therefore, that you wouldn't come upon Rundheim, were you to drive south of Morbach.

IF YOU ENJOYED THE LENGTHENING SHADOW

It would be terrific if you were to leave a short review at the outlet where you bought the book.

Reviews are hugely important as they make the novel visible to other readers, and give them an idea of whether or not they'd like the novel.

In addition, reviews makes it easier for authors to promote their book as many promotional platforms today require a minimum number of reviews. It means that every review gives the novel a better chance of being noticed.

Your words, therefore, really do matter.

Thank you!

THE DARK HORIZON

Each novel in the Linford Series is a standalone, and is complete in itself.

The Lengthening Shadow and the other two novels in the series, *The Dark Horizon*, which is the story of Lily and Robert Linford, and *The Flame Within*, the story of Alice and Thomas Linford, can, therefore, be read in any order.

If you haven't read *The Dark Horizon*, you might enjoy reading the opening chapter, which you can do on the following pages.

THE DARK HORIZON: CHAPTER 1

Oxfordshire,
  December, 1919

Their heads bent low against the blistering cold from a chill December wind, the mourners stood in the small graveyard behind the grey stone church, the veiled women clad in crepe of the deepest black and the men in cashmere.

Their faces white, they stared down at the hand-crafted coffin that lay at the bottom of the steep-sided grave, the final resting-place of Arthur Joseph Linford, aged seventy-one, founder of Linford & Sons, one of the fastest growing building companies in the south of England.

We have entrusted our brother, Arthur Joseph, to God's mercy, and we now commit his body to the ground, the vicar intoned.

Standing slightly apart from the other mourners, Joseph Linford stared at his father's coffin, his face impassive. Then he raised his eyes and looked across the open grave at his son, Robert, and at Robert's wife, Lily. Her face shrouded in a short black chiffon veil, her hand was tucked into her husband's arm.

Joseph scowled.

His gaze moved to his brother, Charles, who was standing next to Lily. Charles's wife, Sarah, stood on his other side, a clear gap between them. That was another rum marriage, Joseph thought.

Glancing sideways, he looked beyond his wife and daughter to the youngest of the three brothers, Thomas, who was at the far end of the grave.

Obviously in a degree of discomfort caused by his artificial leg, Thomas was leaning heavily on his stick, supported by his wife, Alice.

Joseph's eyes rested a moment on Alice, and he felt the same amazement he always felt when he saw her. It was very easy to see why Thomas had married her, but for the life of him he couldn't understand what she saw in him.

It was true that she'd married above her station, but Thomas would not be an easy man to live with, and a woman as good-looking as Alice could surely have done equally well for herself with someone more amenable.

Turning away from them, he looked back across the grave at Robert, and a wave of intense disappointment surged through him.

Followed by anger.

How could Robert, his only son, have been so taken in by a pretty face that he'd blinded himself to the woman's lack of background and education—and then, even worse, how could he have gone and married her? It beggared belief.

He'd been absolutely horrified when Robert had told him that he'd fallen in love with Lily Brown, a Land Girl on

LIZ'S NEWSLETTER

Every month, Liz sends out a newsletter with updates on her writing, what she's been doing, where she's been travelling, and an interesting fact that she's learned. Subscribers also hear of promotions and special offers.

Rest assured, Liz would never pass on your email address to anyone else.

As a thank you for signing up to Liz's newsletter, you'll receive a free full length novel.

To sign up for Liz's newsletter and get a free book, go to www.lizharrisauthor.com.

ABOUT THE AUTHOR

Born in London, Liz Harris graduated from university with a Law degree, and then moved to California, where she led a varied life, from waitressing on Sunset Strip to working for a large Japanese trading company.

A few years later, she returned to London and completed a degree in English, after which she taught secondary school pupils, first in Berkshire, and then in Cheshire.

In addition to the nine novels she's had published, she's had several short stories in anthologies and magazines.

Liz now lives in Oxfordshire. An active member of the Romantic Novelists' Association and the Historical Novel Society, her interests are travel, the theatre, reading and cryptic crosswords. To find out more about Liz, visit her website at: www.lizharrisauthor.com

ALSO BY LIZ HARRIS

The Dark Horizon (The Linford Series, Book 1)

Oxfordshire, 1919

The instant that Lily Brown and Robert Linford set eyes on each other, they fall in love. The instant that Robert's father, Joseph, head of the family's successful building company, sets eyes on Lily, he feels a deep distrust of her.

Convinced that his new daughter-in-law is a gold-digger, and that Robert's feelings are a youthful infatuation he'd come to regret, Joseph resolves to do whatever it takes to rid his family of Lily. And he doesn't care what that is.

As Robert and Lily are torn apart, the Linford family is told a lie that will have devastating consequences for years to come.

The Flame Within (The Linford Series, Book 2)

London, 1923.

Alice Linford stands on the pavement and stares up at the large Victorian house set back from the road—the house that is to be her new home.

But it isn't *her* house. It belongs to someone else—to a Mrs Violet Osborne. A woman who was no more than a name at the end of an advertisement for a companion that had caught her eye three weeks earlier.

More precisely, it wasn't Mrs Osborne's name that had caught her eye—it was seeing that Mrs Osborne lived in Belsize Park, a short distance only from Kentish Town. Kentish Town, the place where Alice had lived when she'd been Mrs Thomas Linford.

Thomas Linford—the man she still loves, but through her own stupidity, has lost. The man for whom she's left the small Lancashire town in which she was born to come down to London again. The man she's determined to fight for.

The Best Friend

Confident that the woman with whom her husband of nine years has run off, wouldn't be one of the three girls who'd been her closest friends since they first started sharing a place in Camden Town eleven years earlier, Caroline walks up to the door of the house where, she's discovered, her husband is living with the unknown woman, and rings the bell.

Reeling from shock when she hears the voice of the woman, her mind sweeps back to Camden Town eleven years earlier, and the reader follows the story of the four girls sharing the house – four girls who became best friends.

The final chapter returns to the present, and the reader then learns which of the three girls has stolen Caroline's husband.

The Road Back

When Patricia accompanies her father, Major George Carstairs, on a trip to Ladakh, north of the Himalayas, in the early 1960s, she sees it as a chance to finally win his love. What she could never have foreseen is meeting Kalden – a local man destined by circumstances beyond his control to be a monk, but fated to be the love of her life.

Despite her father's fury, the lovers are determined to be together, but can their forbidden love survive?

A wonderful story about a passion that crosses cultures, a love that endures for a lifetime, and the hope that can only come from revisiting the past.

'A splendid love story, so beautifully told.' *Colin Dexter O.B.E. Best-selling author of the Inspector Morse novels.*

A Bargain Struck

Widower Connor Maguire advertises for a wife to raise his young daughter, Bridget, work the homestead and bear him a son.

Ellen O'Sullivan longs for a home, a husband and a family. On paper, she is everything Connor needs in a wife. However, it soon becomes clear that Ellen has not been entirely truthful.

Will Connor be able to overlook Ellen's dishonesty and keep to his side of the bargain? Or will Bridget's resentment, the attentions of the beautiful Miss Quinn, and the arrival of an unwelcome visitor, combine to prevent the couple from starting anew.

As their personal feelings blur the boundaries of their deal, they begin to wonder if a bargain struck makes a marriage worth keeping.

Set in Wyoming in 1887, a story of a man and a woman brought together through need, not love ...

The Lost Girl

What if you were trapped between two cultures?

Life is tough in 1870s Wyoming. But it's tougher still when you're a girl who looks Chinese but speaks like an American.

Orphaned as a baby and taken in by an American family, Charity Walker knows this only too well. The mounting tensions between the new Chinese immigrants and the locals in the mining town of Carter see her shunned by both communities.

When Charity's one friend, Joe, leaves town, she finds herself isolated. However, in his absence, a new friendship with the only other Chinese girl in Carter makes her feel as if she finally belongs somewhere.

But, for a lost girl like Charity, finding a place to call home was never going to be that easy ...

Evie Undercover

When libel lawyer, Tom Hadleigh acquires a perfect holiday home - a 14th century house that needs restoring, there's a slight problem. The house is located in the beautiful Umbria countryside and Tom can't speak a word of Italian.

Enter Evie Shaw, masquerading as an agency temp but in reality the newest reporter for gossip magazine Pure Dirt. Unbeknown to Tom, Italian speaking Evie has been sent by her manipulative editor to write an exposé on him. And the stakes are high – Evie's job rests on her success.

But the path for the investigative journalist is seldom smooth, and it certainly never is when the subject in hand is drop-dead gorgeous.

The Art of Deception

All is not as it seems, beneath the Italian sun ...

Jenny O'Connor can hardly believe her luck when she's hired to teach summer art classes in Italy. While the prospect of sun, sightseeing and Italian food is hard to resist, Jenny is far more interested in her soon-to-be boss, Max Castanien. She's blamed him for a family tragedy for as long as she can remember and she wants some answers.

But as the summer draws on and she spends more time with Max, she discovers that all is not necessarily what it seems, and she starts to learn first-hand that there's a fine line between love and hate.

A Western Heart

(a novella)

Wyoming, 1880

Rose McKinley and Will Hyde are childhood sweethearts and Rose has always assumed that one day they will wed. As a marriage will mean the merging of two successful ranches, their families certainly have no objections.

All except for Rose's sister, Cora. At seventeen, she is fair sick of being treated like a child who doesn't understand 'womanly feelings'. She has plenty of womanly feelings – and she has them for Will.

When the mysterious and handsome Mr Galloway comes to town and turns Rose's head, Cora sees an opportunity to get what she wants. Will Rose play into her sister's plot or has her heart already been won?

Made in the USA
Coppell, TX
29 June 2021

58302867R00225